ON MEMOIR

Also by Blake Morrison

Dark Glasses
The Ballad of the Yorkshire Ripper
The Yellow House
And When Did You Last See Your Father?
Pendle Witches
As If
Too True
The Justification of Johann Gutenberg
Things My Mother Never Told Me
South of the River
The Last Weekend
A Discoverie of Witches
This Poem
Shingle Street
The Executor
Two Sisters
Skin & Blister
Never the Right Time
Afterburn

ON MEMOIR

Blake Morrison

b
THE BOROUGH PRESS

The Borough Press
An imprint of HarperCollins*Publishers* Ltd
1 London Bridge Street
London SE1 9GF

www.harpercollins.co.uk

HarperCollins*Publishers*
Macken House, 39/40 Mayor Street Upper
Dublin 1, D01 C9W8, Ireland

First published in Great Britain by HarperCollins*Publishers* 2026

1

Copyright © Blake Morrison 2026

Blake Morrison asserts the moral right to be identified as the author of this work

A catalogue record for this book is available from the British Library

HB ISBN: 978-0-00-876091-5
TPB ISBN: 978-0-00-882760-1

Set in Adobe Garamond Pro Std by HarperCollins*Publishers* India

Printed and bound in the UK using 100%
Renewable Electricity at CPI Group (UK) Ltd

All rights reserved. No part of this publication may be reproduced, stored in a retrieval system, or transmitted, in any form or by any means, electronic, mechanical, photocopying, recording or otherwise, without the prior written permission of the publishers.

'Marked with D' is taken from *Collected Poems* by Tony Harrison (c) Tony Harrison and reprinted by permission of Faber and Faber Ltd.

The villanelle 'Life Writing' is taken from the collection
Shingle Street by Blake Morrison (2015).

Without limiting the exclusive rights of any author, contributor or the publisher of this publication, any unauthorised use of this publication to train generative artificial intelligence (AI) technologies is expressly prohibited. HarperCollins also exercise their rights under Article 4(3) of the Digital Single Market Directive 2019/790 and expressly reserve this publication from the text and data mining exception.

For everyone who writes or reads memoir

If men and women must write, let them leave the great mysteries of art and literature unassailed; if they told us frankly not of the books that we can read and the pictures which hang for us all to see, but of that single book to which they alone have the key and of that solitary picture whose face is shrouded to all but one gaze – if they would write of themselves – such writing would have its own permanent value. The simple words 'I was born' have somehow a charm beside which all the splendours of romance and fairy-tale turn to moonshine and tinsel.

      Virginia Woolf, *'The Decay of Essay Writing'*, 1904

I could inform the dullest author of how he might write an interesting book. Let him relate the events of his own life with honesty, not disguising the feelings that accompanied them.

    Samuel Taylor Coleridge, Letter to Thomas Poole, 1797

You think your pain and your heartbreak are unprecedented in the history of the world but then you read.

          James Baldwin, *Life* magazine, 1963

Contents

Preface	1	Bossiness	33
		Brainard, Joe	34
A	7		
Acknowledgements	7	**C**	36
Addiction	8	Cancellation	36
Adversity	9	Candour	38
AI	10	Characters	40
Anonymity	12	Children	42
Apology	15	Cliché	46
Appropriation	16	Confession	47
Art	18	Consent	50
Augustine, Saint	19	Courage	53
Autofiction	21	Creative non-fiction	55
Automatic writing	23	Crime	56
B	25	**D**	60
Bearing witness	25	Davies, W. H.	60
Beginnings	26	Death	61
Bestsellers	29	Depression	63
Biography	31	Derangement	65

Detail	67	**G**		117
Dialect	69	Ghosts		117
Dialogue	70			
Diaries	73	**H**		119
Didion, Joan	76	Hidden lives		119
Disclosure	77	Humour		120
Diski, Jenny	78			
Distance	80	**I**		123
		'I imagine'		123
E	82	Identity		124
Editors	82	Illness		127
Embarrassment	85	Immortality		129
Equiano, Olaudah	86	Influence		130
Essay	87	Inspiration		131
Ethics	89	Intention		133
Exploitation	92	Interviews		134
F	95	**J**		137
Fact-checking	95	Joy		137
Family history	96			
Faux-naïvety	98	**K**		139
Fiction	99	Knausgaard, Karl Ove		139
Finishing	100			
Flashbacks	102	**L**		142
Food	103	Landscape		142
Footnotes	104	Lawyers		143
Footsteps	106	Length		145
Form	108	Let us now praise . . .		146
Fragments	111	Lies		147
Friends	113	Likeability		149

Loss	151	Persona	194
Love	153	Photos	196
Lyric essay	154	Plagiarism	198
		Plain Style	200
M	157	Planning	202
Me Too	157	Plot	203
Medics	159	Poetry	204
Memoir	161	Point of view	206
Memory	163	Politics	208
Misery	166	Prizes	210
Mission	167	Pronouns	211
Mortality	169		
		Q	215
N	173	Questions	215
Names	173		
Narcissism	174	**R**	217
Nature	176	Rape	217
New Journalism	178	Readers	219
		Reading	221
O	180	Reading aloud	222
Offence	180	Reality hunger	222
Omission	182	Recognition	223
Omniscience	184	Rejection	226
Orwell, George	185	Reliability	229
		Repetition	231
P	188	Research	232
Pace	188	Resolution	234
Passion	190	Revision	235
Performance	191	Roth, Philip	237
Permissions	192	Rousseau, Jean-Jacques	239

Rules	239	**V**	278
		Vengeance	278
S	241	Vignettes	280
Salt Path	241	Violence	281
Schedules	243	Voice	282
Sebald, W. G.	244		
Self-expression	246	**W**	284
Self-publishing	247	What you know	284
Sex	248	Why I write	285
Shock	251	Wolfe, Tom	287
Siblings	252	Wolff, Tobias	288
Similes and metaphors	254	Woolf, Virginia	289
Sport	255	Workplace	290
Structure	257	Workshops	291
Surprise	258	Writer's block	294
T	261	**X**	297
Telling	261	X-rated	297
Tense	262		
Ten(tative)		**Y**	299
commandments	264	'You'	299
Therapy	266		
Trauma	268	**Z**	301
Travel	271	Zzz	301
Truth	272		
Typeface	275	**Bibliography**	305
		Notes and	
U	276	**Acknowledgements**	319
Ugliness	276		

Preface

I've had a life and I've also had a life as a life writer. I didn't plan it that way. There were no youthful ambitions to write about myself and my family. A memoir depends on memory, but there was nothing special or dramatic about my childhood that I wanted to remember. Nor were there many books in the house. My family, I thought, were the opposite of books. Books were my way to escape them.

Then my father died and I found there were things I needed to say about him – about the kind of parent he'd been, and how we'd got on with each other (or sometimes failed to), and what it was like to watch him get ill and die. Five years later, my mother died and, discovering letters the two of them had exchanged as sweethearts long before I was thought of, I found I had things to say about her too – about the enigma she'd been and why she'd hidden her Irish-Catholic roots. A non-fiction book about each parent and another very personal one on the James Bulger murder case, plus a selection of pieces called *Too True* . . . that felt like more than enough life writing. But then my sister died, before her time, just as my unacknowledged half-sister had done (both of them younger than me), and I had to write about them too. It was a must in all cases – a matter of urgency and emotional well-being – to set down the truth.

Urgency can take many forms. In my case the trigger was death. For others it might be a disturbed childhood, or addiction or mental breakdown, or the threat to the environment, or displacement to a new country, or the chaos of the political world. But whatever it is you're trying to make sense of, memoir is the most intimate and direct way to do it. Even poetry can look impersonal in comparison. There's no disguise, no holding back. You're desperate to get things down; to lay them on the line; to level with yourself. Yes, you'll need to shape and edit your story – it's not a splurge. But candour is vitally important: honesty, openness, truth-telling. That's the appeal of memoir: the use of a candid first-person voice. Even if you're a 'journal-er', writing privately with no thought of publication, just an urge for self-reflection and a need to come to terms with difficult stuff going on in your life, even then it's crucial to find the right words. Otherwise the space you've cleared for yourself will remain vacant and the process of discovery will be frustrated.

Life writing undoubtedly serves a therapeutic function: getting things down can be cathartic. It also takes courage: to uncover lies and expose secrets is a painful process. But truth is more honourable than omission, and candour less corrosive than shame. Nor does drawing on first-hand experience make you second-rate. What you worry might be 'strictly personal' material will be universal if you're honest in describing what you've been through and what you've learned. It's worth the pain to relieve the pain, to say the unsayable rather than be lost for words.

I'm not arguing that life writing is superior to fiction or poetry, genres I've worked in too. But it does involve considerations which they don't. Novelists invent and poets imagine; memoirists don't have the same degree of freedom. The row in 2025 over Raynor Winn's *The Salt Path* tells us as much. After an *Observer* article exposed evasions and omissions in the backdrop to Winn and her husband Moth's 630-mile coastal walk, the book became a scandal. Readers demanded their money back on copies they'd bought. The publishers, Penguin, were criticised for failing to fact-check: why had Winn's alleged embezzlement of tens of thousands of pounds from the business where she worked as a book-keeper escaped notice, and how did she get away with calling herself homeless when she owned a property in France? The book became a symbol of a crisis in the publishing industry. Could any memoir be trusted if one of the most acclaimed in recent years (a volume that sold two million copies, was translated into twenty-five languages, and was named by the *Sunday Times* as one of the top 100 books of the past 50 years) was guilty of fabrication?

How far memoirs can be allowed to fabricate, if at all, is a fascinating question. Memoirs, Michael Chabon says in his book *Moonglow*, 'are not true. They are works of fiction . . . Because that's how memory works; memory is a tool of fictionalisation.' James Joyce put it the other way about: 'Imagination,' he told Frank Budgen, 'is memory.' I take the point. We all have unreliable memories. Past events can be mis-recollected or misconstrued. And memoirs have stories to tell, which means they adopt the narrative techniques of novels (I refer to novels quite a lot in this book). But to *dis*-remember, in the sense of knowingly altering the truth, is not the same as unwittingly – innocently – getting things wrong. And the principle of life writing is to get them right, insofar as that's possible.

It's a fraught genre. *All the best stories are true* goes the adage and true stories are certainly stressful: ethically tricky, emotionally taxing and aesthetically troublesome. The genre isn't new: Virginia Woolf used the term life-writing (hyphenated) as far back as 1940. But there has been an exceptionally rich vein of life writing in recent years, in part because previously taboo subjects (to do with abuse, illness, poverty, race, illegitimacy, neurodiversity, gender dysphoria, etc.) are being brought into the open, and in part because talented writers have discovered new ways to exploit the form.

More than other kinds of literature, life writing compels: it leaves no choice. That's how it was for me with my memoirs. And it's the case with this book, too. I've spent three decades as a life writer and now I want to reflect on why the genre matters to me; why it has become so central to our literary culture; how it works and who it's aimed at and why it offers something that fiction and poetry can't. It has occasionally been alleged when I'm introduced at a literary event that I 'established' life writing in the UK, or encouraged its growth, for better or worse. That's bonkers: memoirs have been around for centuries – think St Augustine, Teresa of Avila, Jean-Jacques Rousseau, Nadezhda Mandelstam or (closer to home) Thomas De Quincey, Edmund Gosse, George Orwell, Vera Brittain . . . Still, I do feel protective of the form and anxious to speak up for it. Detractors dismiss first-person life writing as narcissistic, a confessional outpouring of me-me-me – misery memoirs have given it a bad name. But at its best it's the least self-absorbed of genres. You lay yourself open in order to transcend yourself: to get beyond the pain and confusion. You also do it for the benefit of others: reaching readers who have similar stories or who want to learn from experiences radically different to their own. Above all, memoir promises truth-telling, and in a world of fake news, disinformation and conspiracy theory, there's nothing more important than truth.

I feel passionate about the challenges and rewards of the form. Hence this book – a set of ideas, examples and suggestions assembled as an A–Z . The categories kept expanding as I went along; so did my list of books to read. Many people practise life writing, whether as biographers, bloggers, family memoirists or someone keeping a journal, and I hope the book might help them. But I also want to reach the people who consume life writing as *readers*. In particular, I'd like to take up ethical issues that concern us all – issues around consent and privacy and exposure and the conflicts between those who write and those who are written about.

It's not a rule-book or a teaching primer. And the idiom isn't academic – that's why the text is free of citations and footnotes (though the books I discuss are listed in the bibliography). I'm simply raising questions and venturing answers, both for others and for myself.

Blake Morrison, London, January 2026

A

Acknowledgements

I'm starting at the end, not the beginning, with the thank-you pages that come at the close of a book. I say pages, but a page or even a paragraph will often suffice. The author is grateful to everyone who has helped with the book but that doesn't mean *everyone* – not the midwife who delivered them, the primary school teacher who gave Nature lessons, the famous novelist who signed her book for them, etc. 'Thank you to Claire Groden,' Becca Rothfeld writes in the three pages of acknowledgements in her book of essays *All Things Are Too Small*, 'for pressing a tea bag against the roof of my mouth to stanch the bleeding after my disastrous dental surgery.' However lighthearted, is this worth its place? Acknowledgements aren't a roll-call of acquaintances. They're a list of people who genuinely contributed to the book, including those (e.g., librarians and archivists) who helped with research, with no room for cuteness or toadyism. As the travel writer Dea Birkett says, to judge by many acknowledgements pages 'you'll believe a writer's life is characterised by undiluted days of familial and professional joy. Supportive spouses, children who never complain when you don't turn up to sports day, "besties" who reliably "are there for me late at night when I need a shoulder", agents who always answer your calls, editors who turn around proofs in a day . . . ' As if! It's great for an author to have a book coming out but it's not an Oscar ceremony.

Addiction

The expectation is recovery. Addicts don't write mid-snort or mid-bender. They write in the aftermath, as post-addicts, looking back on the occasional joys and repeated degradations (lies, thefts, betrayals and shame) of having been hooked. For the voyeuristic reader, recovery memoirs can't help but end badly because they end well, with the addict restored to health and selfhood. Which is great – except the disease is invariably more compelling to read about than the cure.

Will Self's *Will* intuits that, and though it ends in a rehab clinic called The Lodge, where he has been sent at his mother's expense for rescue from chemical dependency, the book doesn't allow itself, or us, an easy out. He's scornful of his fellow patients, scornful of the staff, and scornful of himself. What finally saves him from heroin addiction is less the treatment or even the fear of killing his mother with grief, but the sudden memory of a fellow user who died young. It's a carefully constructed memoir, beginning with him one morning desperate for a fix ('a snivelling, shitting-his-wack junky, with no money'), then wheeling back through his drug use at school, university and on foreign travels, before returning to the year it began. But the narrative skitters to and fro, resisting smoothness, and the prose is an italic-heavy, high-wire performance, 'a ceaseless and Sisyphean go-round' like addiction. Self isn't even quite Self: he writes in the third person, about a character called

Will, and however autobiographical the story he allows leeway for comic exaggeration.

Leslie Jamison's *The Recovering* is less frenetic but equally exhaustive about the plight of addiction, in her case to alcohol. 'Addiction is a hard story to tell,' she says, 'because addiction is always a story that has already been told', and she's wary of the 'tawdry self-congratulation of a redemption story: It hurt. It got worse. I got better. Who would care. *This is boring!*' To stop the reader's eyes glazing over, she offsets her own over-drinking with analysis of other writers and artists who did the same: Raymond Carver, John Cheever, Billie Holiday, Amy Winehouse, Jean Rhys, John Berryman and many more. She also unapologetically logs her experience of AA, a twelve-step rehabilitation programme in which she firmly believes. Sobriety, she discovers, needn't be a flatline for a writer. The commonality of a first-hand addiction/recovery memoir is precisely what makes it valuable: *I happen to be at the centre of this story, but anyone could be.*

Addicts don't want to know that they are addicts. But when they admit it and, like Self or Jamison, set down their story, they open the door to others, who then feel less alone. The story is shaming and now it's public. Therein lies part of the cure.

Adversity

Where would life writing be without it? We crave happy endings but unless the writer has struggled – with pain, loss, illness, misadventure, risk to life – why read the memoir? A book of ups would be a bore; the downs are more fun. 'Why is the Inferno so much more riveting than the Paradiso?' Margaret Atwood asks in her memoir *Book of Lives*. 'Because when sheep are safely grazing in a field there's not much going on' – but when a wolf appears things get interesting. Even celebs have setbacks. And we've all known heartbreak and disappointment. It's how you get through them that makes the story.

Take Lucy Grealy's *Autobiography of a Face*, which recounts the many treatments and operations she went through, over two decades, after being diagnosed with cancer at the age of 9. The cancer, Ewing's sarcoma, severely disfigured her face and surgery did little to fix the damage. She describes the medical procedures exhaustively, but the greater adversity is being stared at or, worse, being taunted by boys. She puts up a brave defence – 'more often than not I was able to come back with an insult far more sarcastic and biting than their own rather unimaginative Baldy or Dog Girl' – but she can't help but feel ugly and envies what other girls have, not least sex and romance. The epiphany comes at the end, when she accepts that the face in the mirror is hers and that, despite its defects, she's organically whole: 'As a child I had expected my liberation to come from getting a new face to put on, but now I saw it came from shedding something, shedding my image.'

Grealy's adversity is extreme but it's also sharable. You might not have suffered as she did (she eventually died, of a heroin overdose, at 39) but you'll know the feelings she describes: embarrassment, anger, despair, lack of self-esteem. Hardship will always find an audience. It's how well the story is told that counts.

AI

Like the rest of the workforce, writers worry that artificial intelligence will make them redundant. As ChatGPT, Deep-Seek and the rest become more sophisticated, drawing on 'publicly available data' to up their game (i.e., learning from books, sometimes in copyright, by published authors), the day will come when AI produces novels, biographies, translations and perhaps even poems that work perfectly well – that you wouldn't know were written by a bot unless you were told. In 2025, the chief executive of OpenAI, Sam Altman, posted an example of a story created by AI from the simple prompt he'd given: 'Please write a metafictional short story about AI and grief.' Writing in the *Guardian*, Jeanette Winterson hailed the story as 'beautiful and moving'. Others pointed out that a phrase in the story, 'democracy of ghosts', had been swiped from Vladimir Nabokov's novel *Pnin*.

Writers have another reason for feeling hostile to AI: Meta (the company that owns Facebook, Instagram and WhatsApp) has allegedly used a pirated version of the data library LibGen, made up of 7.5 million books and 81 million research papers, many still in copyright, in order to train its AI model Llama. Authors are rightly angry that they're being used in this way and in the UK they have lobbied the government for change. Yes, would-be authors learn from reading published authors, why shouldn't AI do the same? Because AI doesn't buy books and authors earn nothing for the service. (As I write, the September 2025 settlement of the Bartz v. Anthropic copyright lawsuit does promise financial compensation for authors whose books have been used but there's still a long way to go.)

AI does have its uses. Unsure about the title for a book of poems, I asked ChatGPT for suggestions. Within half a second of me emailing the book as an attachment, it came back with six titles that showed every sign of it having read the poems. I asked for more suggestions and one of them, which caught the mood of the collection, greatly appealed – until it emerged that a memoir with virtually the same title had come out the previous year. AI can't always be trusted. In 2025, two US newspapers used it to recommend forthcoming books. Several of those it chose, by Maggie O'Farrell, Percival Everett and Isabel Allende, didn't exist.

Memoir, at least, is safe from AI, which can't speak authentically, in the first person, as an embodied human being. Memoir tells the truth about a real life. And AI isn't alive. It can affect to reproduce human emotions – love, hatred, passion, intimacy, sorrow – but it remains a data-processing problem-solver, not a living person. Sure, AI can invent a plot with people in it but that will be fiction, not memoir. It can record and analyse events that took place but that will be history, not memoir. There won't be an authentic expression of a real life in real time and real place as documented by real human beings on their own behalf.

When AI takes over literature, memoir will be the last genre standing.

Anonymity

Anon has produced more books than any other author. And there have been some classics: *Beowulf, One Thousand and One Nights, The Epic of Gilgamesh, Sir Gawain and the Green Knight*. But Anon has been less productive in modern times. Authors crave recognition and you can't make a name for yourself if you're anonymous.

There have been a few recent exceptions in life writing – memoirs by people whose careers would be jeopardised if their names were made public. Hence *The Secret Footballer, The Secret Barrister* and *The Secret Lecturer* – tales from the dressing room, robing room and seminar room. Workplaces are fascinating but a mystery to outsiders. These pro-cons (professional confessionals) take us behind the scenes. Often the author is a whistleblower hidden behind a pseudonym or a Secret. For civil servants, BBC employees, police officers and social workers, among others, writing candidly about their job and keeping it are usually incompatible. The avoidance of embarrassment is another factor: Gillian Anderson's book *Want*, subtitled 'Sexual Fantasies by Anonymous', collects confessions by women from around the world about what turns them on – they're able to be candid because unnamed.

As well as anonymity, there's pseudonymity. One of the greatest living novelists is a pseudonym: Elena Ferrante. (After it emerged in 2016 that large sums of money had been paid by Ferrante's publisher to the translator Anita Raja, she became the prime suspect, till research via authorship attribution models suggested that Domenico Starnone, Raja's husband, was as likely a candidate. One day the truth will emerge but for now I'd rather not know – let 'Ferrante' enjoy their privacy.) Further back, in life writing, there's W. N. P. Barbellion's *The Journal of a Disappointed Man*. The 'true' author of the book, a tall, skeletal entomologist in his twenties called Bruce Frederick Cummings, took the name Barbellion from a pastry shop on London's Gloucester Road, and the accompanying initials from 'the three most wretched figures in history': Kaiser Wilhelm, the Emperor Nero and Pontius Pilate. The alias gave him the freedom to be intimate – to publish 'whatever is inexorably true, however unpleasant and discreditable'. Writing as himself, he'd have given less away. And his choice of three initials was no accident: he considered himself 'a triple personality' – naturalist, man of letters and lover – all three of them pitted against a common enemy: premature death from multiple sclerosis.

More often, anonymity in life writing will apply not to the author but to one or more of the protagonists, whose privacy is protected with an initial or invented name. Sometimes the people in question will have requested or demanded this; at other times, out of kindness or fear of libel, the author or publisher will have done it voluntarily. In her published diaries, Helen Garner uses the initials M for her daughter Alice, V for her third husband Murray Bail, and F, K, L, G, B, P and R for significant others; Rachel Cusk does something similar in her divorce memoir *Aftermath*, calling her ex-husband and lover X and Y. With books by doctors or psychiatrists, there's the Hippocratic oath factor as well – the obligation to protect clients' identity. Pseudonymity is one way to do this; another is the invented composite case study based on two or more real ones (see, for example, Henry Marsh's *Do No Harm* and Susie Orbach's *The Impossibility of Sex*).

One happy story of namelessness gaining a name comes in Alexander Masters's *A Life Discarded*, a book based on 148 diaries (and five million words) found in a skip in Cambridge. When he began reading the diaries he assumed the anonymous author was dead; the book is as much about his search to find out who she was as about the diaries. When, after five years, he tracked down her name and found she was still alive, he wanted to know if she'd let him publish the story: 'It must be a rule of writing biographies about unknown people that the subject agrees to everything you have put down.' As it turned out, the woman – Laura Francis (b. 1939) – proved surprisingly amenable to Masters, 'as if she had been expecting me all along'. Her life discarded became a life preserved.

Naming names, in that case, was a noble cause. But authors do sometimes have to compromise, especially in a personal memoir. How important is it to identify the teacher who bullied you, the friend who betrayed you, the lover who slept with your sister? Real names will carry a charge for the author but not necessarily for the reader, and it can be fun inventing better ones. A student of mine spent twelve years in an unhappy marriage. Cain, the name she gave her husband, is more evocative than his real one.

Apology

An apology is one thing, an apologia another. In the nineteenth century, John Henry Newman published his *Apologia Pro Vita Sua*, a defence of his life, in response to an attack by Charles Kingsley, who questioned his honesty and disapproved of his conversion to Catholicism. Many memoirs are reputation-saving apologias – not just those with a religious or moral agenda, like the confessions of St Augustine or Rousseau, but those driven by self-justification, often late in life. Apologies are different; the message isn't *I've been maligned and misunderstood* but *I'm sorry for my errors and misdeeds*.

These forgive-me memoirs are often written by grown-up children, who belatedly recognise that the mother or father they didn't get on with had good reason for behaving as they did. I wrote the memoir *Things My Mother Never Told Me* to understand why Mum had been such an enigma. Made aware, after her death, that she'd been the nineteenth of twenty children, and had changed her name, and denied her Irish-Catholic identity, I felt sorry for her where before I'd been mystified and frustrated. 'I wish I had known years ago what I know about her now,' Mary Loudon writes about her sister Catherine in *Relative Stranger: A Life after Death*. John Lanchester expresses similar regret in *Family Romance* – 'I don't think I was ever fully there for my mother' – while allowing that it couldn't be helped: in concealing her years as a nun and shaving ten years off her age, his mother 'was never fully present herself'.

In these and other memoirs, apology and apologia, no matter how different, begin to merge. In their grief, the authors blame themselves for not doing more for the person they've lost. But they also emphasise the lies and secrecy they were up against. Atonement and exculpation join hands.

Appropriation

'We should all be free to write about whatever we like,' Bernardine Evaristo has said. 'I give myself complete artistic licence to write from multiple perspectives and to inhabit different cultures across the perceived barriers of race, culture, gender, age and sexuality.' I'm with her on that. To get beyond ourselves by inhabiting the minds of others and seeing the world as they see it is a fundamental human need. It's empathy. And if writers aren't allowed to empathise they might as well give up.

Still, artistic licence has become a sensitive issue. There's a feeling that writers should stay in their lane; as Kit de Waal has put it, 'Do not dip your pen in somebody else's blood.' A book by a white writer narrated in the voice of a Black person, Asian person or any person of colour won't necessarily fail to find a publisher or, if it does, be panned by readers and reviewers. But it will have to do everything a book should do exceptionally well: convince, delight, offer understanding and insight. Jeanine Cummins agonised about her novel *American Dirt*: 'I worried that, as a non-migrant and non-Mexican, I had no business writing a book set almost entirely in Mexico, set entirely among migrants. I wished someone slightly browner than me would write it. But then, I thought, *If you're a person who has the capacity to be a bridge, why not be a bridge?*' I take her point. But what's permissible shouldn't be as stark an issue as ethnicity-matching (or gender-matching and age-matching). The issue is aesthetic as well as ethical. How good is the book? How well researched, how well constructed, how well written? Is it a bridge or a broken jetty?

Appropriation is an even hotter debate in life writing, where it's less to do with writing from the perspective of someone from a different race or culture than with representing (or misrepresenting) someone closer to home. How far can you go in using the lives of friends, lovers, colleagues and family? Are you prepared for them to rage at you and say they can't forgive you? Will you use words they've spoken or written? Will your right to write trump theirs to privacy? My usual advice to writers I've mentored (most of them conscious of the sensitivities involved) has been to stand firm: there's no sin in honesty; don't be afraid of having your say; while the offence you cause will pass, your book will remain. But however honest you are, even more so when you're *really* honest, you may be accused of betraying your tribe.

Perhaps the most famous example of late-twentieth century appropriation came with Robert Lowell's poetry collection *The Dolphin*, which drew on letters sent to him by the wife he'd recently left, Elizabeth Hardwick, without her permission; in a letter to their friend Elizabeth Bishop she called the collection 'inane, empty, unnecessary'. Justifying his action to Bishop, Lowell said, 'I couldn't bear to have my book (my life) wait hidden inside me like a dead child.' Bishop was having none of it. Sent the book in draft, she pleaded with him to reconsider: 'Lizzie is not dead . . . and you have *changed* her letters. That is "infinite mischief," I think . . . One can use one's life as material – one does, anyway – but these letters – aren't you violating a trust? . . . *Art just isn't worth that much.*'

It's a brilliant line. (Was Lowell tempted to steal it too?) And I like to think that in Bishop's place I'd have said the same – that art isn't worth that much; that Lowell's rapacity went too far. W. G. Sebald was rapacious too, upsetting the family of Philip Rhoades Buckton (in whose house he and his wife were lodgers for a time) when he used Buckton as a model for Dr Henry Selwyn in *The Emigrants*. Sebald's admirers argue that as an autofictionalist he'd the right to embroider (and steal) as freely as he wished. Still, he was obviously conscious of behaving badly: when asked whether he sought permission from the people he wrote about, he lied that he did so *on principle* – showed them what he'd written in advance and if they objected didn't publish. In reality he took stuff without permission, held his nerve and hoped for the best.

Sebald died before controversy arose over his appropriations. Today a life writer as ruthless can expect a lot more trouble.

Art

Can life writing be art or will it always be considered a lower literary form than fiction and poetry? The memoir is a disreputable genre, Angela Carter said, because it uses 'the narrative mode of a good deal of downmarket women's magazine fiction'. That sub-literary-ness might seem to count against it but Carter approved. Annie Ernaux does too: 'This book can be seen as a literary venture,' she says of her memoir *A Woman's Story*, 'And yet in a sense I would like to remain a cut below literature.' *A cut below* rather than a cut above: the memoir as transgressive rather than a failure of the imagination.

In truth, life writers depend on the same methods as novelists: narrative, characterisation, structure, theme, voice and so on. The need to be believed seems to set them apart, but the authors of realist novels have the same aspiration. In short, a well-constructed biography or incisive lyric essay has as much right to be called art as any novel or poem. And the idea that a memoir is simpler to write than a novel because it is based on real events is rubbish. As Joyce Carol Oates has said, a memoir isn't journalism or history, supplying 'a verifiable, corroborative truth', it is a literary text, consisting of words that have been 'artfully arranged'. We might read it in a way we don't read fiction, with authenticity more of a consideration than artistry, but the two are indivisible. Truth in life doesn't automatically morph into truth on the page. And living people don't necessarily come to life in print. It takes creativity – hence the term 'creative non-fiction'.

Still, Annie Ernaux has a point: for a memoir to impale the reader with its truth, it may have to avoid looking too literary. The challenge is to look artless while achieving artistic perfection. 'Memoir done right is an art,' Mary Karr says. You just have to do it right.

Augustine, Saint

He's the paterfamilias of life writing, the daddy of every confessional poet and memoir writer. Unlike most saints, Augustine (AD 354–430) also fathered a *real* child, Adeodatus, whose mother had been his lover for many years. Augustine's *Confessions* are a sustained self-scourging, a humble apology to God for all the sins he committed before seeing the light and converting to Christianity. He's hard on himself, *too* hard. Most of his sins require little atonement.

Sin 1: Crying as a baby. He has no memory of doing so but he knows he must have done and 'It can hardly be right for a child, even at that age, to cry for everything.'

Sin 2: Enjoying the stories of Dido and Aeneas rather than maths or scripture lessons ('it was wrong of me as a boy to prefer empty romances to more valuable studies . . . I squandered the brains you gave me on foolish delusions.').

Sin 3: Stripping a tree of its pears one night with a gang of friends ('Perhaps we ate some of them, but our real pleasure consisted in doing something that was forbidden.').

Sin 4: Falling in love ('My love was returned and finally shackled me in the bonds of its consummation.').

Sin 5: Going to the theatre and being moved by the imaginary sorrows of the characters onstage.

Sin 6: Being distracted by nature when his thoughts should have been focused on God alone.

And so on: love of food, pride in his skills as a public speaker, admiration for scientists and philosophers – there's no end to his self-berating. Meanwhile the God who hears him out and before whom he prostrates himself comes across as a bully ('you broke my bones with the rod of your discipline') and control freak ('The less you allowed me to find pleasure in anything that was not yourself, the greater, I know, was your goodness to me.').

St Augustine sets the pattern for memoirists to record a history of suffering or wrong-doing in order to purge themselves and offer a warning to others. Such narrators are always more compelling when documenting their misdeeds than when advertising their redemption. Too often, though, they leave the reader feeling cheated, because the sins they own up to *don't really seem that bad.* Stealing pears, enjoying plays, loving nature and wanting sex – pah!

The moral for life writers is: if you're going to adopt a confessional tone, make sure you do it justice and confess the worst. There's no point in recalling minor misdemeanours. Readers won't be interested. They won't believe you're levelling with them, either. Julie Burchill once laid into a memoir by Nick Johnstone, *A Head Full of Blue*, about his drinking problem: 'Excuse me! He stopped drinking at 24; that's not an alcoholic, that's a wuss.'

Autofiction

Autobiographical fiction has a long history: D. H. Lawrence's *Sons and Lovers* is more than a century old. Is autofiction just a snazzier name for the same genre? At worst, yes: it's a lazy catch-all term for fiction closely based on the author's own experiences. But at best, no: it denotes a specific literary form, one that's written in the first person, seemingly from the author's point of view, but which has fun blurring the line between truth and fiction. Where memoirists own the truth, autofictionalists question whether the truth matters or even exists.

Most autobiographical novels are memoirs that dare not speak their name. As Annie Ernaux says, many memoirs remain unpublished, 'except in the form of a novel, which succeeds in saving appearances'. Rather than saving appearances, autofiction advertises them. The author is there, in name, and the struggles of authorship are often there too. But there's distance – an avoidance of candid truth-telling. How much of what Rachel Cusk records in her autofictional trilogy, *Outline*, *Transit* and *Kudos*, is based on stuff that she went through or observed? We don't know. But it's a tremendous sequence.

There's little consensus on the definition of autofiction. Perhaps what Thomas Hardy called 'the mixing of fact and fiction in unknown proportions' comes closest. Hardy disapproved of the 'infinite mischief' of the method; 'If any statements in the dress of fiction are covertly hinted to be fact, all must be fact, and nothing else but fact.' But as practised by Cusk, Geoff Dyer, Chris Kraus, W. G. Sebald, Karl Ove Knausgaard, Olivia Laing and Sheila Heti, autofiction has flourished.

Dyer's story 'White Sands', the title piece of a 2016 collection of 'experiences from the outside world', is a case in point. It's prefaced by a short piece of italicised autobiography, as if to suggest that, like most of the other pieces in the book, it's non-fiction. It's set in a car, on Highway 54, en route to El Paso, a journey the narrator is taking with his wife, though her name is Jessica, whereas Dyer's wife's name is Rebecca. The pair pick up a Black hitchhiker, then almost immediately notice a road sign warning 'DO NOT PICK UP HITCHHIKERS / DETENTION FACILITIES IN THE AREA', after which their mood changes from relaxation to paranoia – might he be an escaped convict, even a murderer? When they stop at a gas station and the hitchhiker goes inside to take a leak, the narrator promises him that they won't drive off ('I swear'). You know they will drive off; that because they don't trust the man they picked up, they're lying to him. Trust is the point of the story: you trust that Dyer and his wife drove past that warning roadsign one day, but you're sceptical about the rest. It's autofiction (because it all takes place in a car, doubly so).

There are parts of the world that don't recognise any real division between novels and memoirs: they're all stories, what's the difference? And the teasing, vicarious appeal of autofiction is that, no matter how hard we comb the text and paratext for clues, we don't know what the author personally experienced. If James Frey had published his *A Million Little Pieces* as autofiction, he would not have been pilloried by Oprah Winfrey for taking liberties with the truth. Memoir is different, though:

its claim is that everything it reports did happen – that nothing is knowingly untrue. For the sake of readability, scenes may have been switched round, characters conflated and dialogue approximated rather than meticulously recalled. Readers can live with that. And they know that memory is unreliable and subjectivity unavoidable. But unwitting misremembering is not the same as conscious falsification. Therein lies the difference between memoir and autofiction.

Automatic writing

'I've just come back from India,' I said, when the *Guardian* called one day, inviting me to attempt some automatic writing. 'I'm jet-lagged and spaced out.' 'Perfect,' the editor said. 'You're supposed to do it in a sort of trance anyway.'

Doubtful, I begged for more time. But automatic writing, from which the surrealist movement grew, sidesteps conscious thought: unless I got going right away, I'd start mentally preparing the piece. So I sat down and wrote for about forty minutes. 'Whose are the dreams?' I began. 'A scritch-scratch at the side-window. The car stalled under the flyover where a baby sleeps on a blanket and mother scrabbles for lunch . . . Back home, thousands of miles away, a bird feeder sways in the breeze outside my window. Seeds, nuts, grain, husks, enough to fill the stomach of a child . . ..'

There was a lot more, as bad or worse – I'll spare you. What was the process like? Fun while it lasted, less so when I came to read the results. The surrealists saw automatic writing as a divining rod, or as a pipe to tap the id or collective unconscious. But for me, what came up were recent memories or immediate sense-impressions: an episode the previous day in India, or the view from my desk, rather than thoughts too deep for tears. André Breton believed that automatic writing purged the text of inhibition; its seeming randomness was to be celebrated, as an expression of the 'true' functioning of thought. But to my eyes, a poem such as Breton's 'Soluble Fish' looks suspiciously rational and well-made, orderly in its syntax and lucid in what it imagines. That's the case with many surrealist works: their apparent illogic is oddly coherent, their subversiveness pleasing on the eye, and it's this that makes them enjoyable.

Where automatic writing does have value is as a limbering-up routine. Authors can use it to clear their head and get in a groove. Or limber up by giving themselves a theme, such as might be imposed if they were a student in a workshop. That's not quite automatic: limits of subject matter have been set. But the writing is spontaneous. And, no matter how rough, it's there to return to later, to be developed.

Automatic writing is like walking around in your underwear. An audience deserves something less dishevelled.

B

Bearing witness

Testimony is often the starting point for life writing: the author was there. And false testimony is the death of life writing: if you weren't there, you shouldn't pretend you were. Where what you saw or went through has a historical significance, then bearing witness is crucially important: you've the authority to say what happened.

George Orwell's 'A Hanging', his account of an execution that took place during his time as a policeman in Burma, is a brilliant piece of life writing because it puts us there beside him at the scene. We see what he sees: the 'sickly' morning light 'like yellow tinfoil', the condemned man with a moustache 'absurdly too big for his body', the warders nervously crowding round him 'like men handling a fish which is still alive and may jump back into the water'. The vivid description enforces the moral conclusions he draws. His witnessing is a form of thinking aloud. (See ORWELL for more on him.)

Small and surprising details are what count – the stuff no one would think of unless they were there. In Primo Levi's *If This Is a Man*, which recounts his time in Auschwitz, it's shoes: 'Death begins with shoes,' he says – if they fit badly, and you trudge around in them every day, your feet will develop sores, and once the sores become infected, and you're sent to the infirmary, your chances of survival are poor, 'because it is well known to all, and especially to the SS, that there is no cure for that complaint'.

When his book came out, Levi was attacked on one side for dwelling on the past (the war was over, the camps had been liberated, it was time to move on) and on the other for failing to present a tale of heroic, companionable survival – for revealing, for example, how when anyone went to the washroom in Auschwitz they had to hold their clothes tightly between their knees while they washed, otherwise the clothes would be stolen; and for admitting he himself was guilty of stealing ('if I find a spoon lying around, a piece of string, a button . . . I pocket them and consider them mine'). Levi was another life writer initially patronised for being sub-literary. But his simple prose is perfect for the task in hand – to bear witness to the worst genocide of the twentieth century.

You've probably not observed a hanging or spent time in a concentration camp. But there will be experiences you've been through and events you've seen that are exceptional, no matter how rooted in everyday life. And there may be an emotional or psychological need to write about them, painful though that may be. Orwell and Levi are examples of how to do it. They put us there. They watch and report. And they search out the detail that authenticates what they describe.

Beginnings

'If the book we're reading doesn't wake us up with a blow to the head,' Franz Kafka wrote, 'what are we reading it for?'

The opening of a book may not be as violent as a blow to the head but it does need to grab the reader – to seize attention, as Horace advised with his phrase in *Ars Poetica* 'in media res' (*He always hastens to the matter and hurries his listeners into the midst of things as if they knew it before*) and as Coleridge's Ancient Mariner does when he forces his tale to be heard:

> He holds him with his glittering eye –
> The Wedding-Guest stood still,
> And listens like a three years' child:
> The Mariner hath his will.

The best writers hold you with their glittering eye from the first sentence. Laurence Sterne's *Tristram Shandy*, Charles Dickens's *David Copperfield*, Leo Tolstoy's *Anna Karenina*, J. D. Salinger's *Catcher in the Rye*, Daphne du Maurier's *Rebecca*, Sylvia Plath's *The Bell Jar*, Anthony Burgess's *Earthly Powers*: all have memorable opening sentences, in Burgess's case – 'It was the afternoon of my eighty-first birthday, and I was in bed with my catamite when Ali announced that the archbishop had come to see me.' – more memorable than anything that follows. The priority isn't concision (Sterne and Salinger's opening sentences run on) or quotability. It's to set the tone for what follows – and compel the reader to read on.

Memoirs can be equally adept with first sentences. Among examples that come to mind are Hannah Lowe's *Long Time No See* ('The boy was ten when he discovered his mother had sold him, but by then he hadn't seen her in a year.') and Mary Loudon's *Relative Stranger*: 'On the twenty-seventh of January 2001, while I was skiing fast down a mountain in France, my sister, Catherine, was dying slowly in England, in a hospital I didn't know she had been admitted to, from a cancer I didn't know she had, under an identity I had no idea existed.'

A good example of how *not* to begin a book is Dan Brown's *The Da Vinci Code*. Its clipped US-news-speak, clunky release of information, and pile-up of predictable action verbs are an object lesson in ineptitude, which didn't prevent Brown's novel from becoming an international bestseller (and may even have helped). (If you want to write a bestseller, this novel may, after all, be useful for you to read.) (If you want to write a bestseller, life writing may be the wrong genre.) (But if all you're after is money and fame, then writing isn't how to go about it anyway.)

Brown's instincts are right: what we need from the opening of a book is *who, what, when* and *where* – with the *why* reserved for later. But he crams in too much at once.

By contrast, there's Tobias Wolff's *This Boy's Life*:

> Our car boiled over again after my mother and I crossed the Continental Divide. While we were waiting for it to cool we heard, from somewhere above us, the bawling of an airhorn. The sound got louder and then a big truck shot past us into the next curve, its trailer shimmying wildly. We stared after it. 'Oh, Toby,' my mother said, 'he's lost his brakes.'

What do we learn from the opening? On the face of it not much: that a mother and son are on a car journey across the US. But we read a fair bit between the lines: that the book is a memoir (Toby is the shortened form of Tobias); that the journey has been long and the car is iffy (the word 'again' in the first sentence does a lot of work); that the mother's remark 'he's lost his brakes' means Toby is a child (why else would she need to explain it?). The scene is dramatic – it becomes clear straight afterwards that the driver must have died – and though the two of them are observers not participants, the accident feels ominous, a hint of trouble for them further ahead. The next couple of paragraphs give us the essential facts. It's 1955 and Toby's mother is driving from Florida to Utah to get away from a man she's afraid of. Within a page we have the who, where, when, what and why. But it's done so subtly that we barely notice how much information we're being fed.

Wolff reconstructs the scene from the perspective and psyche of a ten-year-old. The language isn't that of a child: the 'shimmying' of the trailer and (as Wolff writes just afterwards) the 'feathering' of smoke from the crashed truck are the words of the adult writer, whose prose has the texture of poetry. But only a ten-year-old would milk the occasion as Toby does: seeing that his mother's guard is down after the accident, he realises 'that the time was right to make a play for souvenirs . . . I couldn't help myself. When we pulled out of Grand Junction I owned a beaded Indian belt, beaded moccasins, and a bronze horse with a removable, tooled-leather saddle.' A lesser writer would have botched the scene with melodrama; Wolff ends it with humour. The tone is set: darkness and light. We know we're in good hands.

A memoir can't hit the reader with everything at once. It doesn't even need to start with a major episode from the central narrative. But it does have to draw us in, establish a voice and hint at what's to come.

Bestsellers

Word of mouth sometimes enables a memoir by a non-famous writer to become a bestseller; prizes help too. Lea Ypi's first book *Free*, about growing up in Albania, sold 10,000 copies in a month in the UK, an unlikely hit. But only celebs achieve mega commercial success. Non-fiction charts feature recipe and health books more than they do life writing. But rock stars, actors and comedians are sometimes there too, looking back on long careers – household names putting their house in order.

Strikingly, two of the biggest commercial successes in recent years aren't reminiscence so much as self-advocacy – books with an agenda. The title of Britney Spears's *The Woman in Me* says as much: the agenda is to present herself as mature, independent and perfectly capable of taking care of herself, after long years of being coerced by her father, who took out a conservatorship to control her. She became, she says, 'a sort of child-robot. I had been so infantilized that I was losing pieces of what made me feel like myself.' In the book she reclaims herself and reaches beyond her fan-base.

Prince Harry's *Spare* has an agenda too: to explain why Harry and his wife Meghan needed to escape the royal family and hostile British tabloids by starting a new life elsewhere, at the cost (in his view unfairly) of being deprived of security and service on behalf of the Crown. The portrait of the late Queen is affectionate but Harry's father Charles and even more so his brother William come over badly. It's to them, as much as the British public, that he sets out to explain himself:

> *Willy, this was supposed to be our home. We were going to live there the rest of our lives.*
> *You left, Harold.*
> *Yeah – and you know why.*
> *I don't.*
> *You... don't?*
> *I honestly don't...*

I turned to Pa. He was gazing at me with an expression that said: *Neither do I* . . .
I thought: *I have to tell them.*

Unless you're a prince or a queen of pop, you're unlikely to write a bestseller. Not to worry. All that matters is that you write well.

Biography

Brits may be bad at living but we excel at Lives, and it's arguable that the last forty years have been a heyday of biography; literary biography especially, with Michael Holroyd, Hermione Lee, Claire Tomalin, Richard Holmes, Carole Angier, Victoria Glendinning, Peter Ackroyd, Roy Foster, Frances Wilson, Zachary Leader and Jenny Uglow among those leading the way. But literary culture is changing. The era of stellar advances has passed: no biographer today would receive the generous advance Holroyd received in the 1980s for his book on George Bernard Shaw. The era of massive 900-page-plus Lives is passing too: just as cradle-to-grave autobiographies became unfashionable, so big chronologically structured biographies are in decline. There's a pressure, whether editor- or self-imposed, to find other ways of constructing a Life, not least thematically. Dead White Males still predominate. But significant others – those in the shadows or under the sheets – are getting their due. Philip Larkin's companion Monica Jones never published a word but was the subject of a biography by John Sutherland. Women, especially, are being rescued from neglect, especially when, as with Picasso's wives and lovers, they're the victims of misogyny and haven't been given their due.

There's a particularly thriving genre of Them-and-Me biography, where authors insert themselves into the story, playing off their own life against the life of their subject. Nicholson Baker's *U and I*, about John Updike, was one of the first. More recently there have been Azar Nafisi's *Reading Lolita in Tehran*, Nell Stevens's *Mrs Gaskell and Me*, Rebecca Mead's *My Life in Middlemarch* and Lara Feigel's books about Doris Lessing and D. H. Lawrence, which test her own ideas and experiences alongside theirs. Unlike Naomi Wood's novel *Mrs. Hemingway* (about Hemingway's four wives) these books aren't bio-fic. They're bio-non-fic. Bio-auto even.

Where the engagement is intimate and passionate, then the approach works well. Stevens's book describes herself having a crush on an American while speculating on the novelist doing the same; the stories of 'you' (Mrs Gaskell) and 'I' (Nell Stevens) interlock. The risk is self-importance and solipsistic inconsequentiality. 'I know I'm out of step here with current biographical preferences,' Hermione Lee has said, 'but I'm not a biographer who chooses to put themselves in all the way through, or to go on about how I came to find my subject and what they mean to me and how they've changed my life. I don't think biography is the same thing as autobiography.'

Other quasi-biographies follow in the footsteps of famous writers in order to explore the landscape they immortalised – a genre Richard Holmes helped pioneer and which others have followed, not least Nicholas Hunt, who retraces the steps of Patrick Leigh Fermor, from the Hook of Holland to the Golden Horn, in *Walking the Woods and the Water*. A different kind of journey is taken in *Ellmann's Joyce*, where Zachary Leader traces the extraordinary efforts made by Richard Ellmann in putting together his Life of James Joyce. It's a biographer's biography of a biographer but not in the least niche.

'It's always Judas who writes the biography,' Oscar Wilde said, and there's an idea that any Life will be diabolically hostile – as, for example, Roger Lewis's biography of Anthony Burgess was: the chronicler as biogra-fiend, not biogra-friend. 'Attention all Morrisons,' John Crace once wrote in the *Guardian*, 'if you value your privacy, don't even think of dying before Blake.' It's a good joke and there's material in my books about Dad, Mum and my sister Gill that they'd dislike. But a biography can tell the truth and still be affectionate. Commemorative, too, saving the subject from the oblivion gravely summarised in Ecclesiasticus, 44:9: 'And some there be, which have no memorial; who are perished, as though they had never been; and are become as though they had never been born.'

Bossiness

Keats hated poetry that has a palpable design on us. And it's the same with life writing, which is a story, not a harangue from a soapbox. Rather than lecture, authors should let description, dialogue and anecdote carry the message. The risk with pushing an agenda is that you win nobody round (they dismiss you as a bossy-boots) and alienate even those on your side (who feel they've heard it all before). It's better to make room for antagonists or enemies in the text. For there to be conflict. And for authors to send themselves up as uncertain, divided or even unhinged. Then readers feel invited in, not crowded out. We're onside rather than being pushed away by a didact. (See MISSION for more on this.)

W. B. Yeats said it well in his essay collection *The Cutting of an Agate*: 'Only that which does not teach, which does not cry out, which does not condescend, which does not explain, is irresistible.'

Brainard, Joe

Born in 1941 and raised in Oklahoma, Brainard moved to New York as a young man and made a career as a painter, doing set designs for the theatre and mixing with men associated with the New York School, including John Ashbery and Frank O'Hara. He died in 1994. His lasting achievement is less his visual work than his little book *I Remember* and its sequels. The Brainard method couldn't be simpler: single-sentence snapshots from the past, each beginning with the words 'I Remember'. There's no narrative progression and the memories are mostly unconnected. But they're strangely affecting – funny, poignant, fascinating in their recall of the manners and mishaps of his youth.

> I remember fantasies of finding notes in old bottles washed ashore.
> I remember magic carpets and giant 'genies' and trying to figure out what my three wishes would be.
> I remember not understanding why Cinderella didn't just pack up and leave, if things were really all *that* bad.
> I remember getting a car door slammed on my finger once, and how long it took for the pain to come.
> I remember wondering if goats really *do* eat tin cans.
> I remember the fear of 'horror' coming out of my mouth as 'whore', as indeed it quite often did.
> I remember rocks you pick up outside that, once inside, you wonder why.

ON MEMOIR

> I remember hearing once about a boy who found a dead fly in his Coke and so the Coca-Cola company gave him a free case of Cokes.
> I remember thinking how easy it would be to get a free case of Cokes by putting a dead fly in your Coke and I remember wondering why more people didn't do that.

And so on for 150 pages. Brainard thought that his book was 'as much about everyone else as it is about me', and that's part of its success. It doesn't matter if you weren't around when he was – so much is recognisable.

I've sometimes tried the method for myself. It's amazing how much the mantra 'I remember' will release – stuff that you've no memory of till you write the magic words. Brainard's method is a one-off. But stripped of the prefix, the compilation of remembered fragments can enrich and deepen a memoir. Poetry too – here is Ted Hughes in his poem 'Daffodils', about life in Devon with Sylvia Plath:

> Remember how we picked the daffodils?
> Nobody else remembers, but I remember.
> Your daughter came with her armfuls, eager and happy,
> Helping the harvest. She has forgotten.
> She cannot even remember you . . .

C

Cancellation

Cancellation usually refers to a public backlash or social media furore after an author has been accused of offensive behaviour. In some cases, notably that of Kate Clanchy (see CHILDREN), an author may also be also dropped by publishers, literary festivals, libraries and even agents for writing or saying something deemed impermissible. If they encourage rioting, murder or paedophilia, fair enough. But on most issues, let them have their say. That's the basis of free speech. You can argue with them when they're onstage or take issue with them in print or on social media. You can cancel them privately by not buying their book. But don't silence them publicly just because you disagree. 'Cancel culture is bad,' Chimamanda Ngozi Adichie said in a *Guardian* interview. 'We should stop it. End of story.'

Would I want an overtly racist, climate-change-denying or Holocaust-sceptic book to be published? No. And it probably wouldn't be by a serious publisher – its reasoning would be specious and its use of trustworthy sources non-existent. But I wouldn't want a memoir to be cancelled because I dislike the author or their views. I'm ideologically miles apart from Lionel

Shriver but enjoy her humour. And if J. K. Rowling ever publishes a memoir, I'll want to read it.

Cancellation has become more common in recent years. In 2008 I published a novel, *South of the River*, in which one of the five characters, Harry, a young male journalist in south London, is Black. I wrote from his point of view, as I did with the other characters, who are white. Fearful of Black stereotypes, I worked hard to avoid them (drawing on Black friends and the Black newspaper *The Voice* as support), and I don't recall any complaints that it was wrong for a white writer to employ – appropriate – a Black voice. Still I wonder if I'd get away with it now. Whether the book, or Harry, wouldn't be cancelled.

Worst of all, because they're blatant censorship, are library cancellations, especially in the US, where requests for book bans (mostly from pressure groups) rose from an average of 46 titles a year between 2001 and 2020 to 4,190 titles in a single year, 2024. From July 2021 to December 2023, the state of Florida imposed 3,135 book bans, mostly in school libraries and mostly on books that mention, if only in passing, sexual experience, gender identity or race. Any parent in Florida can make innumerable requests for books to be removed (non-parents are limited to one such request per month). The case for such a ban isn't inflammatory speech or licentious authorial behaviour but the inclusion of material that conservatives find uncomfortable. Among the authors banned have been Leo Tolstoy, Ernest Hemingway, Margaret Atwood, Kurt Vonnegut and Toni Morrison. Absurd!

It's not great in the UK either. A 2022 survey found that 26 per cent of school librarians had been asked to censor materials. And in 2024, Index on Censorship reported that of 53 school librarians they consulted, half had been asked to remove books from shelves. Almost all those books had LGBTQ+ content.

As well as going cold on authors accused of serious misconduct (e.g., Neil Gaiman, David Walliams or Blake Bailey), today's publishers employ sensitivity readers to check a text for appropriateness. These pre-readers are often derided. But Hamza Jahanzeb, who is one, defends their role: 'we are not wielding pitchforks,' he says, rather 'we offer honest feedback when we can see lazy tropes or stereotyped characters.' Fair enough: an author can benefit from their intervention, so as not to come over as crass or out of touch. Nevertheless, some gagging does go on.

Memoir writers ought not to be cowed, however challenging their material. If violence and misogyny are part of your story, they should stand. Their presence doesn't mean you're endorsing them – readers will get that and so will publishers. What if an author is recalling an episode when they were racially abused and the n-word was used against them? Author and editor will have to decide. But there's a good case for having the word in full – to be discussed, contextualised and learned from rather than erased.

Candour

'I speak from the grave,' Mark Twain says in his posthumous autobiography, 'for a good reason: I can thence speak freely. When a man is writing a book dealing with the privacies of his life – a book which is to be read while he is still alive – he shrinks from speaking his whole frank mind.' Mostly dictated in his last years, the *Autobiography of Mark Twain* is free of shocking revelations. But he held it back till after he died because he felt he could then be more honest. George Bernard Shaw took a similar line: 'No man is bad enough to tell the truth about himself during his lifetime, involving as it must the truth about his family and friends and colleagues.' Life writing from beyond the grave is an option. But where's the fun in it? Most authors want to be around when their books come out. And despite what Twain says, the more they speak with a 'whole frank mind', the better their writing will be.

There's an idea that candour is an act of hostility – that to write honestly about people is to demean and violate them. But candour can be celebratory. Be brave, I've urged life writing students terrified by what their ex will think, or their siblings, or their grouchy uncle: get that monkey off your back and stop that snake creeping over your shoulder; it's your version of events and if people object, never mind – they can always tell it their way. That's what happened in the McCourt family: after Frank wrote *Angela's Ashes*, his brothers Alphie and Malachy published memoirs too.

It's not just the fear of upsetting family members that makes candour hard. It's conquering the censor inside you who shrinks from writing the very stuff you need to write. As Deborah Levy puts it: 'It's hard to write and be open and let things in when life is tough but to keep everything out means there's nothing to work with.'

Candour takes art: what works as an anecdote told in the pub probably won't work on the page. It needs compression, structure, the right tone of voice. 'The chore for the memoir writer,' Richard Ford says, 'is to compose a shape and economy that gives faithful, reliable, if sometimes drastic coherence to the many unequal things any life contains.' The coherence is 'drastic' because of all that's left out. Say you were beaten and abused by your father in childhood and have many different episodes to call on. Distilling them might seem a cop-out. But one beautifully reconstructed and detailed scene will do the work of twenty. (See REPETITION)

Even with a single episode that stands for related ones, there's still the question of how much to reveal. Not everyone is a tell-all. 'There is nothing at all in England of memoirs, of confessions, of narratives of self,' Madame de Stael observed back in 1799, complaining of 'too severe an abnegation of all that seems to come from personal affections.' The death of Princess Diana was said to show how much Brits have changed – how willing to weep and wail in public we now are. But weeping and wailing on the page is best avoided. The virtue of candour lies in setting down what happened, not in parading extremes of feeling. An author can be open without closing the space for readers, who need room to interpret and explore. To quote *King Lear*: 'Speak what we feel, not what we ought to say.'

Characters

Perhaps that's not the right word. This is non-fiction and they're real people. Still, just like a novelist, a life writer must help us get to know them.

The temptation is to do it all at once, by beginning the story with a big occasion (a party, wedding or funeral, say) at which all the key players, and more, are in attendance. OK, but that means a glut of names among which we'll be lost, unable to take them all on board. Life writers, if they're smart, will save some of the cast for later, when their part in the story really kicks in. They won't overdose on physical description, either. A head-to-toe portrait looks old-fashioned and stilted. A single defining characteristic, repeatable later, should take priority – not something commonplace (his gruff voice, her tilted nose, the old man's liver spots, the child's freckles) but a metaphor that stands out, like the 'inexhaustible charm' of Daisy Buchanan's voice in *The Great Gatsby*, which is 'full of money'.

Michael Frayn's memoir *My Father's Fortune* is a masterclass in characterisation; no doubt his expertise as a dramatist played a part. Despite the title, his mother, who died suddenly when he was 12, is as much a part of the story because of the gap she leaves, which was there even before she died: 'What's our mother like? Not like anything – she's just our mother, as taken for granted and uncharacterised as the air we breathe.' In her absence, Frayn struggles to understand his father Tom, an asbestos salesman, who's hard of hearing, anti-Tory, anti-church and for a time, before disastrously marrying again, a lonely widower. At times the effort to understand his father slides into interior monologue:

> He drives on through the grey South London boroughs, alone with the grey samples on the back seat of the car... Switches his hearing aid on to hear the silence of all the colleagues who know what's happened, but not what to say about it, the joshing of all the customers who don't know, and who are smiling already at the cracks that old Tom Frayn always comes up with. Then at the end of the day, back to the shabby house, with the green gates sagging on the rotten gate-posts. Back to my sister and me. We're his biggest worry, of course. We seem quiet enough. What's going on inside us, though?... What on earth is he going to do?

What's going on inside: here's a shot at catching inner-Tom, a stab of empathy, the son becoming the father who's worried about his children. Tom called Michael 'slow-witted', but the insult didn't rankle. Rather than parricidally vengeful, the memoir is affectionate, not an Oedipal battle or jostle for supremacy, but a book full of joshing, no less mocking of Frayn Jnr than it is of Frayn Snr.

In that respect Geoff Dyer's memoir *Homework* closely resembles it. His father's niggardliness and hard-done-by defeatism exasperated Dyer ('I was home-schooled in notions of acceptance I later found entirely unacceptable,' he says) and, like Frayn, he made his escape through education. But he recalls his father fondly nonetheless: 'yes, he was unbelievably tight but he was also and always, at the deepest level, *honourable.*'

As Frayn and Dyer show, good characterisation doesn't depend on having larger-than-life characters to work with. But Big Dads do often turn up in memoirs, whether a bigamist like J. R. Ackerley's father, a conman like Tobias Wolff's, a bullying drunk like John Burnside's, or a cold fish with a secret past like Germaine Greer's – which isn't to mention the fathers portrayed by, among others, Edmund Gosse, Franz Kafka, Philip Roth, Susan Wicks, Patricia Lockwood, Keggie Carew, Hanif Kureishi and Charlie Gilmour. All were 'characters' in life but it takes skill to make them characters on the page.

What's vital in memoir, no less than in fiction, is that all the characters earn their place. They're real people, which makes it hard, but if they're not central to the story they'll have to be sacrificed. A glut of bit players will muddle the story and annoy the reader. Trim them, blend them, kill them off.

Children

Is it OK for life writers to write about their children? Many a newspaper columnist has done so. And if a child is autistic, say, a book about that, with intimate, first-hand knowledge of the condition and its impact, can be helpful to parents in a similar position, as well as to medics and researchers, and indeed to anyone curious to know more. But children can't consent to be written about. Legally they're too young to do so. And they don't have the maturity to foresee the consequences. At best there *won't* be consequences. But there's always the risk that when they reach adulthood they'll hate having been written about. Here they are, as if in a home movie, running about naked or having a tantrum or getting themselves arrested: *What the fuck did you think you were doing, Dad (or Mum)?*

I've not had that reaction from my kids, but I did write about them; not only in passing in my memoirs, but in a book about the James Bulger murder case. My main preoccupation in that book was how much children can be held responsible for their actions, and at the time of the trial I'd three children at home under the age of twelve. It was a personal book, to which my thinking about my own children contributed; I couldn't leave them out. My wife Kathy agreed but was uneasy about me using their names; she had a background in social work and represented children in court, where names remain private rather than entering the public domain. So I settled for using my children's initials – S, A and G – which echoed proceedings in the Bulger case where, throughout the trial, the two accused were referred to as Boy A and Boy B rather than being named (only at the end of the trial did the judge decide to remove the culprits' anonymity).

I also changed the names of the children of a friend, who'd told me a funny story about an incident at home which seemed relevant to my pondering on how much children know when they're still children:

Mother, doing a crossword: What's an anagram of Lax Rose?
Hannah (12), quick off the mark: Oral sex.
Saul (9): What's an anagram?

My approach in that book wasn't trouble-free. In one passage, I described myself undressing someone of the opposite sex; only at the end did I identify the female as my infant daughter. The point was to show how easily we misread an adult male's bodily interaction with a child as sexual when in truth it's perfectly innocent. Perhaps it was a cheap trick and I deserved what I got – to be attacked as a paedophile by Germaine Greer, who wrote that my daughter, when she grew up, would hate me. Luckily she doesn't. But the episode was chastening. And proves the point: writing about children is a minefield.

I got off lightly compared to Julie Myerson, who was vilified for writing about her son, 'Jake', and his addiction to cannabis in her book *The Lost Child*. 'He knows who he is and I love him,' her dedication reads, and in the afterword she describes how he read her manuscript, made corrections and – with his jokey disclaimer ('Don't you go thinking I approve of what you've done') – gave permission for her to go ahead. In fact the book crosses his story with that of a nineteenth-century watercolourist called Mary Yelloly, who died at the age of 21 – another lost child. But most reviewers ignored the Yelloly sections, saving their venom for Myerson's treatment of her son: how dare she publish a book about him when he was still in his teens and struggling with drug addiction?

No father would have been as demonised as Myerson was. And she wasn't the first mother to give an account of a teenage son's addiction. Two years previously, for instance, extracts from *The Cannabis Diaries*, a blog by Debra Bell (not her real name), appeared in the *Guardian*. Though it covered similar ground, the ethics of publication weren't questioned at the time, nor when the blog was published as a book shortly after Myerson's. Had Myerson concealed her identity like Bell or as she herself had done when writing a weekly column, 'Living with Teenagers', in the *Guardian*, she might have got away with it. But she'd written the book under her own name and was well-known as a novelist. The tabloids were quickly on to Jake, who when interviewed was seemingly upset by what his mother had done (*Daily Mail* headline: '"You're the addict, Mum!" Son of Julie Myerson says she's hooked on exploiting her own children'). For a week or two Myerson was savaged as the Worst Mother in the World: Minette Marrin in the *Sunday Times* called her book a 'betrayal not just of love and intimacy, but also of motherhood itself' and Jeremy Paxman tore into her on *Newsnight*. That she had an honourable motive in writing the book – to raise public awareness of strong cannabis or 'skunk' and how addiction to it could tear apart a family – was overlooked. A cynical press convicted her of cynicism when she'd been, at worst, naïve.

Was Kate Clanchy naïve in writing, mostly with great warmth, about children in *Some Kids I Taught and What They Taught Me*? The book was attacked for its allegedly racist and ableist tropes, and despite it winning the Orwell Prize her publisher, Picador, an imprint of Pan Macmillan, withdrew it. Clanchy eventually owned up to a handful of jarring word choices, and changed them for a new edition of the book with a different publisher, but in the meantime she was hounded. Only in 2025, six years after the book first came out, did Pan Macmillan apologise to Clanchy for the 'regrettable series of events' and the 'hurt' it had caused her. She had taught children for decades and achieved great things with them, especially those who were migrants or from abusive backgrounds. Far from exposing any of them in the book, she changed names, times and places to protect their privacy; moreover, she added, 'I have included nobody, teacher or pupil, about whom I could not write with love.' Still, her case, like Myerson's, is a salutary warning. Unless you've lost children to disease or in an accident, it's a terrible risk to write about them – especially if you're a mother.

Cliché

'All writing is a campaign against cliché,' Martin Amis said. 'Not just clichés of the pen but clichés of the mind and clichés of the heart.' In life writing, examination of the self at intense moments is liable to produce clichés: the accelerating heartbeat, the bitten lip, the sinking feeling in the chest. Minor variations on these are no better – *my head was spinning, my arms and legs went numb, rage was bubbling up, I was blinking away tears, my stomach knotted, I was left weak-kneed* – nor are more convoluted descriptions I've come across – *arousal was already firm in my belly* (what?), *a nagging pit of anger began to simmer in my stomach* (can a pit nag, let alone simmer?). Strong emotion tends to be evoked in old-hat similes, as if a comparison will convey it more vividly rather than (as happens) diminishing its potency: *a pang of jealousy, frightened to death, in the nick of time, a hive of activity, the calm before the storm, a can of worms, licked my wounds, I loved him to bits.* When clichés prevail in life writing, it's not just a case of sloppy prose annoying the reader but of the author losing credibility: if they write this badly can they be believed? Have the experiences they describe been borrowed too?

Second- (or third- or fourth-) hand use of language erodes trust. A memoirist can be simple and direct without being linguistically banal.

Confession

Hostile critics dismiss the confessional memoir as the equivalent of a selfie, a look-at-me snapshot, a glorified ego trip. Take Julie Burchill in the *Guardian*, exasperated by 'the steady drip-drip of confessionals':

> Writers used to take life's little pile-ups and make bad, brilliant or boring novels out of them. But living as we are in a short-term, I want-it-now society and all that, not many people can be arsed to go around the houses any more. Rather, they shoot their bolt in a 'memoir' and sit back smugly to listen to the oohs and aahs of the paying public . . .. While most of us would agree that a pretty good definition of a bore is someone who tells people they don't know their problems, for some reason these jokers – and their ever-willing publishers – think they're pretty damn fascinating.

I enjoy Burchill's wit. But what virtue is there in 'going around the houses' to make a novel out of a personal crisis? What's wrong in telling it straight?

Besides, the confessional genre has a long history: Ovid's *Amores*; St Augustine, Rousseau and De Quincey; the American poets who came to prominence in the 1950s and 60s (Robert Lowell, Sylvia Plath, Anne Sexton, W. D. Snodgrass, John Berryman). And there has been no let-up. The shelves above my desk offer the following random sample: Rachel Cusk's *Aftermath*, recalling the break-up of a marriage; James Lasdun's *Give Me Everything You Have*, which documents the ordeal of being stalked by a former student; Julia Blackburn's *The Three of Us*, which tells how, as a teenager, she became the lover of her mother's lover, who was their lodger; not to mention titles by Jeanette Winterson, Dave Eggers, Lorna Sage, A. M. Homes, Jackie Kay, Dave Eggers, Kathryn Harrison and Karl Ove Knausgaard, all of whom have contributed significantly to the genre.

What confessional memoirs have in common is an intimacy we don't expect – the reader is given privileged access to awkward truths the author feels impelled to disclose. Mortality is often at the heart of it: life-writing often turns out to mean death-writing. But sexual transgression, madness, deceit, crime and addiction can be involved too, with exposure of a messy kind – the equivalent of Tracey Emin's tent (with the names of all her lovers) or her bed (with the detritus of her private life spilled across it).

Why the impulse to write confessional memoir? At least seven possible motives come to mind:

1. Confession as a spontaneous overflow of powerful feelings (Wordsworth) or free association (Freud): *I couldn't help it, it just came out of me, unexpurgated, because the experiences I had were so immense there was no choice.*
2. Confession as an apologia or self-justification, a strategic bid for sympathy and admiration. Owning up to problems, faults and misdeeds as a way to win friends. Show your Achilles heel and, rather than shoot a poisoned arrow at it, the reader will feel protective and on your side.
3. Confession as a desire to shock. It helps if the story is sensational. Or, if it isn't sensational, then you can make it so, by spicing it up, exaggerating, even inventing.
4. Confession as the desire to redefine what's shocking. To nail the hypocrisy or shallowness of polite society.

5. Confession as the drama of the ego, its natural arena not a secret cloister but a soapbox or a stage.
6. Confession as truth-telling – its primary impulse being to set the record straight, to bear witness.
7. Confession as catharsis, cleansing, or purgation. Something bad has happened, and putting it in writing, out there in the world, is a way of feeling better about it.

Of these, I'm especially interested in the idea of confession as a desire to redefine what's shocking – to show that what society deems shameful (which in the past included illegitimacy and mental illness) is actually 'normal' and worth attending to rather than hiding away.

When I showed Mum the draft of a memoir I'd written about Dad, one of the few things she wanted me to remove was a passing reference to her being a Catholic. I did as she asked but, after her death, went on to write a book exploring the backdrop to her request: how disguising her Catholicism was one of the choices she'd made in order to be assimilated into provincial English society. She felt (or was made to feel) awkward about her rural Irish-Catholic background, whereas for me there was no shame attached. The shame lay with the bigots, not with her.

Confession as catharsis is something I understand, too. 'Give sorrow words,' Shakespeare wrote in *Macbeth*. 'The grief that does not speak / Whispers the o'er-fraught heart and bids it break.' Get it on paper. Set it down in words. Writing as therapy.

Ah, therapy – a word generally held to be suspect when associated with literature. (See THERAPY.) *TMI*, people say, *I don't wish to know that*. And it's true that some revelations make us feel uncomfortable: *Ugh, no way,* we think, and refuse to take the author's outstretched hand. But there'll also be readers who feel consoled and affirmed. The therapeutic impulse needn't be damaging. Rousseau said that he wrote to ease his conscience and Virginia Woolf described how writing could 'blunt the sledge-hammer force' of childhood trauma so that it 'lost its power to hurt'. You can write to heal a wound and find the wound isn't just yours – and that others have been healed in the process.

Whatever the motive, intimate life writing is an honourable pursuit. If literature is the enemy of discretion and conformity, if its value lies in breaking the rules by means of truth-telling, then confessional memoirs may be the truest literature of all.

Consent

Some memoirists send drafts of their work to loved ones, or even not-so-loved ones, and where there's a response asking for changes they rework the text. Others see no need for consultation. Either way, when you're immersed in writing it's important to work freely, without anxiety or distraction, uninhibited by the possible fallout of your words. You can worry about people later, when you're editing. In mid-flow, you need the illusion of privacy, not to be anticipating people's reactions (which are, in any case, unpredictable: to protect her identity, I once changed the name of someone I'd had sex with and when the book came out she complained, 'Why couldn't I have been me?'). It can put a curse on a work-in-progress to discuss it with others. And most self-censorship is cowardly. In Elizabeth Strout's *My Name is Lucy Barton*, the writing tutor Sarah says: 'If you find yourself protecting anyone as you write . . . remember this: you're not doing it right.' Michelle Tea, in her book *Against Memoir*, advises going into a kind of trance: 'There is a certain stance you must take to write a memoir, a spell you cast upon yourself at the keyboard. You must not remember that your characters are actual people, people you once loved or maybe still do.'

As you write you need total freedom; once you've finished it becomes more difficult. Who to share your writing with? And how much notice to take if they object? On one side, some writers behave angelically, as it seems Sheila Heti did with her autofictional work *Motherhood*:

> I would never have published this book if I hadn't had the people who are closest to me read it and give me their notes on it. In places that they were concerned, I always responded by changing it. I never felt that there was any compromise in doing that and I think a good work of art can – *should* – be in an ethical relationship to the people who appear in it in certain ways either fictionally or non-fictionally. That's my ethos. I don't want to hurt the people around me in the making of a book and, if I can't make the change to their satisfaction, that's my failure as an artist.

Alexander Masters takes the same line: 'as a biographer of unknown people,' he writes in *A Life Discarded*, 'you must be exceptionally careful not to trash someone who has no capacity to reply. If you cannot reach a version of the book that both you and your subject are prepared to accept, then the whole thing must go on the fire.'

On the other hand there's Anne Lamott: 'Every single thing that happened to you is yours and you get to tell it. If people wanted you to write more warmly about them, they should have behaved better.' Perhaps guilt about behaving badly towards her is why Monique Roffey's ex-partner didn't object to her writing about him in *With the Kisses of His Mouth* – in the Acknowledgements she thanks him for 'giving me the nod'. But he gave the nod before reading the book and when he did read it, and saw how he was portrayed, it seems he regretted his consent.

When I was writing about my father, my mother was still alive. When I finished a draft I showed it to her, resolving to abandon it or put it away in a drawer if she didn't like it. I'd two big worries. First was the intimacy with which I'd dwelt on his last weeks, his terminal illness and bodily decline. But Mum was a doctor and the physical details didn't upset her. I'd also written about his sexual relationship with another woman. Mum was sorry to find that there but, liberal as she was, she let me go ahead. 'It's your story, and if that's how you remember it, so be it,' she said, while resolving to tell inquiring friends who didn't know about Dad's affair that my story was a lurid fantasy.

When I came to write about her I'd no one to consult. Yes, I'd my sister Gill, but I was writing largely about a time before we were born, so there was no risk she'd feel affronted. Some family members *do* object to being written about, even if you are being kind about them. And if you're doing a work of family history, it pays to approach relatives and say, 'I'm writing this book about x, can I come and talk to you?' With my memoir *Two Sisters*, I consulted Gill's grown-up children, Louise and Liam, to make sure they felt OK about the book, which they read in draft; though there might have been parts of it they disliked, they'd no objection to me going ahead.

Maggie Nelson is more ethically scrupulous than most writers, or was when writing about her partner Harry in *The Argonauts*:

> I finish a first draft of this book and give it to Harry. He doesn't have to tell me that he's read it; when I come

home from work . . . I can feel his mood, which one might describe as quiet ire . . . We go through the draft page by page, mechanical pencils in hand, with him suggesting ways I might facet my representation of him, of us. I try to listen, try to focus on his generosity in letting me write about him at all. He is, after all, a very private person . . . .. But nothing can substantively quell my inner defense attorney . . . It's my book, mine! Yes, [he replies], but the details of my life, of our life together, don't belong to you alone . . .

She and Harry worked things out between them. And she had finished a draft before consulting him; she didn't ask mid-composition. With students I used to adapt the Nike slogan: 'Just do it (and worry later).' The feelings of the living have to be respected. But consent is a tricky business. It's a book you're writing, not a relationship you're conducting. And whatever your duty of care, with a private diary or early draft you can't have people butting in.

Courage

How brave, readers sometimes say after reading a piece of life writing. *How did the author have the guts?* By which they might also mean: *how weird to over-share like that – what kind of psycho is the author?* The thought of being judged weird or worse is scary to writers. As Maggie Nelson puts it in *The Argonauts*, 'Most writers I know nurse persistent fantasies about the horrible things – or *the* horrible thing – that will happen to them if and when they express themselves as they desire.'

It does take courage to revisit traumas. You don't want to go there but you do. Stuff you've never talked about to anyone, that makes you well up or wail even to think about, that years of therapy have done little or nothing to alleviate – suddenly, miraculously, it's there, in writing. What's more, you'll force yourself to re-read it to test how true it is to what happened, and perhaps, accordingly, rewrite it. All of which takes grit. As Kerry Hudson says in *Lowborn*:

> When you have grown up in a house where family loyalty comes second only to family secrecy, the act of saying aloud what has happened to you – even to people you love – is hard enough. The concept of writing those same words in a book that will be put into strangers' hands, hearts and potentially judgemental heads is like learning to use your left hand instead of your right (in a situation that involves sawing off your right hand with the edge of a rusty Yale key).

And yet . . . it can sometimes be less painful than expected. Not nerve-shredding or blood-shedding, but a cool re-entry into dark times. It's as if you're absent. The girl you were then isn't the woman you are now. You're on the outside, looking back – remembering not living, writing not experiencing. Afterwards, rereading, you might be upset. But during the writing process you're beyond tears, and you didn't feel brave in the least.

'I used to think that autobiography was a weakness,' Hilary Mantel writes in her memoir *Giving Up the Ghost*, 'and perhaps I still do. But I also think that, if you're weak, it's childish to pretend to be strong.' First-person non-fiction is a vulnerable form: you're laying yourself open, providing evidence that can be used against you. It's a daunting prospect. But it may be less annihilating than you think.

Creative non-fiction

The term isn't an oxymoron but an expression of the obvious: some works of non-fiction are more creative than others (and no less creative than fiction or poetry). A full-length memoir is, or should be, more creative than a brief news item or civil service memo. For some writers, more questionably, the term means a licence to invent – to be creative in the way that accountants are creative when they fiddle the books. It's tricky: only the dourest of Gradgrinds will begrudge the writer some leeway. But there's an understanding that the story, in essence, is true.

Relativists swear it doesn't matter – that there's no real difference between fiction and non-fiction. But is outright mendacity acceptable in life writing? Rebecca Solnit thinks not: 'it's a slippery slope from the things your stepfather didn't actually do to the weapons of mass destruction Iraq didn't actually have'. A little white lie might serve your purpose in shaping the story; a big black one served Bush and Blair's warmongering – do you want to be in the same camp? Brendan Barrington has a thoughtful essay on the subject, based on his experience of editing non-fiction for the *Dublin Review*. 'Some readers' attitude to the non-fiction writer,' he suggests, 'can be summarised as "I am in your hands; do with me what you will." For others, it's more like "I am in your hands; don't you dare lie to me."'

A non-fiction writer can't help but invent, at least a little: false memories, changes of names, omission of material that slows the narrative – they're all fabrication of a kind. But there's a difference between inadvertently getting things wrong and knowingly making them up. I'm with Brendan Barrington in 'hoping never to learn from some future biographer that James Baldwin didn't really get thrown in jail for being in receipt of stolen goods . . . or that Dervla Murphy didn't really cycle all the way to India.'

Crime

From medieval ballads and Shakespeare plays, to detective fiction and Nordic noir, crime has been a great resource for the literary imagination. Its intersection with modern life writing arguably began with *In Cold Blood*, Truman Capote's 'true account' of the murder of four members of a Kansas farming family by Perry Smith and Dick Hickock, who spent over five years on death row before being hanged. The account is indeed largely 'true', despite Capote changing numerous details and allegedly misrepresenting some of the characters. What sets it apart from most *true crime* is its novelistic technique: from documents he read, notes he took (8,000 pages of them) and interviews he conducted with the help of his friend Harper Lee, whole scenes and conversations are constructed (or as some detractors would have it, made up). From the opening description of the Kansas wheat plains and population – 'The local accent is barbed with a prairie twang, a ranch-hand nasalness.' – Capote is at pains to prove that he's no mere crime reporter. The prose is ostentatious, unlike the author, who conceals himself. There's no allusion to his research or extensive interviews with the condemned men. The narrator is omniscient, not first-person. The effect is, as Capote wished, 'immaculately factual', but the book is more a 'non-fiction novel' than a piece of reportage.

John Berendt's *Midnight in the Garden of Good and Evil* – which features four trials for a single murder rather than a single trial for the murder of four people – takes a more transparent approach: Berendt is firmly present from the outset, as a writer in pursuit of his story. In fact, he's present when he wasn't actually present: the opening scene has him meeting the accused man before the murder took place; in reality, Berendt didn't arrive in Savannah and meet him till later – the scene is based on what others told him. Does it matter? The chronological licence makes for a neater structure and stronger opening. And in a Gothic tale of the Deep South, strict adherence to the truth would seem so *dull* – whereas Berendt's had the colour to make it a spectacular bestseller (and to double the tourist trade in Savannah). Still, it's no wonder the book was called a 'non-fiction novel' like Capote's three decades before.

In the UK, the writer who comes closest to matching Capote and Berendt is Gordon Burn, in his books about the Yorkshire Ripper Peter Sutcliffe and the Gloucester murderer Fred West. As an apprentice reporter, Burn was trained to avoid the first-person pronoun and to stick to the facts. But taking encouragement from something John Berger said – that imagination isn't the ability to invent but the ability to disclose what already exists – he brought novelistic flair to non-fiction. For *Somebody's Husband, Somebody's Son*, he spent two years in Bingley, where Sutcliffe grew up and where members of his family still lived. What he got from them was inside knowledge that newspaper reporters hadn't the time, nous or persistence to elicit. *Happy Like Murderers*, his account of the Fred West murders, is equally diligent but more risk-taking, occasionally slipping into the mind of West himself: 'Roll-ups and offers of rides. Lightly, lightly. If it takes a year, it takes a year. He could be tirelessly patient. He was always scouting. Waiting and recruiting. Watching, scouting . . . The *Lustmord*.' Burn also wrote novels but it was non-fiction that best served the novelist in him. The Sutcliffe and West stories gave him plot, character, tension and linearity, which his novels preferred to avoid.

You might not have trained as a journalist (like Burn) or have sat through a murder trial (as I did with the Bulger case), but if a crime obsesses you, that's qualification enough. Virginia Peters, once a PhD student of mine, was taken to sit through court cases as a child by her mother. Decades later, the unsolved murder of Simone Strobel, a German tourist in Australia, caught her imagination, and she spent years trying to crack the case, interviewing key protagonists (including the chief suspect, Simone's boyfriend Tobias), travelling to Germany to talk to both Simone and Tobias's families, and accessing confidential police documents. The difficulties and ethical dilemmas she faced make an absorbing drama, and her PhD, later a book called *Have You Seen Simone?*, allows readers to reach their own conclusion. (Two decades after Simone's death, the case is still unsolved.)

Kate Summerscale is currently the leading exponent of historical true crime in the UK, with books that include *The Suspicions of Mr Whicher* and *The Peepshow: The Murders at 10 Rillington Place*. The historian Hallie Rubenhold is no less compelling, notably with *The Five: The Untold Lives of the Women Killed by Jack the Ripper*, where she concentrates on the serial killer's victims rather than trying to crack the mystery of the man himself. For other writers, crime begins closer to home. Laura Cumming's *On Chapel Sands* explores her mother's abduction from a Lincolnshire beach at the age of 3. The murder of Martin Amis's cousin Lucy Partington by Fred West forms part of his memoir *Experience*. Maggie Nelson's *Jane: A Murder* searches for the truth about the slaughter of her aunt, possibly by a serial killer, back in the 1960s, before Maggie was born; the text is set out as poetry, mostly in couplets, but also draws on diaries, news reports and dreams. In *The Red Parts: Autobiography of a Trial* Nelson picks up the story again, in prose, when a man is tried thirty-five years after the murder.

Nelson persisted with the first book despite the discouragement of her grandfather ('What will it be, a figment of your imagination?') and her mother ('I don't want you to get obsessed with this.'). With crime writing, discouragement is the norm: *you've a sick mind*, you'll be told; *you could end up facing legal opposition* (as happened to Virginia Peters); *you're playing with fire*. But a book that supplements the grim facts with new insights won't be an opportunistic crime-wank. Even the nigglers will be won round.

D

Davies, W. H.

Thanks to the help of George Bernard Shaw, to whom he pleadingly sent a copy of his poems, Davies had made a modest reputation as a poet before writing *The Autobiography of a Super-Tramp*. But as someone brought up in a pub, who left school at 14, lived as a hobo in the US, had his leg amputated after falling from a train in Canada, and spent six years tramping roads and staying in doss-houses in the UK, Davies didn't have a lot going for him – and lived in poverty till his memoir met with popular acclaim. Its appeal is its authenticity: about food, tramp-dialect ('kennel' for house, 'feather' for bed, 'scrand' for food, 'glims' for spectacles), scams to find places to sleep (if need be in a prison), and tips on how to beg. London literati later patronised Davies as a peasant innocent, and though Larkin represented him generously in his edition of *The Oxford Book of 20th-century English Verse* and there's one couplet of his that even non-readers of poetry love to quote – 'What is this life if, full of care, / We have no time to stand and stare?' – he's largely forgotten as a poet. Still his vagrant-memoir, and its sequel *Later Days*, are minor classics of life writing, and they're proof that to have lived as a down-and-out needn't stop you from being up-and-in.

Death

We call it life writing but invariably the subject matter is death: the loss of a loved one (parent, spouse, lover, friend, mentor or, worst of all, child) and the grieving that follows. The challenge for the writer, as for the eulogist at a funeral, is to hold it together: 'Let us disarm Death of his novelty and strangeness,' Michel de Montaigne said. It's important that there be lightness, even laughter, to offset the dark. Writers who recall jokes made round a deathbed won't be thought heartless. The reader will spot their welling eyes.

One notably nerveless performance is Joan Didion's, in *The Year of Magical Thinking*. Didion was a stylish writer and owns up in the opening chapter to having developed 'a technique for withholding whatever it was I thought or believed behind an increasingly impenetrable polish'. When she describes the evening when her husband died, there's polish but no withholding. The single-sentence paragraphs are hammer blows to convince herself that the impossible has happened:

> We had come home.
>
> We had discussed whether to go out for dinner or eat in.
>
> I said I would build a fire, we could eat in.
>
> I built the fire, I started dinner, I asked John if he wanted a drink.
>
> I got him a Scotch and gave it to him in the living room, where he was reading in the chair by the fire where he habitually sat.
>
> The book he was reading was by David Fromkin, a bound galley of *Europe's Last Summer: Who Started the Great War in 1914?*

> I finished getting dinner, I set the table in the living room where, when we were home alone, we could eat within sight of the fire . . .
>
> John was talking then he wasn't.

When she asks at the hospital 'He's dead, isn't he?', she hears herself being described as 'a cool customer'. What would an uncool customer do, she wonders: 'Break down? Require sedation? Scream?' Though she does none of those, we know she's not cool. That telling the story as frankly as possible is her only way of processing the death of her husband. And that no amount of rational thought will prevent magical thinking.

There's a similarly nerveless reconstruction of death, and of the factors leading up to it, in Tim Lott's *The Scent of Dried Roses*, which describes his mother Jean's suicide. The opening chapter is told by an omniscient narrator: Lott wasn't present but so meticulous is the detail, compiled through his father and through his own memories of Jean, it's as though he was. 'That day I remember as being neutral,' he writes, 'without any sense of imminence' – due warning something bad is coming. Suspense comes through small detail. 'Jean had a job to do,' we're told, and when she phones in sick we realise the job in question isn't the one she does as a dinner lady. 'She don't look well', a neighbour remarks, and the unwellness has many causes: her alopecia, her insomnia, her dislike of where she lives (once 'a lovely place'), her loss of self-esteem: 'It was all her fault – so much was her fault.' When she goes upstairs and decides 'to get the job done', the narrator switches attention to her husband Jack, who'll be the one to find her when he returns from work, a blue necklace of rope round her neck. When he cuts her down with a bread knife, she falls into his arms, 'as if they were dancing': thirty-seven years earlier, when they first met, he'd thought her 'lovely, a catch'. She has left a note, which is 'logical and clear, but it made no sense'. Later, with the help of a policeman, he makes a phone call to break the news: 'Jack felt it only proper that he be told what had happened, exactly, and why.' The 'he' is unspecified but we infer it's Tim. Whose book does the same, tells us what happened, exactly, and why.

Both Didion and Lott recite the facts, leaving the reader to supply feeling. Factuality isn't cold-blooded: it's a device to put us there, at the scene. Without the detail, we wouldn't care. Even objects carry feeling. Didion's husband drinking his Scotch, Lott's mother putting on her make-up ('a little foundation, a little mascara, lipstick'); they're deeply poignant. The author need say nothing more.

Death is the 'fairest thing in this world,' the Nobel Prize-winning author Svetlana Alexievich has said, because 'no one has ever managed to buy himself out of it.' William Empson considered it a topic 'people should be prepared to be blank upon'. But the blankness round death – the urge to hide it away, behind screens, and not speak of it – is precisely why it needs to be written about. Death brings grief and everyone's grief is different, as only life writing can convey.

'When a writer is born into a family, that family is finished,' Philip Roth liked to say, quoting Czesław Miłosz. Well, yes, but when a writer is born into a family, that family will have an afterlife.

Depression

First-hand accounts of depression or of bipolar disorder used to be a rarity. To own up to them was to invite prejudice and discrimination; even labels such as 'mental patient' carried a stigma. The other difficulty, still present, is recall. You may have been zapped by medication and ECT or, if you're in hospital, deprived of a writing implement (the pen is an instrument of self-harm, literally as well as metaphorically, and ballpoints are often banned from psychiatric wards). As Norah Vincent says in her book *Voluntary Madness*: 'You know you felt terrible, and you know you don't want to feel that way again. But you don't really remember the details, the quality of suffering.' Nor, when you're at rock bottom, can you conquer your inertia and sense of futility.

The other difficulty lies in making depression intelligible to people who've never experienced it. 'I was feeling in my mind a sensation close to, but indescribably different from, actual pain,' William Styron writes in his 'memoir of madness' *Darkness Visible*, a horror 'so overwhelming as to be quite beyond expression'. His book works hard to make it expressible, dismissing the word 'depression' as insipid ('a true wimp of a word for such a major illness') and finding his own metaphors instead: a siege, a storm, 'a howling tempest in the brain', a 'leaden and poisonous mood the colour of verdigris', a 'merciless daily drumming', a 'poisonous fogbank' that rolled in each afternoon.

It was after a short op-ed piece for the *New York Times* about depression prompted an enormous response from readers who 'had experienced the feelings I had described' but 'for whom the subject had been taboo, a matter of secrecy and shame', that Styron saw the value in writing a book: at greater length (still a modest eighty pages), it would, he hoped, bring an increased understanding of the illness. And it does. He's helped, if that's the word, by the phenomenon of 'being accompanied by a second self – a wraithlike observer who, not sharing the dementia of his double, is able to watch with dispassionate curiosity as his companion struggles . . . There is a theatrical quality about all this, . . . a melodrama in which I, the victim-to-be of self-murder, was both the solitary actor and lone member of the audience.'

The other problem Styron faced in hospital was confinement to a 'laughterless environment'. It was grim, solemn stuff to write about. But he managed it, and several other compelling first-hand accounts of depression do exist – among them Andrew Solomon's *The Noonday Demon*, Kay Redfield Jamison's *An Unquiet Mind*, Susanna Kaysen's *Girl, Interrupted*, Elizabeth Wurtzel's *Prozac Nation* and Stephanie Merritt's *The Devil Within*. It wasn't beyond these authors to write about depression. And they weren't doing it just for themselves, but for the benefit of others; it mattered enough for them to narrate what they'd been through, not deny or repress it.

Derangement

And then there's derangement. How do you describe an out-of-mind experience when at the time it happened you didn't have your mind about you? People who've had out-of-body experiences often describe the sensation of seeing themselves from above, as if suspended. People with depression also sometimes experience a kind of double selfhood (see Styron, above). But when you're inside a frenetic state of consciousness, you don't have aerial omniscience. You're drunk, stoned, demented or psychotic. Or having a panic attack or hallucinations. And so disorientated that when you recover, you recall very little, just the odd image or snatch of conversation.

Then again, it's not quite the same as being asleep and dreaming. You know you went through something *for real*. And it's important to get it down before it disappears. How? As a life writer you rely on memory. In this case, you might have to loosen up and use your imagination.

Perhaps that's why novelists can often do out-of-mind stuff better than life writers. Martin Amis's *Other People* inhabits the head of a young woman in hospital who's suffering from amnesia and nominal aphasia. Jonathan Franzen's novel *The Corrections* has a section which explores mental distress – that of a man, Alfred, on a cruise ship whose Parkinson's and developing dementia is exacerbated by his cocktail of drugs. And Dutch writer J. Bernlef's novel *Out of Mind* is written from the point of view of a man called Maarten who's suffering from dementia: time and place baffle him, as do the identities of those around him: 'Everything happens in jolts and jerks. There is no flowing movement . . . The day is full of cracks and holes.' All three novels approach 'out-of-mind' from within, as do (from personal experience) Antonia White in *Beyond the Glass* and Clare Allan in *Poppy Shakespeare*.

How does a life writer do the same? Only by stifling the inner voice that says *Don't go back there, it's too painful*. Benedicta Leigh's 1991 autobiography *The Catch of Hands* describes a psychotic breakdown that begins with a euphoric visionary experience ('It was as though I had pulled back a curtain from the beginnings of the world'), after which she's sectioned and admitted to a mental hospital, where she assaults staff, hears voices, is confined to a solitary cell and earns her release, some weeks later, by feigning recovery; she then attempts to kill herself by cutting her wrists. Despite some haziness about all that happened, she's able to access key moments, slipping into the present tense as she does:

> Inside me is the shout, and outside me is the bleak whimper of an animal, pulled from me, and take me home,

take me, take me. The shadow slips away to his covert, but my skin creeps still, and I am marked as prey, since I am gentry, a captive, and have wet myself with fear. And I know that nothing need ever be heard of me, nothing revealed.

This isn't a measured backward look, but panicky, syntactically disordered and intense. What James Joyce said about dreams, while defending the language of *Finnegans Wake*, applies to derangement too: 'This area of experience cannot be rendered by the use of wideawake language, cutandry grammar, or goahead plot.'

Though their language is more measured, John O'Donoghue in *Sectioned: A Life Interrupted* (less a story of locked wards than of hostels, soup kitchens, sheltered housing, drug addicts, well-meaning charity workers and relentless poverty), Tom Lee in *The Bullet* (about his parents' mental illness and his own anxiety and depression) and Joanne Limburg in *The Woman Who Thought Too Much* (about her Obsessive Compulsive Disorder) have also written powerful stories of mental distress. It can be done if the writer finds the right idiom – a mindful way to describe out-of-mind experience.

Detail

'Go in fear of abstraction,' Ezra Pound said. God – or the Devil – is in the detail. Most young writers, James Agee said, 'roll around in description like honeymooners on a bed'. Good writing immerses us in the senses: sight, sound, smell, taste and touch (the sixth sense, too, if you believe in it). Detail is how an author puts us there. It's life – and the essence of life writing.

Of poetry too. William Carlos Williams's kitchen, with plums in the icebox, 'so sweet and so cold', and a tap he turns to 'watch the water plash / into the clean white sink. / On the grooved drain-board.' Philip Larkin's 'awful pie' eaten on a railway platform and 'the deep blue air' beyond the high window of his library 'That shows / nothing, and is nowhere, and is endless'. Elizabeth Bishop's bullfrogs ('slack strings plucked by heavy thumbs') and pelicans that crash into the water ('like pickaxes, / rarely coming up with anything to show for it'). Seamus Heaney's spade ('the coarse boot nested on the lug, the shaft / against the inside knee levered firmly') and tinsmith's scoop ('sunk past its gleam in the meal-bin'). Ted Hughes's pike ('green tigering the gold') and snowdrop ('her pale head heavy as metal'). Sylvia Plath's cut thumb ('The top quite gone / Except for a sort of hinge // Of skin, / A flap like a hat, / Dead white. / Then that red plush') and Christmas balloons ('Guileless and clear, / Oval soul-animals'). It doesn't matter how idiosyncratic the detail is. On the contrary, the odder it is, the more it shows how closely the writer has been paying attention.

When my sister Gill died self-destructively, I lamented how she had deprived herself of the sensory world I was still able to inhabit: 'The sensation of soft sand between my toes . . . The slap of seawater . . . The sound of wood pigeons . . . The music of Mozart's clarinet quintet . . . The taste of nectarines and greengages . . . The smell of sausages on a barbecue'. To me that list of what she could no longer perceive was a better way to convey tragedy than to say her death was a tragedy.

The same with my dad when I listed all the stuff he'd hoarded in his garage:

> crumpled cans of Simoniz, paint tins with a crust-hard quarter inch in the bottom, hanging saws with their teeth torn

out, garden shears open like lobster claws, the drum circle of an extension lead, a knapsack weedkiller spray, a paraffin wick road-lamp, an oil can with its plunger jammed half out.

The list says a lot about him: his hoarding instincts, the mix of clutter and orderliness, the wartime mentality which told him that any object, however old or broken, might prove useful one day. The objects were only his tools, the kind you might find in any garage. But they became *my* tools – for conveying his character and my grief. My descendancy too: 'Some day,' I ended that passage, 'all these will be mine.'

Dialect

Most of us grow up with dialect, whether family idioms or slang picked up at school. Older members of the RP brigade – sticklers for Received Pronunciation or old-style King's English – might disapprove of regional accents and urban street-talk as 'common', but it's great to find them in a book. Work-talk, the special language of a job or profession, is always fascinating too and often includes the kind of compounds you get in Anglo-Saxon verse, whether applied to corporate malpractice – *jizz mopper, fuck booth, puke tank, fight pit, grill jockey, nut bag* – or to business bullshit – *cloudify, cross-platform, core-competent, hyperscale, intermandated, quality-vectored, virtualised, user-centric.*

In *Brothers and Keepers,* John Edgar Wideman offsets his elevated, university-educated idiom with his imprisoned brother's hustler ebonics: 'Wasn't nothing going down like it spozed to. Shooting. A dude running. We was in a mess and Cecil still holding them Kramer brothers lined up behind the truck . . . I'm scared but they scareder than me. And mad. Don't say shit but they mad.' The language of homeless Stuart's speech in Alexander Masters's *Stuart: A Life Backwards* is less slangy but it's essential in helping us know how he's lived (and brawled): 'Chin down, look up. If you can get hold of the fella it helps, then push off and fucking whack back. Breaks his nose every time if you do it right.' Or to go full-pelt there's Tom Wolfe's 'kandy-coloured' version of how the women in a detention centre yell 'Harry' to a man in the street below, which for economy's sake here (*his* vowels stretch to three lines) goes 'Hai-ai-ai-ai-ai . . . ai-ai-ai-ai-ai-aireeeeeeeeee!' Vibrant language is a treat for the reader. The only rule is to avoid phonetic spelling for regional or international accents – don't have a Frenchman saying 'Ze weather is fine zis morning' or a northerner going 'ee-bah-gum'.

I used some of the dialect I'd grown up with in 'The Ballad of the Yorkshire Ripper', a long poem about Peter Sutcliffe, while also adding words from an old dialect dictionary: the poem was about misogyny and, revealingly, misogyny was inscribed in the language I found in that dictionary, not least in words denoting a 'loose' woman: *lad-loupin' moll, gadabout, flappysket, drabbletail, goer, buer, slag*. However obscure the dialect words a writer uses, the context will make them intelligible or there can be a glossary at the end. In *The Stopping Places: a Journey through Gypsy Britain,* Damian Le Bas does both, noting usages along the way ('By my teens I knew four traveller words for "punch", five for "money" and seven for "police"') and compiling an extensive list at the end.

Dialogue

How do life writers accurately recall conversations that took place decades ago? Unless they're freaks (and some writers are:

Beryl Bainbridge claimed to recall family rows from childhood word-for-word), they can't. Most of us even struggle to recall conversations that took place last week. The compromise is to approximate. It's something we all do in recounting anecdotes. We know the people, the peculiar expressions they used, their tone of voice, accent and gestures. We know the context (slanging match, marriage proposal, coming-out announcement, etc.). We know what we thought and felt. It's enough for a writer to go on. Someone who was also there (a sibling, say) might dispute the version of events – or add to them. But it's what the author took away that matters.

The convention of using spoken words, rather than reported speech, is as integral to life writing as to fiction. Dialogue has the virtue of immediacy. It puts us there. We clock what's not being said as well as what is. A well-chosen snatch of dialogue will save pages of description and explication. The exchanges Linda Grant has with her mother in *Remind Me Who I Am Again* movingly capture the ravages of multi-infarct dementia:

'I won't be able to come in next Sunday because I'm going to Nice for a long weekend.'
'That's marvellous! Where did you say you were going?'
'Nice.'
'How long for?'
'For a long weekend.'
'But you haven't told me where you're going yet.'
'Nice.'
'Ooh. I'd love to go there. How long will you be away?'
'For a long weekend.'
'And where did you say you were going, again?'

If it's a run of dialogue, the best writers stick with 'said' – he said, she said, they said – rather than choosing fancier options such as pronounced, opined, declared, commented, vocalised, uttered, hypothesised or (for heaven's sake) ejaculated. And if it's a run of dialogue between two people, and it's obvious who's speaking, there's no need to identify the speaker each time.

> 'I hate you,' Donna said.
> 'That's a cruel thing to say,' Roland said.
> 'It's true.'
> 'It's mean.'
> 'I'm serious.'
> 'You're just in a bad mood.'
> 'Fuck you, Roland.'

Another choice for the writer is how to set out dialogue. There are a couple of common ways. First, as above and below, the most traditional and formal, with quotation marks.

> *'I'm feeling exhausted,' she said, sinking into the nearest armchair, 'I didn't sleep a wink last night.'*

Second, there's a looser, more contemporary usage, which dispenses with quotation marks – this can get confusing when there's description as well as speech but here it works fine.

> *I'm feeling exhausted, she said, sinking into the nearest armchair, I didn't sleep a wink last night.*

The modernist variation was to use dashes, as James Joyce did in *A Portrait of the Artist as a Young Man*, though it now looks old-fashioned.

— *You'd think butter wouldn't melt in your mouth*, said Heron. *But I'm afraid you're a sly dog.*
— *Might I ask you what you are talking about?* said Stephen urbanely.
— *Indeed you might*, answered Heron.

Should Joyce have bothered with 'urbanely'? And does he need 'answered Heron', when it's clear that Heron is speaking? I'm only asking, not disparaging a literary giant.

Diaries

Here's the most intimate form of life writing: entries dashed down in the heat of the moment and not intended to be seen by anyone else. They're unmade beds or unswept floors, not tidied up for public consumption. Except that diaries are rarely as spontaneous and private as they seem. They're often written to schedule, nerdily so, at a fixed time each day. And however hidden away, they've half an eye on being discovered – by some nosy parker in the same house (parent, lover, offspring) or (it's vain of writers to think like this but they do) posterity.

Some diaries have half an eye on publication from the start. Did Joan Didion intend the ones she kept about sessions with a psychiatrist, addressed to her husband, to come out one day, as they did in 2025? Perhaps not. But why then did she preserve them, typed up and chronologically organised, in a filing cabinet next to her desk? Celebrated as she was, she surely knew anything she left behind might one day be published. Then again, the file was a set of notes, unpolished, and Didion was always polished; would she have liked to be seen in workaday clothes? (Similar doubts arise about the posthumous publication of Harper Lee's *The Land of Sweet Forever*, short stories and journalistic fragments she had chosen not to bring out, and Gabriel García Márquez's *Until August*, which he was working on while suffering from dementia: the books do the authors no favours.)

The best diarists are performers. Life's a play in which they cast themselves as the lead, bigger and bolder than they are in reality. 'There is a shadow writer at work in a diary,' Deborah Levy says in her memoir *Real Estate*. 'Reaching for her truest thoughts, like a shadow she sees herself extended on the page, taller than her physical self.' At their best, diaries aren't a transcription of days but an assembly of observations, ideas, confessions, jokes, meals, character sketches, anecdotes, ecstasies and regrets. *A funny thing happened to me on the way to . . . This great story I heard went . . . The graves in the churchyard where we were having a piss-up looked like . . . ..* It helps a diarist to hobnob with the famous. Or to be as alert to nature as Dorothy Wordsworth. Or to have lived through a plague or in a war zone. But it's not essential.

Diaries are also an invaluable source – raw material to be developed into a book. They're memory-keepers and memory-joggers. Annie Ernaux put the experience of a love affair into a novel, then looked at the diaries she'd kept at the time and published them too, at a later point; the life writing was truer to the experience than the fiction. The seductiveness of diaries lies in the sense of trespass: you feel they've come into your hands by default (or theft) and that if you were an honest broker you'd hand them back, unread. But there's probably no one to hand them back to: however vividly alive to you, as they record their transgressions, the authors may have been dead for several centuries. The aliveness of Pepys's journal is that he records every crisis, with nothing spared:

and, after supper, to have my head combed by Deb, which occasioned the greatest sorrow to me that ever I knew in this world, for my wife, coming up suddenly, did find me embracing the girl with my hand under her skirts; and indeed, I was with my hand in her cunny. I was at a wonderful loss upon it, and the girl also, and I endeavoured to put it off, but my wife was struck mute and grew angry, and as her voice come to her grew quite out of order, and I do say little, but to bed, and my wife said little also, but could not sleep all night, but about two in the morning waked me and cried, and . . . she went on from one thing to another till at last it appeared plainly her trouble was at what she saw, but yet I did not know how much she saw, and therefore said nothing to her. But after her much crying and reproaching me with inconstancy and preferring a sorry girl before her, I did give her no provocation, but did promise all fair usage to her and love, and foreswore any hurt that I did with her, till at last she seemed to be at ease again, and so towards morning a little sleep . . .

Few writers who have published books of their diaries are up there with Pepys, though Alan Bennett, Simon Gray and Helen Garner aren't far behind. Nor is W. N. P. Barbellion with his *The Journal of a Disappointed Man*, which 'keeps open house to every kind of happening in my soul' and is exuberant and self-affirming even when despondent: 'nothing can alter the fact that I *have* lived; *I have been I*, if for ever such a short time. And when I am dead . . . my dust will always be going on, each separate atom of me playing its separate part . . . Death can do no more than kill you.'

That's where journal entries make a greater impact than any other kind of writing: I *have* lived, *I have been I*.

Didion, Joan

One of the great life writers. Her reportage in the 1960s dissolved the line between inner world and outer. If she was falling apart, as she seemed to be (*The White Album* includes a psychiatric report describing her as 'a personality in the process of deterioration'), that's because the country was falling apart too. An attack of vertigo and nausea was her 'response' to the summer of 1968; a marriage crisis was played off against the Vietnam war and a tidal wave heading to Honolulu; she was in such pain writing *Slouching Towards Bethlehem* that she stayed awake for 21 hours at a stretch, drank gin-and-hot-water to blunt the pain and took Dexedrine to blunt the gin. Her form was the fractured essay – snapshots of a world of disorder, 'flash pictures in variable sequence', which she left for the reader to connect.

She changed tack in 2003 with her first memoir, *Where I Was From*, an exploration of her Californian ancestry in all its confusion; it's there that she passes on a great motto for life writers, 'Imagine your remembering'. That book might have been her only memoir but for the deaths of her husband and daughter, which led to two more: *The Year of Magical Thinking* and *Blue Nights*, both examinations of grief. 'We might expect that we will be prostrate, inconsolable, crazy with loss,' she writes in the immediate aftermath of the first death. 'We do not expect to be literally crazy, cool customers who believe that their husband is about to return and need his shoes.'

Later she talks about wanting to be present at the autopsy: 'I needed to know how and why and when it had happened.' Her book is a need-to-know-and-report-the-truth. A forensic examination of death and grief. Not an outpouring of emotion but a containment.

You sit down to dinner and life as you know it ends.
In a heartbeat.
Or the absence of one.

Disclosure

As well as the question of how *much* to reveal (see CONFESSION), there's the question of *when*. As readers we need easing into a narrative and it takes time to get to know the people involved. Then again, we can't be kept waiting for too long. There needs to be development. To hell with the hooks and cliff-hangers. We can't be tantalised indefinitely.

The question is, what's gained by holding back key information? Perhaps a lot – the Big Reveal may turn the story on its head, forcing us to re-appraise both the narrative and the narrator. Perhaps not much – what the writer thought a Big Reveal may prove to be No Big Deal. *So what?* we'll shrug, *Is this all it amounts to? Why didn't you tell me earlier?* I was guilty of that in an early draft of a book about my sister Gillian, keeping the fact of her alcoholism a secret till halfway through the book. As my agent pointed out, the postponement stymied the narrative and wrecked the tone. She was right. I changed it.

'When the writing is successful,' John Gardner says in *The Art of Fiction*, 'the reader senses that the climax is coming and feels a strong urge to skip to it directly, but cannot quite tear himself from the paragraph he's on. Ideally, every element in the lead-in passage should be a relevant distraction that heightens the reader's anticipation.' The writer can prolong the delay, to jokey effect, as Laurence Sterne does in *Tristram Shandy* and Samuel Beckett in *Waiting for Godot*. But when you're writing from life, and the disclosure is a key moment in that life, jokey procrastination will be unwise.

Jo Ann Beard offers a remarkable series of 'relevant distractions' in her 40-page story 'The Tomb of Wrestling', from the collection *Festival Days*, which describes a 'she' (a plausible version of herself) who's brutally attacked at home by an intruder but then recovers to hit him over the head with a shovel. It's an extremely tense piece because we're unsure whether the blow she strikes is fatal and, equally, whether the 'she' will survive. To add to the tension, the narrative is delayed and broken into by the inclusion of sections about her childhood, father, first husband and dogs, not to mention a heron, a frog and a literal yardstick. And there's the further complication or enrichment of sections written from the point of view of the intruder. It's a bravura feat of postponement, tempting the reader to skip ahead to the denouement yet doing just enough to hold us back.

A successful memoir won't give away too much too early nor withhold too much for too long.

Diski, Jenny

She's an author who deserves to be much better known, not least for her reflections on life writing. 'There are infinite ways of telling the truth, including fiction, and infinite ways of evading the truth, including non-fiction,' she writes in her first great memoir, *Skating to Antarctica*, a paradox she expanded on in her second great memoir, *In Gratitude*. 'I write both fiction and non-fiction, but it's almost always personal . . . I may not make things up in fiction, or tell the truth in non-fiction, but documentary or invented it's always been me at the centre . . . I lie like all writers but I use my truths as I know them in order to do so.' There's paradox for you. But Diski did have a sense of boundaries; she wasn't a shrugging relativist; she'd probably not have liked her fiction to be categorised as autofiction, however much it drew on her life. Her work is notable for its intimacy, the access we're given to what she's thinking and feeling, the courage of her honesty. Then again, she'd have denied there was anything courageous about it: she was just being herself – or playing at being Jenny Diski (an invented name). The role she most enjoyed was that of contrarian: an author who presented herself as bone-idle, 'a connoisseur of sleep', but who was hugely productive; who wrote very personally ('I start with me and often enough end with me') but 'never . . . had a sense that my writing is "confessional".'

To her, writing was about exploring the unsayable. Which included her positing that a woman might be complicit in abuse and take pleasure in being beaten by a man (as happens in her novel *Nothing Natural*). She didn't use the word *traumatic* of her rape at the age of 14, when a stranger she met in the street, an American, lured her into his recording studio and had sex with her. In her account, she says she was *embarrassed* into the sex (embarrassment would also be her first reaction when diagnosed with cancer), that she didn't think of it as the worst thing that had ever happened to her, that she didn't even feel particularly violated. By today's standards her level tone and lack of indignation are shocking. But it's not as if she lets her rapist off the hook: anger is there in the showing, if not the telling. And when she says it's not the worst thing that ever happened to her, that's in the context of all the other stuff she went through – extremes of neglect, rejection, mental breakdown and suicidal despair – not that the experience wasn't awful.

Where does Diski fit as a life writer? Nowhere. She didn't want to fit. I can think of writers she might have approved of and could be compared with – for their fearlessness in exploring their own lives, Annie Ernaux and Tove Ditlevsen; or for their essayistic flair, Deborah Levy, Maggie Nelson and Olivia Laing. But her sense of humour sets her apart. However dark the paths she leads us down, there are always jokes.

Distance

How removed do you have to be from the experience you're writing about? The common wisdom is that it takes several years to achieve perspective. Just as the bereaved are told that *it takes time to heal*, so life writers are told they need to *process*. The novelist Bernice Rubens said of one of her books, 'It was good therapy for me, but a rotten novel. You should always write in yesterday's blood.' Byron felt the same: 'To write so as to bring home to the heart, the heart must have been tried, – but, perhaps, ceased to be so. While you are under the influence of passions, you only feel, but cannot describe them, any more than, when in action, you would round and tell the story to your next neighbour! When all is over, – all, all, and irrevocable, trust to memory – she is then but too faithful.'

Yesterday's blood. When all is over. I'm not so sure. Great books have been written quickly, in the heat of the moment. Jack Kerouac was fibbing when he said he wrote *On The Road* in three weeks (that was the typing up; there'd been several earlier drafts). But Samuel Johnson's *Rasselas*, composed after his mother's death to raise money to pay for her funeral, was written in a week, and William Faulkner's *As I Lay Dying* and Dickens's *A Christmas Carol* in six weeks. Even if you're grieving (perhaps *especially* if you're grieving), as Johnson must have been, you can feel energised, as if you've entered a new world.

ON MEMOIR

What counts is the ability to see yourself as a character from the outside, which brings objectivity instead of lachrymosity or twaddle. I like J. R. Ackerley's description of how he operates in *My Father and Myself*, as if 'this life I am prowling about in were someone else's and I its historian'. A line on the first page of Susan Sontag's novel *Death Kit* voices a similar sentiment: 'Some people are their lives', she says, others 'merely inhabit' them.

A degree of watchfulness is essential: a capacity to stand outside oneself, or float above. There's a brilliant example in Sharon Olds's poem 'First', from her collection *The Wellspring*, when, as a naïve teenager, she's coerced into giving a blow-job in a steam bath to a much older man, and then turns his abusive and unfounded taunt – 'You've been sucking cock since you were fourteen' – into a compliment, an 'unmeant gift'. Rather than feeling soiled by his insult, she rises above it, cleansed and empowered.

To look down from above at your past self can be enriching: you're older and wiser; you know what's coming; you see what you didn't see at the time. But there has to be immersion as well as detachment – the writer then (when it happened) as well as the writer now. The most powerful passages in memoir don't pull out of a scene to pass judgement in hindsight, they keep us in the moment, as if it's still happening, and leave judgement to us. That takes detachment. But it isn't distanced from the event.

E

Editors

Nabokov called them 'pompous avuncular brutes'. Henry James said that they practised 'the butcher's trade'. Byron associated editing with emasculation and would, he said, 'have no gelding'. D. H. Lawrence compared it to trying 'to clip my own nose into shape with scissors' and John Updike said 'It's a little like going to the barber', adding, 'I have never liked haircuts.' In short, editors get a bad press. They're seen as bullies and bigots, in thrall to the current ethos of their publishing house and insensitive to their authors' integrity. There they sit, with their blue pencils or keyboard delete buttons, wilfully hacking away. They come in many different guises – from fact-checkers and OK-ers (as they're known at the *New Yorker*), to line-editors who niggle, and creatives who grasp the big picture. But in popular mythology they're lumped together as meddling middlebrows. 'Invisible behind his arras,' one Victorian critic wrote, 'the author's unsuspected enemy works to the sure discomfiture of all original ability – this fool in the dark who knows not what he mars.' Those who can, write; those who can't, edit – that seems to be the line. I prefer T. S. Eliot: asked if editors were no more than failed writers, he replied, 'Perhaps – but so are most writers.'

Mine may be a rare and lucky case but the editors I've known, far from bullying and squashing, have done the opposite, elucidating and drawing me out, or, when I'm exhausted and on the point of giving up (like a marathon runner hitting the wall), coaxing me to go the extra mile. Far from being bullies, editors can be quiet, nurturing sorts who tread so gently-gently that when they do tamper with the text you barely notice and can kid yourself they did no work at all. Frank O'Connor compared his editor William Maxwell to 'a good teacher who does not say "Imitate me" but "This is what I think you are trying to say".'

It's true that, just as some writers write too much, some editors edit too much. As the *New Yorker* writer Renata Adler acerbically puts it, there are those who 'cannot leave a text intact, eating through it leaf and branch, like tent caterpillars, leaving everywhere their mark'. When he edited the magazine *Granta*, Bill Buford was sometimes accused of overbearing interventionism – in his spare time he hung out with football hooligans, and he was accused of bringing the same thuggishness to editing. Personally I never found him brutal. He edited *And When Did You Last See Your Father?* and it's down to him that the book begins as it does: not (as I originally had it) with my father ill in hospital, but with him years earlier at his most alive and exasperating. In that way readers get to know Dad when he's fully himself – and can sympathise as he becomes less himself.

William Golding came to dislike *Lord of the Flies* but he'd no wish to see it republished without the cuts suggested by his editor at Faber, Charles Monteith. For Raymond Carver, it was a different story. Though grateful to Gordon Lish for helping with his breakthrough short story collection *What We Talk About When We Talk About Love,* he also felt humiliated. Critics and creative writing students might applaud his pared-down prose but it was Lish who'd done the paring. And he didn't just cut to the bone, he sometimes sawed right through and (so Carver felt) spilled the life-blood: 78% of the text cut from this story, 45% from that one. Was ever an author more savagely truncated? Lish re-titled the stories, re-paragraphed them, put in section breaks, changed the names of characters, modified the tone, created new endings (in one case, a murder becomes a double murder) and tampered with motive and psychology.

A more typical example (and more pertinent to life writers) was the editing of Roger Deakin's *Waterlog* at Chatto & Windus. It was fifty-something Deakin's first book and twenty-something Rebecca Carter's first big editing job, and as Patrick Barkham describes in his biography of Deakin, *The Swimmer*, they worked together to give the book shape and momentum. But Deakin felt 'short-changed' in the process and told Carter that 'the very heart of the book is in danger of being taken out', a complaint which she found 'upsetting because I'd emotionally and creatively engaged with the book', tightening its structure and persuading colleagues that 'a little book about swimming' could be a big success (which it was). When she proposed cutting a sentence about moorhens walking like little girls at a party trying out their mothers' high-heeled shoes, Deakin objected; its lyricism was the essence of the book, he said. It's a good image – Carter might have been right about everything else but he was right to want to keep it.

Many agents now double as editors, getting a text in order before they try to sell it. The reader doesn't notice if it has been through endless drafts and that's how it should be. But a published book relies on many different hands and life writers should be grateful for the care and work involved: their material is personal and often sensitive, and they depend on others to do it justice. With memoirs, a good editor will play a safeguarding role as well as tinkering with the text.

Embarrassment

For a couple of years I 'collaborated' with Paula Rego: she illustrated some poems of mine for a book called *Pendle Witches* and we spent many hours discussing children, sexuality and violence. (I'm putting 'collaborated' in quotes because she always interpreted the poems in uniquely Rego-ish terms.) We'd meet in her studio and she'd also talk about her paintings and how adding some quirky or outrageous visual detail, even if only in miniature or in a corner of the canvas, could make an impact. *The more you embarrass yourself, the better*, she thought.

I agree. Life writers should be willing to embarrass themselves, especially if they're depicting others in an embarrassing light. In my memoir of Dad I describe myself masturbating in the bath round the time of his death. When a reviewer in the Sunday papers picked up on this, I remember feeling embarrassed that something I'd made public was now *more* public – a feeling made worse when I blushingly walked into work next day and had to face colleagues. Perhaps readers of that passage felt equally discomfited, but if so that's fine. In his book *Keats and Embarrassment*, Christopher Ricks argues that 'one of the things for which we value art is that it helps us to deal with embarrassment, not by abolishing or ignoring it, but by recognising, refining and putting it to good human purposes'; to him 'the nobility of Keats' lay in seeing how embarrassment is 'inextricably involved in important moral concerns'.

In a memoir, embarrassment stems from putting on paper what polite society regards as too shaming to be said; you breach etiquette to challenge a prudish or repressive moral order. In 1993 a passing reference to masturbation, especially in the context of death, was thought dodgy. These days wanking is old hat. But there'll still be embarrassments an author remembers – things done or said, or not done and not said – which are part of the story they're writing. And if they're brave they won't worry about including them.

Equiano, Olaudah

Born in Nigeria in 1745, kidnapped from his family home as a child and sold into slavery, Equiano began serving on ships from the age of 12. Temporarily onshore in his teens, he was sent to live with his master's cousins – two sisters, the Guerins, who had a house in Greenwich and who paid for him to be educated. After buying his freedom, for a second time (the first time he was cheated), he worked as a hairdresser, took up the French horn, converted to Christianity, went to sea again many times and published his autobiography, *The Interesting Narrative of the Life of Olaudah Equiano, or Gustavus Vassa the African,* in 1789. It became a bestseller and, along with his own vigorous campaigning, played its part in the abolition of slavery. He married in 1792 and had two children, before he died in 1797.

Equiano's isn't the first book by a former slave to be published: ahead of it, in the UK, are the *Letters of the Late Ignatius Sancho, An African* in 1782, and the little memoir by Ukawsaw Gronniosaw ten years earlier. (Surprisingly there's no record of the three men having met, though Equiano, as the youngest, would certainly have heard of Sancho, a famous figure in his day.) But I'm giving pride of place to Equiano, because his is the angriest and most abolitionist book, published nine years before the first slave narrative in the US. None of it takes place in a plantation; its vibrancy lies in its stories of adventures (and catastrophes) at sea and in foreign lands. Nor is it so polemical in its campaigning that all white men are presented as tyrants; he's grateful for whatever decency and kindness he can find. But his account of the dishonesty, cruelty and inhumanity of those working in the slave trade is devastating – worst of all are the overseers, 'human butchers' as he calls them, 'who cut and mangle slaves in a shocking manner'. His account of a world in which 'Tortures, murder, and every other imaginable barbarity and iniquity, are practised upon the poor slaves with impunity' is an engrossing and instructive read – especially for anyone thinking of writing a story about cruelty or abuse.

Essay

In scholarly circles the form used to be thought of as impersonal, with the use of the first-person pronoun discouraged. But as Virginia Woolf puts it, essays can't help being 'essentially egotistical . . . Almost all essays begin with a capital I – "I think", "I feel" . . . to express one's personal peculiarities, so that under the decent veil of print one can indulge one's egoism to the full.' Montaigne's essays were candid, open, unafraid of the first person. And whether Orwell is writing about *Gulliver's Travels*, boys' comics, the poetry of the 1930s or the idiocy of Tolstoy's criticism of Shakespeare's *King Lear*, you always hear the same voice – somebody freely sharing his thoughts, even if they're out of step with current opinion. Among recent writers who have added enjoyably to the form are Geoff Dyer, Rebecca Solnit and Sinéad Gleeson.

Because of its association with school homework or university coursework, the essay form sounds unappealing, as if a matter of anguished duty not pleasure. But at best, essays are a journey of discovery. Unless they're hack-work, authors write them to find out what they think. They don't push strident opinion but admit to uncertainty, complication, the difficulty of arriving at the truth. There's a Philip Larkin poem I'm fond of called 'Ignorance', from *The Whitsun Weddings*, which puts this well:

> Strange to know nothing, never to be sure
> Of what is true or right or real
> But forced to qualify *or so I feel*
> Or *Well, it does seem so:*
> *Someone must know.*

Well it does seem so: in an essay that kind of exploratory tentativeness works better than a cocksure, no-room-for-argument *That's how it is.*

Montaigne described his essays as attempts to show 'some traits of my character'. They also expressed his thoughts on politics, religion, morality, love, sex, parenthood, death, the whole lot. But they were unashamedly personal and this is what made them radical. 'The target of my thoughts has been myself alone,' he writes. 'I study nothing but me, and if I do study anything else it is to apply it at once to myself.' Sounds narcissistic, doesn't it? But in 'applying' the issues to himself he took in the world at the same time. And he's right to say that essays can't help but be subjective.

The American novelist Jonathan Franzen has suggested that what defines the essay – the expression of opinions or the narrating of personal experiences (or some combination of the two) – is now a staple of social media: of blogs, posts and tweets. 'Should we be mourning the essay's extinction?' he asks, 'Or should we be celebrating its conquest of the larger culture?' Unlike essays, social media posts have little room for nuance. But as first-hand testimonies or thoughts derived from personal experience, blogs belong to the essay genre.

Where life writing is speculative, more enquiry than narrative, more an exploration of ideas than story-telling, the essay is the right form – though when it's pushed from rational argument towards poetry it's something else again. (See LYRIC ESSAY.)

Ethics

I've touched on this already (see CONSENT) but it's worth emphasising what a huge issue the ethics of life writing has become. For example, all universities now have ethics committees and in most of them creative writing is treated much as sociology or anthropology are, with informed consent an essential requirement for any PhD student working on a memoir. A key question is whether the 'participants' (i.e., any living persons who appear in a memoir, however briefly) have given their permission to be written about – as if they were interviewees contributing to a research project. Even before student life writers begin writing, they may be grilled by a committee, at times so dauntingly that some give up.

I had a student who at one point in her PhD made innocuous passing references to her two siblings. 'Have they consented for you to write about them?' she was asked by the Ethics Enforcers. The suggestion was that where she wrote, 'My sister smiled and squeezed my hand', she would need a signed consent form permitting that description. And if she quoted her brother asking 'Would you like a cup of tea?', she'd need the same from him. Common sense suggests this is ludicrous.

Another PhD student I worked with was the writer and ethics expert Anna Derrig, who argues that it's important to seek informed consent (a writer like Sheila Heti would agree). She drew up a helpful guide on how to write ethically:

- Aim for written permission before you publish.
- Be prepared for changes. Consent is a process.
- Agree if a right of veto is allowed and clarify details.
- Remember the written-about have rights too.
- Aim to balance your right to free expression with their right to privacy.
- Change identifying details & conflate events, if requested/as necessary.
- Share the rewards, if writing collaboratively or about others and publicise.
- Give credit where it's due for ideas, as well as published material used.
- Avoid plagiarism and check copyright on and offline.
- Be transparent – name your sources, e.g. letters, emails, Facebook etc.
- Tell the truth…as you perceive it! Take legal advice if unsure.
- Decide when it's more ethical to publish: immediately or after events.
- Weigh up the costs and benefits of disclosing painful/sensitive information.
- Consider using an impartial advocate if your subject is vulnerable.

- Write well and with empathy.

Anna's is a thoughtful and sensitive approach. Our stories are our most precious possessions, she argues, and other people get hurt if we tell them carelessly. But she presses the need for consent further than I would. I'm more in the *publish and be damned* school. The memoir of my father would be poorer without passages I used without seeking consent – from his lover Beaty, for instance, one of whose letters, which I quoted, tells me to stop pestering her for information about their affair ('Please leave me one last small piece of the jigsaw – it's mine.') It's a great letter. But I didn't think of asking her permission to reproduce it. And if I had, she might have refused.

When the Australian writer Helen Garner was considering publishing diaries she'd written, she told friends and family; their reaction was Feel free, go ahead, I trust you. She did some editing but didn't sugar-coat. Morally, she thought, it was fine to go ahead, provided she was as tough on herself as on others: 'The only way it's ethically doable is if you bring to bear on yourself the same amount of sharp, biting criticism and examination of your own foolishness or cruelty or harshness or indifference. It just seems like a fair deal.'

As I see it, unnecessary work and worry have arisen because of a mis-categorisation of life writing as a 'research' activity, in which any living person alluded to is treated as a potentially litigious interviewee. Memoirs can be a minefield and when you're writing candidly about others the stakes are high. That's why some publishers use libel lawyers. But editors should use their own judgement about the ethics of what they're publishing. None of the classics of life writing would exist were they made to meet the requirements of Ethics Enforcers.

Exploitation

'Every journalist who is not too stupid or too full of himself to notice what is going on knows that what he does is morally indefensible,' Janet Malcolm famously wrote in *The Journalist and the Murderer*. 'He is a kind of confidence man, preying on people's vanity, ignorance or loneliness, gaining their trust and betraying them without remorse.' Do life writers go high where journalists go low? Joan Didion didn't think so: 'Writers are always selling somebody out,' she wrote in *Slouching Towards Bethlehem*. For memoirists drawing on their own experiences, the discomfort won't only be guilt about 'using' others or *speaking ill of the dead* but the shame of *self*-exploitation. The shame of thinking themselves worth writing about. And the shame of treating their life as 'material'.

Karl Ove Knausgaard had these feelings in the aftermath of his father's death. They'd had a difficult relationship and hadn't spoken for some years. But when he came to the house where his father had been living ('bottles everywhere, on the floors, up the stairs, on all the tables and sideboards') and saw him in his coffin (his nose broken and his face clogged with blood), he was overwhelmed by grief. Nevertheless, 'In the midst of this emotional chaos, one thought remained unaffected . . . that I had to write about all this. That it was a great story.' It took him many years to find the right way. But when he did, he found himself 'flaring with shame and a burning sense of freedom. Only rarely did I think about anyone ever reading what I wrote.'

People did read it. He considered *A Death in the Family* (the first of his six-volume sequence *My Struggle*) to be a book 'about myself' but sent the manuscript to people who appeared in it. And all hell broke loose: his father's family – in particular his father's brother – were enraged and brought a lawsuit to prevent publication. They didn't succeed. On the contrary, when news of the lawsuit got out, Knausgaard found himself in the middle of a media storm and his book became a bestseller.

He's not the only celebrated life writer to be accused of exploitation and to cause severe distress. Primo Levi upset Lello Perugia, the real-life model for the man he calls Cesare in *If This Is a Man*. They were fellow prisoners in Auschwitz and Levi's portrait is affectionate. But Perugia felt betrayed because Levi made him a barrow boy, not the book-keeper he had been. Sandro, a character in Levi's *The Periodic Table*, was similarly portrayed (to his family's annoyance) as coming from a poorer background than he did. Even Levi, the great truth-teller of the twentieth century, was apt to fictionalise, or 'fake', if he thought that would better serve his story. In the words of a Tuscan proverb that he liked to quote, 'The tale is not beautiful if nothing is added to it.'

W. G. Sebald is guilty not just of commission but omission. A man called Peter Jordan felt resentful that an unpublished memoir by his aunt Thea Gebhardt which he lent to Sebald (and which became the story, in *The Emigrants*, of Luisa Lanzberg) wasn't acknowledged. Susi Bechhöfer was even angrier at Sebald's unacknowledged use of her memoir *Rosa's Child* in depicting the childhood of Jacques Austerlitz; she felt her identity had been stolen. Sebald was similarly high-handed in his exploitation of the life and work of the painter Frank Auerbach, the model for Max Ferber (originally, in the German version, Max Aurach) in *The Emigrants*. Auerbach knew nothing of the book until it was due to come out in English. He objected to the name, to the reproduction (without permission) of one of his drawings, and to the inclusion of a photo of his eye. The name was duly changed and the two illustrations were dropped but Auerbach remained angry, writing that he found Sebald's 'presumptuous/humourless solemnity repellent', and that he 'deprecate[d] the use of other people's misunderstood biographies to lend weight to what appeared a narcissistic enterprise'. Sebald wasn't narcissistic (other people's suffering affected him deeply) but in gathering material he was ruthless.

You can upset people by tampering with the truth. And you can upset them by sticking to it. You can't predict how they'll react. I once wrote a friendly piece about Dorothy Pilley Richards (widow of the critic I. A. Richards) who'd been a pioneering mountaineer in her youth. She was furious when it came out because I'd revealed her age. It's tricky getting things right. Going too carefully can be as self-defeating as upsetting people or ripping them off. What Elizabeth Strout said (in a *Guardian* interview) about fiction applies no less to memoir:

> You can't write fiction and be careful. You just can't. I've seen it with my students over the years, and I think actually the biggest challenge a writer has is to not be careful. So many times students would say, 'Well, I can't write that, my boyfriend would break up with me.' And I'd think 'Well, OK, I'm sorry, I don't really have much more to tell you.' You have to do something that's going to say something, and if you're careful it's just not going to work.

Writers do generally care about the people they write about. But they also have to care about the writing. And caring about the writing comes first.

F

Fact-checking

Even in a novel, it makes no sense to have your protagonist catch a train to Edinburgh from Charing Cross. Or for swallows to nest in Barnsley in December. Or for the sun to set over the sea at Great Yarmouth. In a work of non-fiction, no matter how creative, it's doubly important. 'Take nothing for granted if you can check it,' Kipling advised, even if it 'seems waste work . . . There are always men who by trade or calling know the fact or the inference that you put forth. If you're wrong by a hair in this, they argue, "False in one thing, false in all".'

False in one thing, false in all. Unless life writers are making a play of their unreliability, which very few do, they want readers to trust them. And that means checking facts and period detail, the nitty-gritty of clothes, idiom, food, prices, music, brand names, television shows, bus routes, etc. Memories can't be relied on. And it's better for a writer to avoid mistakes than to be called out by an affronted reader. It's not pedantry to get the facts right, it's evidence that you want to be truthful. And you can't rely on publishers to fact-check for you. It's not that they're lazy or lack the resources, it's the nature of the game. If you're the one telling the story then you're the authority, the expert witness, the person that readers depend on. Facts are only part of the truth but they count.

Family history

A growing number of people are writing works of family history for the benefit of relatives, children and grandchildren. If you're in that category your priority will be getting the facts down, so there's a record of origins and future generations will know where they come from. But much archival material is dry and you don't want to be boring. What you've found in your research is important. But so is shaping the story. You have to make it readable, not just serve up genealogical data. Narrative, characterisation, structure, tone – these matter as much in a work of 100 privately printed copies as in a mainstream publication. You can't use a limited readership as an excuse for not telling the story to the best of your ability.

Sometimes the story is a gift, or will seem to be. Your father was a Japanese prisoner-of-war. Your grandmother was a cabaret artist. Your great-uncle helped to build the *Titanic*. Great material. But key facts are missing and you can't rely on stories passed down in the family, which may be fanciful. The research will be exhaustive – exhausting too. The gift isn't a poisoned chalice but there's more to telling the story than you imagined: more graft is required and more patience too.

'You are now the keeper of the family archive,' Edmund de Waal's father jokes at the start of *The Hare with Amber Eyes*, as he hands over a small cache of photos. It isn't much to go on. But photos put flesh on people. And de Waal is determined to unearth the human history behind the collection of 264 Japanese *netsuke* (delicate wood and ivory carvings) he has inherited. Two or three months should be enough time to put together the story, he thinks, and other material soon emerges. But the quest lasts two or three years, taking him to Paris, Vienna and Japan, and into the posthumous company of Renoir, Proust, Laforgue and Rilke, among others. It's family history on a grand scale, as affluent domestic life intersects with war and antisemitism, and the *netsuke* miraculously survive Nazi appropriation, despite the loss of so much else. To do it justice took more time than expected. It always does.

Source material for family history might be diaries, letters, postcards, passports, wills, maps, paintings, inventories, invoices, manifests, legal writs, microfiche, receipts, ledgers, documents from an archive or anything relevant that comes to hand. When I read the letters my parents exchanged during the Second World War, years before I was born, I learned many things about them I'd not known, which may be why Dad had taken such trouble to keep them. It was tempting to let the letters stand alone, much as the wartime letters of the actors Hugh Williams and his wife Margaret Vyner, parents of the poet Hugo and actor Simon Williams, stand alone in the book *Always and Always*. But I decided they needed a context. *Things My Mother Never Told Me* quotes liberally from the letters, but my reaction is also part of the story, not least the shame of reading highly personal material:

> The letters weren't grenades. And my parents couldn't explode at me. It felt dangerous handling them all the same . . . The still, small voice of conscience told me: 'This is none of your business.' But it was my business. Family business. The legacy I'd come into. The love to which I owed my life.

Lorna Sage is similarly self-accusing and self-inclusive in her memoir *Bad Blood*, as she reads through her womanising grandfather's diaries and his wife's angry marginalia. 'Reading these diaries turned out to be a bit like eavesdropping on the beginnings of my world,' she writes, though the shock for her was as much 'the record of a pottering, Pooterish, almost farcically domesticated life' as it was the confessions of a sinful vicar. When a confrontation of source material is dramatic – emotionally, ethically, as an illustration of a generation gap or for other reasons – it deserves to be part of the story.

Multiple narration can also be useful – stories from others (friends and family you've consulted, letters you've discovered, criminal or military records, etc.) to complement your own. I was recently sent a privately published book about a young woman who died at the age of 25. She'd had no time to realise ambitions or forge a career because she'd been ill since her teens. But she'd left a mark on those who knew her and the book brought her to life – through photos, through her own drawings and letters, and through the memories of family and friends. The book came out many years after death. That doesn't matter. She has her memorial.

Faux-naïvety

A *faux-naïf* tone is a kind of pact with the reader, allowing them to see things that the author now knows but didn't understand at the time: the child didn't realise her dad was a drunk, the girl thought the man offering her a lift in his car was simply being kind, the teenage boy warned about chlamydia thought it was a house-plant, etc. Overdone, the *faux-naïf* can make a narrator look credulous and pathetic, a mere victim. But skilfully managed, it's a rich device. Andrea Ashworth speaks as a *faux-naïf* child early on in her memoir *Once in a House on Fire*, in the wake of her father's death: 'Scuffing along the pavement, my red sandals jumped the cracks by heart,' she writes and notices 'purple-grey clouds, bellies full of rain'. These seemingly random childish details aren't random at all: there are cracks in her life (and heart) as well as on the pavement; those clouds are an augur of her mother's belly, which within a year, thanks to the new man in her life, will be 'swollen full of a third child', leaving Andrea with an unwanted new name (Andrea Clarke-Hawkins) or, as she puts it, 'an ugly new tail'.

Hilary Mantel's *faux-naïvete* in her memoir *Giving Up the Ghost* is hilarious: 'I am waiting to change into a boy. When I am four this will occur', 'I used to be Irish but I'm not sure now', 'My grandfather is a railway man and has been to Palestine, though not on the train', 'Tibby is Mrs Clayton's cat. He lives at no. 68, and flees along the wall. I do not know him. He is a Protestant cat.' The method works for her early years, till the getting of wisdom at five: 'We sing he [Davy Crockett] killed a bear when he was only three. Somehow I doubt it. Even I didn't do that.'

Fiction

How far fiction is allowable in life writing is one of the great debates (see AUTOFICTION). I'm of a school that believes non-fiction means not making things up. But minor adjustments to time and place are inevitable. And memory is often a liar (see MEMORY). I like George Szirtes's line on it in his memoir *The Photographer at Sixteen*, where he says 'that any knowledge is partly invention, that memory is mostly invention, and that knowledge of another is invention in the highest degree . . . I invent nothing factual. I don't make it up, but the person at the core of it all still has to be constructed and understood in terms of invention. The trick is to invent the truth.'

There's a motto for any life writer: *the trick is to invent the truth*. It's an axiom that sees off the idea that life writing is an easy-peasy genre, where the only task is banal transcription – jot it down, spew it up. As Szirtes says, to tell the truth means being inventive. Which doesn't mean fictionalising but does require imagination.

Finishing

How do writers know when the memoir, essay, poem or novel they're writing is finished? When they're thoroughly sick of it would be one answer – when they've reworked it so many times they feel they can take it no further. But chances are they'll have had that sensation when it *wasn't* finished: after leaving it a few days, or getting feedback on it, they'll realise there is more to do. So what's the difference this time? 'A poem is never finished, only abandoned,' W. H. Auden said. He was condensing Paul Valéry, who said in a 1933 essay 'In the eyes of those who anxiously seek perfection, a work is never truly completed – a word that for them has no sense – but abandoned; and this abandonment, of the book to the fire or to the public, whether due to weariness or to a need to deliver it for publication, is a sort of accident, comparable to the letting-go of an idea that has become so tiring or annoying that one has lost all interest in it.'

ON MEMOIR

Is finishing, as Valéry suggests, more an accident than a decision? Perhaps the truth is that authors finish several times:

- They finish the final draft then find, on re-reading, that it's only the penultimate draft, or pre-penultimate draft.
- They finish the final draft but their best friend, or most trusted reader, or agent, tells them it needs further revision.
- They finish the final draft (duly revised) and their agent sends it out and a publisher's editor who's interested says it needs some reworking.
- They finish the final draft (duly reworked) and the publishing editor likes it and accepts it but suggests a few structural adjustments.
- They finish the final draft (duly restructured) and it goes to a copyeditor, who has some queries.
- They finish the final draft (with the queries answered and any necessary corrections made) and then there's the cover design to think about, and the blurb, jacket quotes and author's photo and biog.
- They finish the final draft and the book is published and a couple of readers point out factual mistakes, which are corrected for the paperback edition.

And even when all the publicity, talks, readings, etc., are over, it's not that the author has abandoned the book; on the contrary *it* has abandoned *them*. It was a love affair while it lasted (with all the heartache) but now they're through and out the other side they can't remember much about it. In fact it's a blank, a book they perhaps never look at again. And *that's* when it's finished.

Flashbacks

Is there any point to them in life writing? If a book's a memoir, it's *all* flashback: scenes recalled and made sense of. Ditto back story: a memoir *is* back story, a recounting and re-examining of the past.

Still, life writing invariably consists of parallel narratives: there's the author now and there's the author (imaginatively) then. It's as common a structure in memoir as the sonnet is in poetry. In *Bad Blood*, Lorna Sage's account of her grandfather's promiscuity, surreptitiously documented in his diaries, is supplemented by the story, among other things, of her own teenage pregnancy ('my mother's worst insult was to say "You're just like your grandfather." . . . I took it as a great compliment'). In *The Lost Child*, the back story – about a young nineteenth-century painter – alternates with Julie Myerson's present-day story about a teenage addict (her son).

The back story, in Myerson's case, is relatively dull; more often in parallel narratives the problem is the *front* story. Say it's a memoir about a woman who discovers the diaries her mother kept from adolescence through her broken marriage up to her suicide in middle age. This back story is compelling. But the author's account of her own life, in the present day – writing, cooking, talking to friends on the phone – is boring. There's all the potential for a powerful parallel narrative, since her own marriage, she tells us in passing, has just ended in divorce. And she's exploring her mother's life, in part, to combat her own drift towards unhappiness and depression. But she can't bring herself to deal with that.

I remember a story in which a troubled young woman fantasises about having sex with her father, whom she never knew but whose story she reconstructs. In passing she alludes to having had difficult experiences with men – brother, boyfriends, husband. The emotional-psychological thrust of the narrative cries out for these to be explored but she doesn't go there.

In short, where authors are making themselves part of the present-day story, which is almost inevitable in a piece of life writing, they shouldn't shirk self-examination. The now may be a smaller strand than the then but it has to earn its keep.

Food

I'm not a foodie. I once horrified a magazine editor by choosing skate as a favourite main course – she thought it was a misprint for steak. And my reluctant contribution to a writers' and artists' cookbook was a recipe for red cabbage, chosen because my three-year-old grandson liked how I made it. That's how infantile my relationship with food is and why I've few book recommendations to make on the subject. If recipes and restaurants are your thing, fine, the weekend newspapers are full of ideas for them, along with shopping, holidays and interior design. But don't make me read food memoirs. Unless the author is a genius (at writing as well as eating or cooking), I'll be bored.

Still, food can play a crucial part in memoirs, even when they're not about food. The childhood pleasures of eating (choc ices, sherbet fountains) and childhood agonies of being forced to eat (spinach, cabbage, semolina); the refusal of food (in anorexia memoirs); the life-changing dramas that happen during a meal. Sathnam Sanghera's *The Boy with the Topknot* is more about madness and ethnicity than food, but his mother's chapattis are integral to it.

For a behind-the-scenes story from restaurants you won't do better than Anthony Bourdain's *Kitchen Confidential* and Bill Buford's *Heat*. (Buford also has a good memoir about football fandom, *Among the Thugs*.) But my pick of food memoirs is Nigel Slater's *Toast: The story of a boy's hunger*. It's organised as a set of short sections, each about an item of food (Tinned Ham, Lemon Meringue Pie, Prawn Cocktail, etc.). Each has a slice of narrative from his childhood and adolescence: school, class and sex are there as well as home cooking. Slowly a larger, tragic story emerges, about the death of his mother and his father's unwise re-marriage to Joan, the family cleaner. Food is at the heart of every section but the 'hunger' of the subtitle is for love and happiness as well. And Slater is brilliant (and very funny) when describing food and everything associated with it: chops so overcooked 'I might as well be eating the sole of my father's brown brogues', thin sausages 'like little pink rodents', the music of an ice-cream van, 'wobbly, like a music box running down', his dad carving the roast as if he has 'clubbed the animal to death and dragged it home through the snow like a caveman with a mammoth'.

Food, as Slater shows, can play a huge part in the family dynamic. Memoirists shouldn't avoid it. But nor should they curry favour (hah) by gourmandising the text.

Footnotes

Footnotes in life writing can be fun. As a quasi-scholarly device, reserved for stuff that will distract from the main narrative but which deserves a passing reference in small print, they can enhance a memoir – not just to supplement or qualify but to lark about. The footnotes in Adam Kay's *This Is Going to Hurt* explain potentially baffling medical terms. They also make jokes: 'Much like your drunk mate insisting you go on to one more club even though she's already got vomit in her hair, pregnancies sometimes keep going longer than is wise.'

In *Experience,* Martin Amis uses footnotes from the off, sometimes three or four to a page. They range from the purely informational ('The novelist Elizabeth Howard: my stepmother from 1965 to 1983'), through the jokey-pontifical ('It's not the case that in the future everyone will be famous for fifteen minutes. In the future everyone will be famous all the time – but only in their own minds') to the farcical ('in astrology everything is 110 per cent false except everything about Scorpios [his own star-sign], which is 100 per cent true'). The difficulty for Amis lies in finding a balance between (to borrow his own phrase) 'foppery and overearnestness'. In a book that's in part about the murder of his cousin, foppery would rankle, but when it's also about having a comic novelist for a father, overearnestness is equally no-go. The footnotes help to strike a balance between light and heavy.

In *Memories of a Catholic Girlhood,* Mary McCarthy uses an alternative method: appendices to each chapter. They're correctives to material she first published independently in magazines, using comments from members of her family and her own revisions. As though a Catholic in a confessional, she contritely admits to misremembering or over-dramatising or (to be harsher about it) telling lies. 'There are several dubious points in this memoir', 'This account is highly fictionalised', 'There are some semi-fictional touches here', '[I cannot] vouch for the exact words or the exact order of the speeches', etc. What's interesting about McCarthy's annotations is how *long* they are, sometimes running to several pages and becoming stories in their own right.

Notes are also helpful if friends and family have read a book in draft and the author wants to acknowledge their gripes without absorbing them in the main narrative. Tara Westover has two pages of footnotes at the end of her memoir *Educated*, when she qualifies her account of accidents to her brothers Luke and Shawn by acknowledging other people's different memories of what happened. She then adds a further 'Note on the Text' to reflect on this 'carousel of contradiction' and to reconsider how well or badly her father behaved during the two crises: 'Either my father sent Luke down the mountain alone, or he did not; either he left Shawn in the sun with a serious head injury, or he did not. A different father, a different man, is born from those details.'

What's at stake for Westover is the decency or otherwise of her father. It's a big issue and she doesn't minimise it by putting it in a footnote.

Footsteps

More than any other biographer, Richard Holmes has made it a principle that, to understand whoever it is you're writing about, you need to stand where they stood, walk where they walked, eat, drink and sleep where they ate, drank and slept, etc. As he puts it in his book *Footsteps: Adventures of a Romantic Biographer*, biography, for him, means 'a kind of pursuit, a tracking of the physical trail of someone's path through the past, a following of footsteps'. The landscapes and buildings may have changed beyond recognition, especially if the subject is long dead (as were, in his case, Shelley, Coleridge and Robert Louis Stevenson). And the figure being pursued will always remain just out of reach. Nevertheless, they'll be understood in ways they wouldn't have been understood if the author hadn't made the journey: 'You stood at the end of the broken bridge and looked across carefully, objectively, into the unattainable past on the other side. You brought it alive, brought it back, by other sorts of skills and crafts and sensible magic.'

The footsteps premise holds true not just for biographers or family chroniclers but for life writers whose subject is themselves. If you're writing about childhood you need to revisit the places where it happened. So much gets triggered just by being there – stuff you wouldn't have remembered otherwise, stuff you might not *want* to remember but is essential to the story. I was fortunate, in writing memoirs of my parents, that they'd moved only yards away from where I grew up, into a house they built on the field at the back of our old house. They'd also taken everything with them – the same furniture and domestic items. Objects of that kind are never just objects; they hold memories. And, for me, seeing or holding them again – that dining table, those knives, the faux-French print showing dogs queueing to piss on a lamp-post – allowed numerous lost memories to return.

Footsteps can be a source of understanding too. At the trial of Robert Thompson and Jon Venables in 1993, it became clear, from witness statements, that the boys had walked little James Bulger back into the neighbourhood where they went to school and where one of them lived. Why do that if, as the prosecution alleged, they planned to murder him clandestinely? What chance did they have of getting away with it, when people they knew saw them? And why tell passers-by the little boy was lost and they were taking him to the police station? The court process shed little or no light on this. So I walked the walk. At the end of the alley where their journey finished, they could have turned right to the police station or turned left to Robert's home. Both were close by. But both would have meant them getting into trouble. So they took a third option, a scramble up onto the railway line where, rather than abandon James, they killed him. Footsteps told me why they'd ended up on the railway line. However brutal, what they did was opportunistic – the kind of decision a ten-year-old would make. Childish panic rather than adult premeditation.

Life writers can't just sit at home. They need to get out. To revisit the sources. Walking itself can free up thoughts. And where an author is walking with a purpose, as part of a quest, it can bring even greater rewards. Margaret Forster puts it brilliantly at the end of her memoir *Hidden Lives*, where she talks of walking through Carlisle:

> The past – my grandmother's, my mother's, my aunts' – did not seem a foreign country to me as I daily walked its streets. I passed over again and again the places where they lived and worked and shopped until the empathy with them was strong, and the recollection of my childhood self so sharp, that we all walked together. But that perhaps is the point of any memoir – to walk with the dead and yet see them with our eyes, from our vantage point.

Form

Form has to mirror content, the adage goes, and it can in numerous ways. There's onomatopoeia, the sound words make echoing the things they describe, as in Tennyson's 'The moan of doves in immemorial elms, / And murmuring of innumerable bees' (a run of *m*s may seem less apt for evoking bees than doves, but hum the letter to yourself and it does create a buzz). There's significant structure, for instance the numerological principle whereby the number of stanzas in a poem or chapters in a book reflects the theme (Anthony Burgess was incensed when American publishers tried to cut the last chapter of *A Clockwork Orange*, because he'd divided the novel into three sections of seven chapters each to mirror the hero Alex's progress – rise, imprisonment and then redemption at the age of 21). Or there's unfinishedness, as in Mike McCormack's *Solar Bones*, a novel written in a single incomplete sentence: its last words are 'keep going' and it does, as do Bernardine Evaristo's *Girl, Woman, Other*, the concluding Molly Bloom section of *Ulysses,* and the novels in the Norwegian Jon Fosse's *Septology* sequence, all of them composed without full stops. These formal innovations are like mirrors, reflecting what the books are about.

Form needn't always mirror content, though. Sometimes they work in opposition. My poem about Peter Sutcliffe, the Yorkshire Ripper, is written as a ballad, a form which by the twentieth century was mostly treated as comic. The poem's subject matter – serial murder and misogyny – is anything but comic. But in earlier centuries ballads told stories of violence, bloodshed and crime. While working against the current grain, in verses that readers found discomfiting, the Ripper ballad was also restoring the form to its origins. I've read memoirs that work in the same way, exploring dark and tragic material in a comic, or seemingly comic, voice. In *A Truce That is Not Peace*, Miriam Toews grieves for her sister, but many passages in it are hilarious.

That's also the intention in *And When Did You Last See Your Father?*, where I mourn my father while remembering him as comically larger than life. The form of the book is past-present: chapters in which he's exasperatingly alive alternate with chapters in which he's terminally ill; both implicitly address the question of the title. The binary form arrived by itself, without forethought. Nor did I plan the fluctuating tenses in *Things My Mother Never Told Me*, where the 'present' moment of the book, after Mum's death, is narrated in the past tense, whereas the recreated 'past' of their romance, before they married, is told in the present tense, to convey its drama and immediacy. The book's coda uses the future tense, imagining a sequence of events, round the time Mum died, that have already happened, as if to ward them off. The tenses are integral to the book's form. (See TENSE for more on this.)

As to the idea that a literary work should be formally disordered so as to mirror social or psychic disorder, it's given short shrift in Tobias Wolff's autofictional *Old School* by no less a poet than Robert Frost, during a visit he pays to the all-boys private school that Wolff (or his protagonist) is attending. After Frost has recited 'Stopping by Woods on a Snowy Evening', a young teacher pompously asks him 'whether such a rigidly formal arrangement of language is adequate to express the modern consciousness' and whether 'more spontaneous forms of expression' aren't better suited to evoking world war, concentration camps, the threat of nuclear annihilation, etc. Frost gives him hell:

> Don't tell me about war. I lost my nearest friend in the one they call the Great War. So did Achilles lose his friend in war, and Homer did no injustice to his grief by writing about it in dactylic hexameters . . . Would you honour your own friend by putting words down anyhow, just as they come to you – with no thought for the sound they make, the meaning of their sound, the sound of their meaning? Would that give a true account of the loss?... Such grief can only be told in form. Maybe it only really

exists in form. Form is everything. Without it you've got nothing but a stubbed-toe cry – sincere, maybe, for what that's worth, but with no depth or carry. No echo. You may have a grievance but you do not have grief, and grievances are for petitions, not poetry.

Frost's isn't a fogeyish defence of traditional form. He's arguing that strong emotions such as grief need form to contain them – that without the discipline of rhyming quatrains, say, all you get is a *stubbed-toe cry*, a wail or whine rather than a work of art.

Frost's premise applies as much to life writing as to poetry. However compelling the story, the author needs to find the right way to tell it – the right idiom, the right structure, the right tone of voice, the right form. And that can be a long haul.

Fragments

Robert Frost doesn't believe in disorder as a device. Would he be more responsive to fragmentation? Probably not. But life writing sometimes works best when it's episodic, fractured, broken up. And it suits a certain kind of writer, who's resistant to fluent narrative. The philosopher Galen Strawson, in his essay 'Against Narrativity', argues against a consensus summarised by Oliver Sacks's claim that 'each of us constructs and lives a "narrative" . . . this narrative *is* us, our identities'. On the contrary, Strawson says, 'There are deeply non-Narrative people and there are good ways to live that are deeply non-Narrative.' He calls these people Episodics and says he's an Episodic himself: 'I have absolutely no sense of my life as a narrative with form, or indeed as a narrative without form.'

An enterprising example of fragmentariness is Carmen Maria Machado's *In The Dream House*, a memoir about a toxic relationship in which she wants to make room for reflection as well as event and to convey the disjunctions she experienced. 'You begin to experiment with fragmentation,' she writes of her approach. 'Maybe "experiment" is a generous word; you're really just unable to focus enough to string together a proper plot . . . You feel like you can jump from one idea to the next, searching for a kind of aggregate meaning . . . You will spend the next few years of your career coming up with elaborate justifications for the structure . . . You can't bring yourself to say what you really think: I broke the stories down because I was breaking down and didn't know what else to do.'

I broke the stories down because I was breaking down: no arguing with that. In memoirs about illness, addiction and mental turmoil, the narrative can fragment to mirror a fragmented mind.

Jenn Ashworth's incapacity to see her life as narrative followed a traumatic, blood-strewn medical procedure, though a disruptive childhood contributed too. Struggling to construct a memoir, because 'pieces of the story are missing', and unable to think (as novelists do) in terms of epiphany, she embraced apophany, the impulse to find connections where none exist – random configurations, intrusive thoughts, leaps of association. The book that ensued, *Notes Made While Falling*, includes material ranging from a lecture on *King Lear* to an 'off topic' analysis of her own 'derailment'. There's no narrative line, since she can't see her life in linear terms, but the book works as a 'braided essay', a frame for disorder, 'a form that's all about interruption and rupture, about disconnection. And also about repair and recuperation, without the flattening out of coherence.'

Elena Ferrante names one of her books after a dialect word her mother used: *frantumaglia*, a jumble of fragments, 'a word she used to describe how she felt when she was racked by contradictory sensations . . . a miscellaneous crowd of things in her head'. A book needs to be more than a jumble of fragments. But for writers who're Episodic not Narrative by nature, fragmentariness makes sense.

Friends

If they've helped with the book, as readers or mentors, they deserve to be acknowledged. But like family, friends are unpredictable. And if they're depicted in a book, they'll be sensitive about how they come across. In *A Moveable Feast*, Hemingway recalls Scott Fitzgerald with affection. But his friend wouldn't have liked the portrayal of his hypochondria, let alone the scene when, after he confesses 'Zelda said that the way I was built I could never make any woman happy', Hemingway has to reassure him that his penis is not, after all, disastrously small. Fitzgerald had been dead for over twenty years when the memoir came out. Even so.

Worst of all is when friends feel they've collaborated on a piece of writing and haven't been given any credit. Take the relationship between Langston Hughes and Zora Neale Hurston. For a time, during the Harlem Renaissance, they were the closest of friends and told each other so: 'honey', 'darling' and 'lovingly yours' was how she addressed him in her letters; 'my darling', 'the nearest person on earth to me' is what he called her. Then they fell out over a play they were writing together, *The Mule-Bone*, and had, what Henry Louis Gates Jr called, 'the most notorious literary quarrel in African-American cultural history'. Hurston felt, with justice, that the play was her invention and that she'd written almost all of it: 'It was my story from beginning to end. It is my dialogue; my situations.' Hughes exaggerated his part in its composition but resented her dumping him when they'd agreed to collaborate: 'Zora chooses to be not only contrary and untruthful, but malicious and hurtful as well.' There were complications involving a wealthy, white 'godmother' patron they shared, Charlotte Mason, and a young woman, Louise Thompson, with whom (so Zora jealously believed) Langston was having an affair. Their acrimonious row dragged on for years, with lawyers involved and bitter letters exchanged. The two of them never got over it but nor, in their memoirs, could they address it. Hurston omits Hughes entirely from her autobiography *Dust Tracks on a Road*; even in a chapter on her many friends (dropped on the advice of her publishers and printed as an appendix in a later edition) he doesn't appear. Hughes does talk about Hurston in his autobiography *The Big Sea* but condescendingly and, in relation to *The Mule-Bone*, with self-serving dishonesty. Having once shared similar ideas and aspirations, they went separate ways, he towards Communism and she to write her novel *Their Eyes Were Watching God*. Sundered from each other, they also divided later generations of Black writers, with some championing his achievement and others hers.

On a smaller scale of literary achievement, there's the more recent episode of Dawn Dorland and Sonya Larson, who fell out after the latter wrote a story about a woman who donates a kidney, which the former had done; Larson took words Dorland had used; lawyers representing them became involved in a dispute about the rights of a writer to use whatever material they choose, without consultation. 'There are married writer couples who don't let each other read each other's work,' Larson said. 'I have no obligation to tell anyone what I'm working on.'

ON MEMOIR

Like Hurston/Hughes, Dorland/Larson was a spat between rival writers. But friendships can suffer in more humdrum ways. I once offended an old schoolfriend because of a scene I'd written in a memoir after I'd seen his brother on a train. I mistakenly thought he was flirting with a teenage girl; in truth, I later realised, many years having passed since I'd last seen him, he was chatting with his daughter. The joke was on me but my old friend didn't think so. I suspect he objected to another passage where I wrote about him (not his brother) as a peer we'd envied for his self-assurance, a passage I'd written in admiration but which he might have found embarrassing. *Je ne regrette rien*. Or so I tell myself. But I am sorry to have upset him. That's the risk when you write about old friends. (See OFFENCE.)

Overall, I've got off lightly. But I did write a villanelle, 'Life Writing', about the risks:

You're trying to bring to life what's in your head,
a story that's discomfiting but true.
Your interest in inventing stuff's long dead.

You know that all worth saying's all been said
but strive to tell it straight and make it new.
You want to bring to life what's in your head.

The names of all the ones you took to bed,
the triumphs and disasters you lived through:
you'd like to set this down before you're dead.

You comb your troubled past from A to Z.
You drag forgotten memories into view.
Your memoir brings to life what's in your head.

But Tim, best mate at school, was really Ted,
and Tania's nut-brown eyes were turquoise-blue.
They phone you late at night and wish you dead.

The humour and affection go unread.
Your candour earns you merciless reviews.
Don't try to bring to life what's in your head.
It's safer telling lies about the dead.

G

Ghosts

If someone's telling their own story it's rare for them to use a ghost writer. But occasionally it's unavoidable: either they don't have the capacity to write or they're so rich, successful and busy that all they can do is throw out ideas for a ghost to work up on their behalf. Mark Twain didn't exactly ghost the memoir of his friend the former President Ulysses S. Grant, which came out just a month before Grant died of cancer, but he encouraged, revised, promoted and published it – without Twain, there'd have been no book and no royalties for Grant's widow. There have been some excellent ghost 'collaborators' in recent years, notably J. R. Moehringer, who helped both Prince Harry and André Agassi with their memoirs. And now AI ghosts have arrived, whose assistance, so it's claimed, will allow you to self-publish a book on Amazon within 24 hours – just 'generate a prompt template' and write 'iteration guidance' and your novel or poetry collection will follow. Hmm. I don't recommend it for life writing, a genre where authenticity is the *raison d'être*.

Jennie Erdal's *Ghosting* is worth reading not just for a laugh, as she relates how she worked as a ghost writer for the flamboyant publisher and would-be, couldn't-be novelist Naim Attalah, but for her insights into what makes good writing. 'Concealing your identity can actually be a strange sort of liberation,' she found. 'It can even be self-affirming, since eventually you work out who you really are by being who you are not.' She doesn't name Attalah in the book, just calls him 'Tiger', whereas he called her (and all the Selinas, Devinas and Sabrinas in his employ) 'Beloved'. To begin with, she took the tapes of his 250 interviews with famous women and turned them into a 1,200-page book. Fired up, he then proposed a romantic novel, by which he meant an erotic novel, and bullied her to come up with the goods ('Have we done the fucky-fucky yet?... Beloved, we need the jig-jig!'). The sample quotes she gives from the novel are excruciating, but Attalah was ecstatic with the results and bumped up her salary. For his second novel, he wanted a scene where a man gives two women simultaneous orgasms, though he is in the room with only one of them . . . After that it was time for her to quit.

'Can one write from another person's heart?' Erdal asks. 'It is difficult to see how it can be meaningful or eloquent. You have to write from inside your own skin.' She duly did so, writing her own novel. But she took pride in the ghosting nonetheless: 'I did and I did not feel responsible for the words on the page, I did and did not feel that they belonged to me... but there is plenty of personal ambition involved in trying to do the job well.' The job she does in *Ghosting* is brilliant, and the portrait of Tiger one of the funniest you'll ever read.

Hidden lives

Family history is most exciting when there are secrets to uncover or little-known lives to bring into the open. In Margaret Forster's family there was a taboo about discussing her orphaned grandmother's early life and the daughter she wouldn't acknowledge. Stories and hearsay filtered down nonetheless, and Forster became convinced that her grandmother's history 'was somehow essential to understand better not simply my own but that of a whole generation of working-class women.' Her 1995 memoir *Hidden Lives* breaks through the silence and she writes with affection and insight about three generations of women, ending with her own marriage and career. 'Everything, for a woman, is better now,' she concludes, 'even if it is still not as good as it could be.'

Nine years before Forster, Carolyn Steedman published *Landscape for a Good Woman*, an equally passionate attempt to document two lives (her mother's in Burnley, and her own in south London). What defines Steedman's mother is a 'sense of unfairness, her belief that she had been refused entry to her rightful place in the world', and Steedman is angry too, bringing feminist and psychoanalytical theory to her analysis. It's an unusual book, not least for its subversion of stereotypes: though 'a good woman', Steedman's mother is not a good mother, attributing her frustrations with life to the burden of having two daughters – which is probably why the visit Steedman paid her mother two weeks before she died was the first in nine years.

The secret in J. R. Ackerley's family was that his father had a second family: a mistress with three daughters. Ackerley learned of it in two letters his father left him, which he opened, as instructed, 'in the case of my death'. 'The discovery of my father's duplicity gave me, I suppose, something of a jolt,' he writes with beautiful understatement in his classic memoir *My Father and Myself*. The jolt didn't make him detest his father: though Ackerley was gay he shared the same 'sexual incontinence'. The hidden life the book exposes isn't just his father's but his own; his self-absorption, his sexual roaming and his disquietingly intimate relationship with his Alsatian bitch Queenie.

The trick when uncovering hidden lives is not to gasp with horror or sensationalise. These books don't patronise the lives of their subjects, they contextualise, they explain, they forgive.

Humour

When professional comedians write memoirs, their routines are often disappointing – less funny on the page than onstage. It's better when they do the unexpected. Alan Davies's *Just Ignore Him* is exemplary in that respect, recalling his paedophile father's molestation of him as a child and his frustrated efforts to bring him to justice; the humorous episodes – which include a fantastical chapter about going to the local police station to report his dad (but not really) – are tinged with sadness, even despair. Other comedian-memoirs that attempt the same mix shout it out in the title (Jennette McCurdy, *I'm Glad My Mom Died*; Frankie Boyle, *My Shit Life So Far*).

It helps when comedians have an earlier career to draw on, as Adam Kay does. *This Is Going to Hurt* contains 'the secret diaries of a junior doctor' in the NHS. We see Kay stressed by long hours and difficult procedures ('Hugo took me outside for a cigarette – we both desperately needed one after that. And I'd never smoked before.'); coping with gormless patients ('explain[ed] to a couple in the fertility clinic that massaging semen into her navel isn't quite going to cut it'); and extracting a bewilderingly large number of objects from vaginas and anuses. The humour, by his own admission, is gallows humour. He loves his colleagues and he's devoted to his work, but the NHS is on its knees and, after a tragedy when he's the senior person in charge, he hangs up his stethoscope. There are other near-tragedies. Many tears are shed. The humour doesn't make light of all this. It's won against the odds.

Novelists and poets who bring humour to life writing also work against the grain: what might look grievous is given a twist. The refusal of Jackie Kay's Nigerian birth father to tell his family about her, or to allow her to see him when she has travelled close to where he lives, is a brutal second rejection, the kind adopted children often go through. In other hands the story of her eventual encounter with him and (separately) her mother, Elizabeth, might have become a chastening tale about the risk of tracking down birth parents. But *Red Dust Road* opens hilariously with an eleven-page chapter, set in Abuja on the one occasion when she does see her dad. White-robed, born-again and manic, he dances around for two hours in a hotel room in a vain effort to convert her to Christianity and cleanse her of the 'sins' of illegitimacy and lesbianism.

> He starts up again, more whirling and twirling and shouting to God Almighty. More clapping and foot tapping and spinning and reciting. A whole big wad of the Bible rolls out of his mouth like ectoplasm. 'For the grace of God . . . repent of your sins. Allow me to purify and cleanse you . . .' I try to think of all my sins. True, there are a lot of them. But the fact that I was born out of wedlock? That is not my sin.

Thanks to the love of her adoptive parents, Kay is able to laugh where others would weep. 'There is still a windy place at the core of my heart,' she writes, but her resilience wins through and she achieves revenge on her birth father when she makes contact with his two sons, who accept her warmly.

Memoirists who let in light to offset the pain include Simon Gray, who does it triumphantly in his 'Smoking Diaries' trilogy and *Coda*, and Howard Jacobson in his mournfully comic *Mother's Boy*. Others go for broke and it's comedy (by which I don't mean fart jokes) all the way. David Sedaris, Nina Stibbe and Caitlin Moran are obvious candidates for laugh-out-loud but there's no shame in going back to Gerald Durrell's *My Family and Other Animals* either.

'I imagine'

Just because they're writing non-fiction doesn't mean authors can't imagine. Often they're forced to imagine. In a work of family history, say, there'll be gaps in their knowledge: they weren't there or don't have the documentation; odd details have come down that need to be pieced together. Authors can be frank about that – but also make clear that their imagining is an approximation of the truth, not some freewheeling fantasy. Biographers necessarily speculate at times, with a *probably*, *possibly* or *perhaps*. Forewarned, the reader will take it on board.

In my memoir *Things My Mother Never Told Me* (a title that gives due warning), there's a section where I imagine my mum, back in Ireland, going out on a drive with her father to visit a sheep farm (which he often did in his job as a wool trader) and stopping off seeing friends and relations. I knew from letters she sent my father that she was back home for a longish spell that summer and spending time with her parents. And I thought it worth filling in her family background and evoking a little of County Kerry at that time: the annual Puck Fair in Killorglin, the bachelor farmers, the character of her father, Patrick O'Shea. The section runs to five or six pages, after which 'I confess to a little embroidery there' but also insist that 'what I've set down scarcely qualifies as fiction. With fiction you can let go, constrained only by the logic of your inventions. With my mother . . . there's a demand for honest reporting. I can feel her over my shoulder, scanning the page for stuff and nonsense.'

That's something else that will hold an author back: the desire to do right by the people they're writing about. *I imagine* – but what you imagine needs some grounding in fact.

Identity

Some of us write to find out who we are. We don't know where the writing is leading us but as it takes shape we take shape too. We start out unaware of what we want to say and by the end we've said it. Samantha Harvey puts it well in her book about a 'year spent in search of sleep', *The Shapeless Unease*: 'I proceed from some open and elusive subconscious formlessness roughly called "me" . . . Then words . . . And somehow, I start to see myself out there in the words I've made, out in their many worlds, scattered and free.'

If you've been adopted, identity is always an issue: who has shaped you, your birth parents or your adopters? A. M. Homes addresses this in *The Mistress's Daughter*, a book that's no less comic than Jackie Kay's adoption story *Red Dust Road*, especially when her birth father, Norman, tells her that he's not circumcised ('We've just met and he's telling me about his dick.') and again when she concludes that she's *definitely* his daughter: 'I am watching him and I'm thinking: There goes my ass. That's my ass walking away . . . He is an exact replica, the male version of me.' The book is angry as well as comic. 'To be adopted is to be adapted,' Homes concludes, 'to be amputated and sewn back together again . . . There will always be scar tissue.' Martin Rowson's *Stuff,* another sad-and-comic book by an adoptee, challenges that view, dismissing the 'temptation to talk up adoption as if it's something more than it really is, almost as if it's a bid to recruit the adopted to the legions of other victims who trumpet their victimhood.'

In recent years, explorations of identity have been a staple of writers from underrepresented groups – including writers of colour, LGBTQ+ writers, neurodivergent writers and disabled writers. They describe experiences and feelings which seem to them uniquely theirs but which readers with a similar background or condition feel heartened to find set down in words – and which readers *un*like them can connect with and learn from too. It's an important aspect of recent publishing, with autoethnography (a narrative that often highlights an author's ethnicity) or autopathography (first-person stories of illness and disability) at its heart. If white, middle-class heterosexuals feel marginalised by this trend, that's their – our! – loss. Even those in a privileged majority know what it's like to feel misunderstood, unheeded, out on a limb. So what's to stop us engaging with a writer who feels they have been born in the wrong body, as Jan Morris did (she writes about it in her 1974 memoir *Conundrum,* published after gender reassignment surgery), or with one assigned to the wrong racial group, as Rachel Doležal felt she was (a woman born to white parents but identifying as Black, she recounts the story in her memoir *In Full Color*)?

Audre Lorde's 1982 memoir *Zami: A New Spelling of My Name* is a classic example of an identity memoir. 'To whom do I owe the woman I have become?' she asks at the outset and goes on to explore the childhood influences and later friendships that shaped her as a Black, gay feminist at a time, in the McCarthy era, when to be any of those things was to court trouble and abuse. She subtitles the book *A Biomythography*, her own coinage it seems and an indication that she grew up with myth, not least about her family and origins. It's a book about loneliness but also solidarity: 'Lesbians were probably the only Black and white women in New York City in the fifties who were making any real attempt to communicate with each other,' she says, 'we learned lessons from each other.' A poem of hers emphasises the importance of conquering reticence:

> when we speak we are afraid
> our words will not be heard
> nor welcomed
> but when we are silent
> we are still afraid
> so it is better to speak.

Learning to speak was no less a challenge for Camilla Balshaw, the daughter of a Jamaican mother and Nigerian father. In her memoir, *Named*, she recounts how she was called Camilla (at her father's behest) on her birth certificate but brought up as Mandy (her mother's preference after the marriage broke up). The book is a fascinating reflection on how names define us. It also touches on the difficulties an unfamiliar forename or surname can cause, for instance to people being interviewed for a job. For Balshaw to ditch Mandy and become Camilla took years but she got there in the end, thereby reclaiming (as she saw it) her core self.

Illness

'Illness,' wrote Proust, 'is the doctor to whom we pay most heed; to kindness, to knowledge, we make promise only; pain we obey.' Pain must be obeyed but can it be written about? Virginia Woolf thought not: 'English, which can express the thoughts of Hamlet and the tragedy of Lear, has no words for the shiver and the headache . . . let a sufferer try to describe a pain in his head to a doctor and language at once runs dry.' Today the drought is long over: many fine books about illness have appeared in recent years.

Josie George's *A Still Life* is one of them, describing her life as a single mother with mobility problems: a mysterious chronic fatigue that laid her low in childhood has persisted with intermittent severity ever since. An invisible illness, her condition is called. But by telling us what it looks and feels like, she makes herself visible in the process. Robert Douglas-Fairhurst's *Metamorphosis*, about his multiple sclerosis, is equally powerful. Both memoirs are, in part, about the consolations that offset suffering (whether through reading, the natural world or companionship), with pain, in Josie George's words, 'a doorway not a fist'. The narrators *learn* stuff, about themselves as well as about their illnesses. They've a heightened awareness of why life is worth living. Neither dependably upbeat (sure of a cure) or bleakly self-pitying (why me?), they win us over with their honesty. As Van Gogh said, 'one perhaps learns how to live from the sick'.

Further back, Robert McCrum's *My Year Off* is a compelling account of the stroke he had at the age of 42, which left him paralysed down one side and with his speech impaired. Many stroke patients, doctors and nurses have found the book invaluable, both for its honesty and for its lightly worn neurological research; drawing on diaries kept at the time, it has the immediacy of front-line reportage, with the body as a battleground and the outcome, if not a total victory, a triumph against the odds. (More recently, after a fall in broad daylight that left him acutely aware of his mortality, McCrum published *Every Third Thought*, a reflection on 'Life, Death and the Endgame'.)

Also on my list of insightful illness memoirs are *Patient: The True Story of a Rare Illness*, by the musician Ben Watt (the illness is Churg–Strauss syndrome); Hanif Kureishi's *Shattered* (tetraplegia); Lucy Grealy's *Autobiography of a Face* (and her friend Ann Patchett's companion volume *Truth & Beauty*); Siri Hustvedt's *The Shaking Woman, or A History of My Nerves*; Paul Kalanithi's cancer memoir *When Breath Becomes Air*; John Diamond's *C: Because Cowards Get Cancer Too* (throat cancer); Simon Boas's *A Beginner's Guide to Dying* (ditto); Jenny Diski's *In Gratitude* (lung cancer); Ruth Picardie's *Before I Say Goodbye* (breast cancer); Tom Lubbock's *Until Further Notice I Am Alive* (brain tumour); Sheila MacLeod's *The Art of Starvation* (anorexia); Mary Cregan's *The Scar* (depression); Raymond Antrobus's *The Quiet Ear* (deafness); Sheila Hale's *The Man Who Lost His Language* (her husband's stroke); Graham Caveney's two books *On Agoraphobia* and *The Body in the Library* (oesophageal cancer); Alice Jolly's *Dead Babies and Seaside Towns* (miscarriage, IVF and surrogacy); Sarah Moss's *My Good Bright Wolf* (eating disorder); Fred D'Aguiar's *Year of Plagues* (prostate cancer); and Christina Patterson's *Outside, the Sky is Blue* (acne, lupus, polyarthralgia and breast cancer).

Forgive the long list. There's much more to these books than accounts of illness: Patterson's explores childhood and family, Diski writes about her relationship with Doris Lessing (who took her in as a teenager), D'Aguiar's is set during the Covid pandemic and around the murder of George Floyd. Illness doesn't stop authors engaging with the world. It may even help them (and us) learn more about it. Maggie Nelson's book on her illness (mouth infections and jaw pain) is called *Pathemata*, which in ancient Greek means *learning through suffering*.

Immortality

It's a common human instinct: the desire to leave something of yourself behind. Having children arguably serves that purpose but not everybody has children or thinks human lineage is enough. The narrator of Rebecca F. Kuang's 2023 novel *Yellowface* shouts her aspirations from the rooftops: 'I want my books in stores all over the world . . . I want to be eternal, permanent; when I'm gone I want to leave a mountain of pages that scream, Juniper Song was here, and she told us what was on her mind.'

The drawback with immortality is that you're not around to enjoy it. Kafka, Emily Dickinson and Herman Melville had no idea how revered they would become after their deaths (nor did Van Gogh). And success in your own lifetime is no guarantee either; countless authors acclaimed in their day are now unread and unheard of. (See Christopher Fowler's *The Book of Forgotten Authors* for ninety-nine of them.) Nor does rejection and failure give grounds for hope of posthumous reprieve: if you're not liked now, there's only a modest chance you will be in the future. That's if there is a future: should the planet and the human race expire, immortality will itself be mortal.

The only virtue in craving immortality is if it makes you work harder at what you're writing. And the benefit of memoir is that it's not just any old book you leave behind. It's the book of your life. Or the book of someone else's life that would otherwise (in Keats's phrase) be 'writ in water'.

Influence

Writers find their way through other writers. They're looking to be themselves but can't get there on their own. Boccaccio influenced Chaucer, who influenced Shakespeare, who influenced Milton, who influenced Dryden, who influenced Pope, who influenced Byron, who influenced Browning, who influenced T. S. Eliot . . . and so on. Authors don't just take from other authors, they measure themselves against them. 'I want to be able to do anything with words: handle slashing, flaming descriptions like Wells, and use the paradox with the clarity of Samuel Butler, the breadth of Bernard Shaw and the wit of Oscar Wilde,' Scott Fitzgerald wrote, and after *The Great Gatsby* he talked of aiming for something 'really NEW in form, idea, structure – the model for the age that Joyce and Stein are searching for, that Conrad didn't find.' Harold Bloom, in *The Anxiety of Influence*, traces how writers 'swerve away' from their predecessors rather than replicating them; other critics talk of intertextuality. For life writing, it's the same as with other genres: what authors read seeps into what they write.

With memoir the pathways are less obvious than with novels and poetry. The stuff of your life takes priority over literary precedent. Still, you need to have some knowledge of the genre; how writers before you handled voice, tone, momentum and structure will be instructive. In particular, perhaps, you can learn how a memoir needn't be *earnest*, even when the subject matter is grim. Jackie Kay's *Red Dust Road* and Dave Eggers's *A Heartbreaking Work of Staggering Genius* show the way – Eggers even has a list of rules to be followed.

At Goldsmiths, like most creative writing mentors, I hoped to be an influence on the students I worked with, not to make them write like *me* but to make them write like *them*. It was one of the best things about the job – seeing someone develop a particular voice or style and find the way to tell their story. That said, there were a few who needed very little help at all. With one PhD student we broke all the rules: instead of coming to me for supervision sessions several times a term, which was the university guideline, she worked on her own for three years then turned up with a book that needed little or no revision. She had already published books before coming on the course; what she wanted was the qualification (to improve her salary and job prospects), not my input. Her book did well and was adapted for television. I'd have liked to pretend I *taught her all she knows*. But she did it by herself.

Creative writing teachers *can* be an influence, and so can family, friends and lovers, even if they never read a word you've written. In my case, the debt is at least threefold: to the Irish school teacher Paddy Rogers, who introduced me to Modernist writers; to Karl Miller, who as my PhD supervisor at University College, London, taught me how to write passable English; and to my dad, who thought that reading was a criminal waste of time (instead of sitting with a book, I could and should have been outdoor *doing* something), who failed to persuade me to follow him and become a doctor, and who had his revenge on me when I ended up writing a book about him, which proved that I hadn't escaped him after all.

Inspiration

Poets call it their Muse (female), an infrequent and fickle visitor. Kipling called it his Daemon (male) and spoke of the 'good care I took to walk delicately, lest he should withdraw.' A writer can't summon a Muse or Daemon. They come out of nowhere, impelling you to embark on a new project or moving your current one in unexpected directions. If you're wise, you go with the flow, follow the lead and are taken. (Hemingway: 'The story was writing itself and I was having a hard time keeping up with it.') The words may not feel like yours and that's what's exciting: you've been handed a gift. The afflatus won't be with you forever. You'll feel bereft when it departs. But with luck you'll have been left with pages of writing you'd have thought yourself incapable of – courtesy of who-knows-who.

The force was the term Zora Neale Hurston used: 'the force from somewhere in Space, which commands you to write in the first place, gives you no choice. You take up the pen when you are told and write what is commanded. There is no agony like bearing an untold story inside you.' Inspiration makes you excavate – the archaeology of selfhood. Or it takes you through the back of the wardrobe: you start in darkness and come out in the light. When writers talk of *expressing the inexpressible*, this is part of what they mean: words for difficult-to-express feelings that you don't expect to write; sentences that come out of the blue; ideas you didn't know you had.

Another word for it, which Miranda France uses in her autofiction *The Writing School*, is *synchronicity*, 'when everything in life magically responds to the work in progress': an overheard conversation, the colour of a flower, a spilled coffee – even the most trivial of experiences will feed into your writing. As France says, 'It may be that such coincidences are happening around us all the time and it takes the heightened state that comes with a book in full flow to reveal them.' Whether they're coincidences or Muse-ly offerings, a writer does well to make use of them.

I'm not a mystic. The pragmatist in me sides with the nose-to-the-grindstone ethos of Dr Johnson and Orwell, who didn't believe in hanging around for heaven-sent gifts. If you don't keep actively writing, you won't have the facility to capitalise when inspiration or synchronicity strike. That said, I've had two experiences of a voice that wasn't mine taking over, first with a long poem 'The Ballad of the Yorkshire Ripper' (the narrator has a broader northern accent than mine), and again when I was writing a novel about Johann Gutenberg – I'd hit on the idea of having him dictate his memoirs to a scribe (the kind of person his printing press made redundant) only to discover that the scribe was me: I sat there taking dictation from him; he was a ghost and so was I.

Twice in a long writing career isn't much. In gloomy periods when I'm not writing, I berate my Muses for deserting me. But they're blameless. They come and go as they please. I've written books without them. Waiting for their blessing is an excuse for indolence. I stay grateful – and listen in the rare moments they appear.

Intention

Imagine you're writing a portrait sketch of your mother that's meant to be benign – a celebration of her energy, passion and commitment. But when you show it to a friend she asks why you're so hostile towards your mother: that description of her 'sly' smile and 'outsize' nose, the embarrassed account of an affair she had, the stories of her being 'loud and obscenely drunk' at parties – they're disrespectful, you're told, even matricidal. What?! You're shocked, hurt, quietly indignant. You thought your love for your mother overrode these unflattering passages. And you set out to be honest – to paint her in the round, not compose a hagiography.

What's at stake here is the difference between *intention* and *reception*. There's what authors think they're doing. And what readers make of it. The two don't coincide.

Chances are, in the case above, you can take the feedback on board and adjust the passages without compromising yourself. Maybe 'sly' isn't quite right – 'wry' or 'ironic' is closer to what you meant. And let her nose be 'Roman': that too is nearer the mark. With a few small changes you'll be over your upset. Be *grateful* to that friend. You've been spared committing matricide.

Interviews

Like journals and letters, interviews can be an integral part of life writing. Often, they're implicit, a contribution to research, people you talked to while gathering information, fully credited in the acknowledgements. But sometimes interviews are worth reproducing as extracts in the text. For a conversation with a professional (lawyer, doctor, therapist) there'll need to be permission, sometimes hard to obtain.

John Edgar Wideman wasn't allowed a tape-recorder when visiting his brother Robert in prison. But as he explains in *Brothers and Keepers,* they evolved a collaborative method which allowed Robert a voice in the book: 'Robby would tell his stories. I'd listen, take notes, reconstruct the episodes after I'd allowed them time to sink in, then check my version with Rob to determine if it sounded right to him. Letters and talk about what I'd written would continue until we were both satisfied.' The result was a work of co-authorship.

Some life writing consists entirely of interviews. One great exponent has been the Nobel Prize winner Svetlana Alexievich, whose interviewees talk about the experience of war or, in the haunting monologues of *Chernobyl Prayer*, about catastrophe at a nuclear power station. Before her, Studs Terkel was the US master of interviews, while in the UK it was Tony Parker, whose final book (which included interviews) was about Terkel. Before that, Parker published numerous books featuring people from the fringes of society, whether lighthouse-keepers, miners or criminals; though he affected to 'record without comment or judgement' he was, as Anthony Storr put it, a 'mouthpiece of the inarticulate and counsel for the defence of those whom society has shunned and abandoned'. He had, in Duncan Campbell's words, 'an ability to persuade people to talk to him without restraint and to reproduce what they have said like a beautifully crafted short story'.

In his efforts to come across as a neutral oral historian, Parker deleted his questions: he couldn't be seen as leading people on. But while he pretends to be a mere functionary with a tape-recorder, as though the interviewee is calling the shots, he's an active presence. Take his book *The People of Providence*, about the tenants of a south London housing estate. In the introduction, Parker effaces himself, leaving four tenants to do the talking. He has told them why he's there ('Going to what? Bloody hell, write a book, well good luck to you, mate.') and thereafter, for over 350 pages (based on interviews with 200 people and 340 hours' worth of tape), the stage is theirs. But he's there, too, made visible by them, whether being handed treats ('Please eat as much of the cake as you can my darling, I made it specially for you coming.'), being given a guided tour ('Then straight ahead of us through this glass door.'), returning on a second visit ('I said I'd have a think for you after you'd gone didn't I?'), or taking his leave ('It's been a pleasure to talk to you dear, you call in when you're passing any time.'). Only at the end, in the acknowledgements, does he unashamedly appear, expressing hope that his book conveys 'something of the peopled world that exists behind the outward appearance of anonymity and characterlessness of a modern housing estate'.

The book is a model of *how to do voices*. It's idiomatic, with lots of *I think*, *I feel* and *I hope*. But it's tightly edited and punctuated, to show respect not patronise. Anyone working on dialogue in a book can learn from it. And it shows what can be done with a book about a community, workplace or large family – how authors can accommodate other voices without obliterating their own. Mary Loudon achieves something similar in the stories she weaves together from interviews in *Unveiled: Nuns Talking* and *Secrets & Lives: Middle England Revealed*.

'It's not just the tape recorder I can't switch off,' Studs Terkel said, 'it's me I can't switch off either.' That's the secret to Terkel, Parker and Alexievich: they're indefatigably attentive listeners.

J

Joy

The famous Henry de Montherlant quote 'Happiness writes white' has been overused, not least by me. When you're enjoying life, you don't pick up a pen: that's the gist. But it's untrue. There are many novels and poems which do evoke happiness. Jack Underwood has a collection of poetry with that title, the title piece of which begins 'Yesterday it appeared to me in the form of two purple / elastic bands round a bunch of asparagus, which was / a very small happiness, a garden variety'. There's also a Raymond Carver poem called 'Happiness', which locates it in the silent companionship of two boys delivering newspapers early one morning: 'Happiness. It comes on / unexpectedly. And goes beyond really'. And I have a poem of that title, which ends 'Two deckchairs in the shade of a weeping birch. / Everyone you love still alive, last time you heard.'

Happiness often sneaks in, joy less so. It's briefer and more provisional. And there's even less of an impulse to write when life's a beach. 'My best poems were all written when I felt worst,' Langston Hughes says in his autobiography *The Big Sea*, 'When I was happy I didn't write anything.'

Worse still, full-on joyful books – especially happy-clappy memoirs – have little appeal. There has to be trouble. Adversity. Disaster, desperation and dismay. A common pattern in memoir is *look-I-have-come-through*, from desolation to fulfilment, from illness to health. Trouble is, the reader may prefer the gutter or the hospital bed – the rags of cancer rather than the riches of good health. It's perverse. But a life writer has to allow for it. There's no duller content than contentment.

Langston Hughes is a case in point. When *The Big Sea* describes him working on boats, or living on the breadline, or battling against racial injustice, the memoir is riveting – less so when he talks of his success. Ditto Anthony Burgess's pair of memoirs. The first, *Little Wilson and Big God*, takes him from childhood to early adulthood and ends magnificently, after he has been given a year to live (a false prognosis). The sequel, *You've Had Your Time*, gives us the career thereafter – a gossipy account of his rise to international celebrity. The unmediated record of a child and adolescent can't help but be more fascinating than the self-congratulations of an ageing author.

Which is to say (though I feel guilty for saying it), a life writer can't skimp on the bad stuff and shouldn't overdo the good.

Still, it's important to give your reader a sense of joy – whether through jokes, images or delighted storytelling. When a reader wrote to the great American showman P. T. Barnum to say how much she enjoyed his Life, he replied, 'My dear madam, that is nothing to the way I enjoyed living it.'

K

Knausgaard, Karl Ove

No discussion of contemporary life writing can ignore Knausgaard's six-volume masterpiece *My Struggle*. Life writing? Some class it as fiction. Masterpiece? Many readers dispute that too. I'm a fan, but even if I weren't he would be here. His work raises all the great life writing issues: how strictly do you need to tell the truth? How much authenticating detail should you put in, even if it's banal? How far can you go in writing honestly about people without being sued?

Born in Oslo in 1968, Knausgaard began his career as a novelist and his first two novels were well received. But he changed course in 2009 with *A Death in the Family*. In an essay on his work, he refers to it as a 'non-fictional novel'. Perhaps something has been lost in translation and what he means is a non-fiction narrative – or even a non-fiction non-narrative. It certainly feels like that in his account of how the work came about. What began as an attempt to write a novel about his father's death only took off when he dropped the camouflage of fiction and 'found a language for my non-narrative, day-to-day existence':

I didn't believe in what I myself was writing all the while I was trying to tell my story in the form of a novel. I didn't want to write about the relationship between a father and a son, I wanted to write about my dad and me. I didn't want to write about a house where a man lived with his aged mother, like some variation on Ibsen's *Ghosts*, but about that particular house and the concrete reality that existed inside it . . .

I was a novelist, I wrote novels, and to the extent I made use of experiences from my own life, they were camouflaged, part of the fiction. The option of abandoning that had never existed for me as a writer. I could bring the events of the novel as close to reality as I had experienced them, but to take that final step and write, 'I, Karl Ove', 'my brother, Yngve', or 'my father, Kai Åge', was something that had never as much as occurred to me. It wouldn't be literature any more, would it?

Every life writer will recognise the doubts Knausgaard had about the value of what he was doing: 'Who would want to know that I had stood and pissed up against a pile of snow while listening to Talking Heads on a Walkman one night in the 1980s?' His breakthrough came when he saw that the episode *could* be interesting if documented in detail. His work became literature once he stopped worrying about it being literature. And the transgressiveness gave his writing its energy:

> If I went in that direction, simply writing down things I had experienced, using my own name, it was as if all concerns about style, form, literary devices, character, tone, distance, at once ceased to exist and the vestments of literature suddenly became unnecessary posturing: all

ON MEMOIR

I had to do was write. But it wasn't only the freedom of this that now fuelled the writing, it was also the unprecedented nature of it, the fact that to a large degree what I was doing was forbidden.

Few authors have Knausgaard's courage to tell all. But he's an inspiring example of the artistic breakthrough that's possible when, to tell a personal story, you dispense with the camouflage of fiction.

L

Landscape

I'm thinking not so much of nature or travel books but of books where the author has a psychological or emotional investment in a particular landscape – one that offers escape, memory, reassurance, fear, elation or recovery. Noreen Masud's *A Flat Place* describes how, as a child confined to home in Lahore by an autocratic father, she would gaze in wonder at the flat landscapes she'd see when he drove her to school. Escaping to England as an adult, lonely and unable to socialise, she began to ask herself 'Why do I love flat landscapes so much? . . . It's hard to imagine anything really exciting happening there.' In the flatness of Ely, Orford Ness, Morecambe Bay and Orkney she finds herself 'mirrored and validated' as someone who's a 'damaged landscape' and who realises that 'the quiet presence of a flat landscape – refusing to rise to anything – gives me permission to be numb, to be without feeling or desire.' By the end she is coming to terms with her PTSD.

For Amy Liptrot in *The Outrun*, the healing-through-landscape happens in Orkney, where she grew up and to which she returns after alcoholism and a ruinous boho lifestyle in London have all but wrecked her. Hard work on drystone dykes is the start: 'I'm repairing these dykes at the same time as I'm putting myself back together.' Lambing, birding, swimming, cloud-watching, star-gazing, reconnecting with her parents and living alone on a small island complete the process. 'High on fresh air and freedom', she embraces extremes that nourish rather than deplete: 'I might have been washed up but I can be renewed . . . The powers are churning inside me.'

In *Lowborn* the landscapes are urban as Kerry Hudson returns to the places where she spent her impoverished and neglected childhood – Aberdeen, Liverpool, Canterbury, Airdrie, North Shields, Hetton-le-Hole, Coatbridge, Great Yarmouth. As well as turning up child protection documents and medical records, she interviews people living in her old neighbourhoods to see whether life is better for them than it had been for her. Often it's not: places leave damage; so does the class system. But Hudson's a survivor and her book offers hope that a difficult childhood in bleak surroundings needn't condemn an individual to silence and defeat.

Lawyers

With luck there'll be no need for lawyers. But life writing raises delicate issues about free speech on the one hand (Section 10 under the Human Rights Act) and the right to privacy (Section 8) on the other. And there have been cases with lawyers involved and a writer forced to self-censor after a heavy outlay on legal fees.

In 2009, Rachel Cusk was sued for a travel book she had written, *The Last Supper: A Summer in Italy*. According to her, 'You don't have to lie – no-one said I lied – but if you describe people and they recognise themselves they can sue.' The book was pulped soon after publication following an uncontested breach of privacy suit; it reappeared with several passages and phrases removed. The key offending chapter, 'A Game of Tennis', ran to nineteen pages in the original version and to sixteen in the re-jig. The people affected by it were an English couple running a hotel in Italy, to which Cusk, holidaying nearby, was invited to play tennis. Gavin and Mary (not their real names), rechristened Roger and Amanda (even less their real names) in the edit, had a number of objections to Cusk's portrayal of them.

Were Faber & Faber (Cusk's publishers) unduly weak in pulping the book? 'Gavin' might reasonably have argued that the unflattering portrait of him wasn't only a breach of privacy but a threat to business: potential guests might be put off staying. But it's possible to imagine a defence lawyer making the case for Cusk's right to free expression, since she says no one disputed the truth of what she wrote. The publishing compromise was to save face and settle the matter out of court.

It's not as if Cusk's book depended on her portrayal of 'Gavin' and 'Mary', who play only a minor role. But there are cases when the person depicted *is* central to the story, as, say, the liar, philanderer or abuser who wrecked the author's life. In 2008, Constance Briscoe, one of the UK's few Black women judges, whose autobiography *Ugly: The True Story of a Loveless Childhood* had sold 400,000 copies, was sued for libel by her mother Carmen Briscoe-Mitchell, who – accused of mistreatment by her daughter – retaliated by accusing her of writing a 'piece of fiction'. (See UGLINESS for more detail.) Briscoe won the case. 'I didn't believe for a split second that I owed my mother a bond of silence,' she said. 'I had a story to tell and that story really is that I, someone who from dirt poverty, from absolutely nowhere, with absolutely no assistance whatsoever, who faced adversity at every turn, could come through . . . You just have to believe in yourself.'

ON MEMOIR

It's hard to believe in yourself when the subject of your book has set her lawyers on you, but Briscoe's background in law ('you do not have to be posh or privileged to be at the Bar') may have helped. At any rate her book had the last word – as did Knausgaard's, and as did James Rhodes's *Instrumental*, despite efforts from his ex-wife to block it. (See VENGEANCE.)

Length

There's no right length for a book. It depends on the story. And it depends on the nature of the storyteller. Around 80,000 words is reportedly the average for literary fiction and memoir. But if everything can be said in 50,000, why go longer? *The Great Gatsby* is only 47,000 words and its slimness does it no harm.

Anything over 100,000 may be more of a problem. Kipling deplored the return of three-decker novels, 'quivering to their own power, over-loaded with bars, ball-rooms and insistent chromium plumbing'; a similar prejudice against bagginess persists today. With a memoir there's all the more reason for concision: it's meant to be a slice, not the whole cake. Tove Ditlevsen did write a triple-decker memoir, which Penguin brought out as *Childhood, Youth, Dependency* in a single-volume English translation in 2020. It totals a mere 360 pages – an average of 120 pages for each part – and is notable for its epigrammatic succinctness. For example: 'Childhood is a long and narrow coffin, and you can't get out of it on your own.'

I've known students who've kept such copious diaries that when they contemplate a memoir they think of it comprising several volumes. Beyond day-by-day documentation, though, their memoir has little shape or momentum. They've equated what's happened to them with what will fascinate the reader. And even if elements of their life writing *are* fascinating, they've not yet identified which those are, let alone boiled them down to a coherent narrative.

I'm a serial offender, in having written three memoirs (and a fourth book with elements of memoir). But I like to think the books are distinct. And they're more about other people than about me – people who deserve a full-length volume each, though were I a student on a creative writing course I can envisage a tutor (my alter ego) telling me otherwise.

Let us now praise . . .

James Agee's account of three sharecropper families in the Deep South, *Let Us Now Praise Famous Men*, commissioned as a piece of journalism (with photographs by Walker Evans) and worked up into a 400-page book, has been described as a 'documentary classic'; Agee himself called it 'an effort in human actuality'. Yet no one coming fresh to it today would categorise it as a work of documentary realism. Not that it isn't realistic; not that Agee isn't painfully preoccupied with telling the truth about sharecropper families in 1930s Alabama. But with its Modernist experimentalism and textual paraphernalia (footnotes, quotations, snatches of dialogue, reading lists, newspaper cuttings, etc.), it's not how documentary is meant to behave. Above all, there's the presence of Agee himself, laying open his doubts and self-recriminations. His lack of boundaries – as when he discloses his dangerous fondness for the young, unhappily married Emma Woods ('if only Emma could spend her last few days alive having a gigantic good time in bed . . . with Walker and with me') – is partly what the story is about.

He describes it as 'obscene and thoroughly terrifying' that he and Evans should have been sent 'to pry intimately into the lives of undefended and appallingly damaged human beings'. Scruple did make him change the names of the families (Gudger, Woods and Ricketts were really Tingle, Fields and Burroughs) but he does the business of factual reportage nonetheless. We learn exactly what these tenant families earn, the objects they own, the food they eat, the clothes they wear, the idiom they use, the education they receive, and the 'simple and terrible' work of planting and picking cotton. And when Agee moves in with the Gudgers (shedding the last vestige of reportorial detachment), we too feel the 'thinness and lumpiness of the mattress and the weakness of the springs'.

The local community resented the book (some there still do). They thought it exploitative of the sharecroppers' plight and saw the book as an indictment of the victims, not of government policy. To Agee the book was redemptive – a Christian-Marxist celebration of the meek and poor; a hymn of praise for unfamous working men and women. But when it was finally published in 1941, the American public – on the verge of entering the Second World War – wasn't much interested in learning about the social conditions of the rural South, nor in wrestling with a hubristic Modernist text. Still, it's an inescapable piece of life writing, one of the oddest and most intrusive ever written. And proof, in its meandering, that life writing doesn't need to be straight.

Lies

Do lies have any place in life writing? Isn't the contract that you tell the truth? It's fair enough when an author misremembers, or makes minor protective adjustments with names, dates and settings. But when a life writer knowingly deceives on a large scale is that forgivable? The American nature writer Barry Lopez thinks not. In his essay 'Landscape and Narrative' he extols the intimate trust between authors and readers, which untruthfulness destroys: 'Lying is the opposite of story. Every storyteller falls short . . . but to make up something that is not there, something which can never be corroborated . . . to knowingly set forth a false relationship, is to be lying, no longer telling a story.'

Lauren Slater's memoir *Lying* was published in 2000. Its first chapter consists of two words, 'I exaggerate', and the afterword ends with the boast (or admission) that 'there is only one kind of illness memoir I can see to write, and that's a slippery, playful, impish, exasperating text, shaped, if it could be, like a question mark.' Because 'Illness has claimed my imagination, my brain, my body, and everything I do I see through its feverish scrim', she struggles with truth: 'I have written a book in which in some cases I cannot and in other cases I will not say the facts.' Rather than facts, she gives us metaphors. The book may not be hand-on-heart accurate, she says, but it's 'heartfelt'.

Lying describes Slater's epilepsy, and the different treatments she had for it, and the creativity that stemmed from it, which led her to writing. And it does seem that TLE, temporal lobe epilepsy, is one of the diagnoses she was given to explain her seizures and auras. The book documents her illness. But it also documents her history of deceit. She steals. She fakes seizures to win sympathy. She joins an AA group and pretends to be a recovering alcoholic. She plagiarises swathes of writing ('the pages in this book, maybe? I won't say.'). And having developed Munchausen's syndrome (a compulsion to fabricate illness) at the age of 13, she says 'perhaps Munchausen's is all I ever had. Perhaps I was, and still am, a pretender, a person who creates illness because she needs time, attention, touch.'

Maybe. Perhaps. Either Slater knows but isn't saying. Or she doesn't know and is giving voice to her disorientation. Either she's a postmodernist tease or she's too feverish to know the truth. 'I have epilepsy. Or I feel I have epilepsy. Or I wish I had epilepsy.' It's up to the reader to decide which.

If you feel messed about by Slater, you'll hurl the book across the room. If you sympathise with her, you'll stick it out. It's worth sticking it out for Chapter 7, which consists of a (spoof?) memo sent to her publishers on 'How to market this book'. 'Sell it as non-fiction,' she pleads, while laying out four possibilities for the authenticity of her tale: a) she does have epilepsy and the book is 99 per cent accurate, b) she does have epilepsy but has exaggerated how badly and we should believe her only selectively, c) she doesn't have epilepsy but does have Munchausen's, and d) she has neither epilepsy nor Munchausen's but did have an awful mother.

I'm choosing b) but the choice is irrelevant. When an author advertises herself as a liar, how can you tell when, if ever, she's telling the truth? Why interest ourselves in a partly or wholly made-up story posing as memoir? Why care that she had a self-abasing affair with a creative writing tutor called Christopher? Who's to say it ever happened? And why believe anything in her previous book, *Prozac Diary* (1998), which mentions the many symptoms and psychiatric disorders that led to her taking Prozac but doesn't mention epilepsy or seizures?

Lying is fun but self-defeating. And so, in a memoir, is lying.

Likeability

It's ridiculous for a play to be panned or a novel rejected on the grounds that the main character isn't likeable. Are Iago and

Macbeth likeable? Is Gatsby? Is Humbert Humbert? Is Milton's Satan? Half the enjoyment in a novel or play is watching the villain pull the strings. We may have a sneaking admiration for their obnoxiousness and deviance from the norm but we sure as hell don't like them.

With life writing it's more of a problem. Say you're writing a story that's personal and true. Since you're the first-person narrator, eager for the reader to trust you, you probably *do* want to be likeable. In life it could well be that you *are* likeable – popular, admired, the soul of the party. But that won't make you so in memoir. With a book, you're not among friends but talking to strangers. And winning them over isn't straightforward.

One sure way for a narrator to be dislikeable is to be squeaky-clean: Ms Perfect, smugly delighting in her probity; Mr Exemplary, dishing the dirt on others. You can't be a paragon or we'll hate you. And you can't be a blank page or we'll wonder what you're hiding. The likeable narrator owns up to flaws: 'Autobiography is only to be trusted when it reveals something disgraceful,' Orwell thought. 'A man who gives a good account of himself is probably lying.'

I used to tell students: *Be vulnerable, tentative, unsure of yourself* (they usually were anyway). *A bit of haplessness does no harm. And don't be so solemn. Send yourself up. We all love a clown. You can't be straight-faced. Or strait-laced. An endless splurge of guilt and self-accusation will be off-putting. Ruefully negative self-appraisal is more appealing. The less you like yourself, the more we'll like you.*

Dave Eggers reckoned as much when he prefaced *A Heartbreaking Work of Staggering Genius* with a list of his failings and foibles.

The author offers the following:
a) That he is like you.

b) That, like you, he falls asleep shortly after he becomes drunk.
c) That he sometimes has sex without condoms.
d) That he sometimes falls asleep when he is drunk having sex without condoms.
e) That he never gave his parents a proper burial.
f) That he never finished college.
g) That he expects to die young.
h) That, because his father smoked and drank and died as a result, he is afraid of food.
i) That he smiles when he sees young black men hold babies.

One word: appealing.

In both fiction and life writing a refusal to conform is generally seen as a 'good' quality, even if it isn't 'nice'; few readers will take against a narrator who fails to shower each day or doesn't go to church. More is at stake if there's a serious crime or appalling behaviour within a family or marriage. But even then readers may find themselves drawn in. Antiheroes are hard to resist.

Loss

'The art of losing isn't hard to master,' Elizabeth Bishop wrote in her poem 'One Art'. But the art of writing about loss *is* hard to master. How to offer the reader something more than grief for what's gone? 'I lost my mother's watch,' Bishop goes on, and 'three loved houses.' Worse still:

> I lost two cities, lovely ones. And, vaster,
> some realms I owned, two rivers, a continent.
> I miss them, but it wasn't a disaster.

Sometimes loss is a disaster, or worse than, as it was for Rob Delaney when his son Henry, not yet three, died of a brain tumour. His book *A Heart That Works* begins with a quote from Mary Shelley's *Frankenstein*: 'Pardon this gush of sorrow.' He gives due warning. But the book isn't a gush, it's tough, witty and when it comes to evoking sorrow too idiosyncratic to be called sentimental: 'you sit there like a decaying disused train station while freight train after freight train overloaded with pain roars through you.' He doesn't spare the medical detail: the vomiting, the tracheostomy, the bodybag when Henry died. And he's angry: he'd like to meet the God he doesn't believe in so he can kick his teeth in.

Lu Spinney has every reason to be angry too: her son Miles suffered brain damage after a snowboarding accident at the age of 29, then survived for five more years, catastrophically injured and minimally conscious, with no quality of life. That his mother's memoir, *Beyond the High Blue Air*, is beautifully written and, against the odds, emotionally composed, makes the story all the more poignant. In his losing battle against spasticity, it's clear to Spinney and the family that Miles would be better off dead. But British law is stacked against it. The grief is that Lu Spinney loses her son not once but twice.

'I am forty-three years old and haven't the first clue about how to grieve,' Decca Aitkenhead writes in *All at Sea*. 'I am an expert in grief avoidance . . . a total amateur at feeling sad.' But sadness overwhelms her when her partner Tony drowns while saving the older of their two small boys off a beach in the Caribbean. She had turned Tony round from criminality and crack addiction to a youth worker with a first-class degree. Some of the grief in what follows is Aitkenhead's guilt, 'the inexplicable appeal of self-blame': she should never have booked the holiday; they shouldn't have stayed by the sea; 'for him to survive so much jeopardy only to die on my watch feels like a damning indictment'. The book describes her defencelessness and slow recovery.

'The thing to remember about this story,' Aitkenhead says, 'is that every word is true. If I never told it to a soul, and this book did not exist, it would not cease to be true.' These books move us because memoir, unlike fiction, doesn't invent. *The loss is real*, we think. *It could have been us.*

Love

You go to a book about war and find it's a love story. Many a distraught memoir turns out to be a love story too (see LOSS, above). Love for the child or parent who died; for the partner who disappeared; for the person the author was before adversity, age or illness came along. If there's no love in a book, it's doomed. But love can take many forms, including (as acerbic memoirists have shown) love of vitriol.

Or alcohol. Louisa Young's *You Left Early* tells the story of her long on-off love affair with the composer and pianist Robert Lockhart, whose addiction to booze, along with other health problems, led to his death at 52. 'Our love story, while idiosyncratic, is universal,' she says, and the universality, at the start, is the unrequitedness of her love: after a 'revelatory' night together he disappears. She's terrified of her desire for him ('I saw what I could lose myself in; what could take me from myself, enthral and imprison me, keep me from my own free life.') but later, as his illness worsens, they're together and while he lies in a coma, on a life support machine, she slips wedding rings on their fingers.

The less predictable the love, the more powerful. In *Maggie and Me* (2013) Damian Barr offers love, or, at any rate, gratitude, to Margaret Thatcher. Despite all her misdeeds, which he lists (everything from milk-snatching to the Poll Tax), she has saved his life: 'You made it OK for me to run away and never look back. You offered me certainty, however grim, when I had none at home. You threw me an escape ladder.' In Sathnam Sanghera's *The Boy with the Topknot* (a book that bravely breaks taboos about schizophrenia in an Asian family) romantic love vies with filial love. After more than one secret relationship with a *gori*, a white English girl, Sanghera writes his mum a heartfelt letter ('I want you to stop insisting I marry a Punjabi Jat.') in hope of winning her round. We don't know who will triumph. That's what love in good memoirs is like – deep, complex, contradictory.

There have been some brave shots at love in recent life writing, including several books that reached a mass audience, among them Dolly Alderton's *Everything I Know About Love* (comedy and guidance), Natasha Lunn's *Conversations on Love* (interviews with experts), and Sheila Hancock's *The Two of Us*, about her marriage to John Thaw. Further back there's the marvellous Nora Ephron. The challenge for memoirists is how to write about love without sounding soppy or smug. Google 'memoirs about love' and you'll find they're mostly biographies of the famous or, where they're first-person, that the author is writing about a relative, not about themselves. Love isn't quite a blank page in memoir but it struggles to speak its name. Novelists and poets find that invention loosens the tongue.

Lyric essay

It's a form said to combine poetry, essay and memoir, with practitioners including Anne Carson, Claudia Rankine and Maggie Nelson. But that doesn't get you very far. Nor does the suggestion that the genre is restricted to American women writers. The term was invented by Deborah Tall and John D'Agata in 1997 and the closest they come to a definition is that 'The lyric essay partakes of the poem in its density and shapeliness, its distillation of ideas and musicality of language. It partakes of the essay in its weight, in its overt desire to engage with facts, melding its allegiance to the actual with its passion for imaginative form.' More helpful is to think of the genre as a series of not quites: it's not quite an essay, if that suggests a scholarly paper; it's not quite a prose-poem, if that suggests something short; it's not quite pedagogic, since it prioritises art over information; it's not quite *music before meaning* because it's a representation of lived experience. What can be expected of a lyric essay is sensuousness and a more-than-usual reliance on metaphor – which is why Montaigne, say, isn't really a precursor.

If it's a piece of writing that's not a chronological narrative so much as an exploration of an idea, written in language as close to poetry as to prose, then 'lyric essay' may be the right term for it. A spirit of levity also helps. To essay something is to have a go, and in his famous *Dictionary* Samuel Johnson defines the essay as 'a loose sally of the mind, an irregular indigested piece, not a regular and orderly composition'. Lyric essays put forward a bright idea or series of bright ideas, not fully formed perhaps, but stimulating and provocative: *Here's what I think – how about you?* In recent years, Irish writers have been among the finest proponents, Emilie Pine (*Notes to Self*) and Sinéad Gleeson (*Constellations*) among them. More prominently, there's Claudia Rankine, whose *Citizen*, subtitled *An American Lyric*, consists of fragments set in rectangular blocks (and a few images), with racial injustice the predominant theme.

Good luck if it's your genre. But be aware that a) it's a form mostly found in anthologies and magazines, rather than as a full-length book, and b) you won't come across a Lyric Essay section in bookshops. 'Booksellers and customers often complain about the difficulty of knowing where to stock or find my books,' Geoff Dyer complains. That's what happens if you're a genre-buster.

M

Me Too

The phrase was used by the activist Tarana Burke as early as 2006 but it didn't become a viral hashtag till 2017. The movement took off in the US after women reported abuse at the hands of Donald Trump, Harvey Weinstein, Brett Kavanaugh and Bill Cosby, then it quickly became a global phenomenon. One crucial contribution came in the victim impact statement made by 'Emily Doe' before the sentencing – for a mere six months – of her sexual attacker Brock Allen Turner. When her statement appeared on Buzzfeed it had over 15 million viewings within days and drew support from, among others, Joe Biden and Hillary Clinton. She ended it by addressing 'girls everywhere': 'I am with you. I fought everyday for you. So never stop fighting.'

'Emily Doe' was the pseudonym used by Chanel Miller before, during and immediately after the trial. She outed herself three years later in her memoir *Know My Name*, which recounts the many obstacles she faced in getting justice. It's a stylistically adventurous book (not least in its use of italics) and, like Suzie Miller's play *Prima Facie*, it spells out what sexual assault victims are up against when their cases come to court.

She'd been drinking and had passed out when Turner dragged her over the ground to a dumpster, half undressed her, stuck his fingers in her vagina, then ran off when two passing cyclists interrupted him. Though Turner owned up, he never apologised, presenting himself as the victim: Miller, he claimed, had given him consent and 'enjoyed' the experience. He was supported by family, teachers and an expensively hired defence attorney, who spoke of his record as a top athlete and upright citizen – an irrelevancy, as Miller says: 'Bad qualities can hide inside a good person.' The jury agreed, unanimously finding him guilty on three counts of serious sexual assault, but the judge was lenient and gave Brock 'something that would never be extended to me: empathy. My pain was never more valuable than his potential.'

Miller's anger is uncompromising but lucid, redemptive, super-intelligent – unlike the anger in Rose McGowan's memoir, *Brave*, which is raw. Her book, which appeared a year before Miller's, is less about exposing Harvey Weinstein, who she says raped her in the hotel room to which she'd come expecting a business meeting, than an assault on Hollywood ('a small, myopic, self-fellating town') and its rampant misogyny. It was two decades before she called out the offenders. But, as she says, to have kicked up a fuss against Weinstein (whom she never names, calling him simply 'the Monster'), and against all the other abusive male directors, producers, agents, journalists and film crews she came across, would have ended her career before it took off. As it was, she had already earned a reputation for trouble-making and was blacklisted.

You could argue that Me Too was anticipated thirty years earlier by Betty Friedan, Gloria Steinem, Kate Millett, Audre Lorde and Germaine Greer, and in particular by Andrea Dworkin, whose book *Intercourse* in 1987 argued that phallocentric representations of the sex act, as one of possession and violation, normalised the subordination and abuse of women. Dworkin wasn't saying that all heterosexual intercourse is rape, though angry critics took it that way ('sheer raving lunacy,' 'a hate-mongering tantrum'), the same kind of critics who later disbelieved her account of being drugged and raped in Paris in 1999. Today her book would have a better reception.

It's tough for a heterosexual man to read Me Too books. We might not be Trump or Weinstein but we recognise the misogyny that produced them. If not within us, it's certainly around us – a primitive strain of male dominance and sexual aggression that ought to have perished long ago but which incels keep alive.

Medics

There's a long list of doctors who were also writers, among them Keats, Schiller, Bulgakov, Chekhov and William Carlos Williams. But a medical career isn't easily compatible with a literary career: in both, long years of apprenticeship are followed by long daily grind. Chekhov made light of the division: 'Medicine is my lawful wife and literature my mistress. When I get tired of one, I spend the night with the other.' These days it's harder to double up: a medic will have to work part-time, take leave or retire to find the space to write. Some terrific books by medics have appeared nonetheless. In recent years in the UK, Henry Marsh, Gabriel Weston, Gavin Francis, Adam Kay and Rachel Clarke have all written brilliantly as surgeons, hospital doctors or GPs. Christie Watson's book about her twenty years as a nurse, *The Language of Kindness*, was a bestseller. And Carla Valentine's *Past Mortems*, about her job as a 'death professional', opens the mortuary door. Moreover, the rise of 'narrative medicine' – the recognition of the importance of patients' stories in diagnosing and alleviating their sickness – has contributed to the genre: as Andrew Solomon has written, 'In telling the stories of illness, we need to tell the stories of the lives within which illness is embedded,' and to do that both patients and doctors need words. Narrative medicine alleviates the ancient sore that Voltaire diagnosed: 'Doctors are men who prescribe medicines of which they know little, to cure diseases of which they know less, in human beings of whom they know nothing.'

I've a soft spot for medic-mems because I'm the son of two doctors. Or because a couple of serious operations (prostate and kidney) have made me eager for knowledge. Or perhaps it's because I'm haunted by the poem 'In the Theatre', four stanzas written by Dannie Abse, a poet as well as a GP, about a neurological operation performed on a patient who was fully awake and who cried out, as the surgeon probed around with a scalpel, 'Leave my soul alone, leave my soul alone' – a poem that evokes an eerie religiosity in an operating theatre. It may also help that I'm not squeamish when I read passages such as those in Gabriel Weston's *Direct Red*: 'I lifted up Mrs Mbele's blanket and coated her anal mass with the jelly. It shone after this smearing and her haemorrhoids looked giant.' Lucy Grealy's experience as a patient in *Autobiography of a Face* didn't gross me out, either: 'I vomited up large amounts of blood I'd swallowed during the procedure. I began to welcome the deep, lungy urge to release the sweet-tasting fluid from deep within me. It tasted almost pleasant. Drainage tubes drifted down onto the pillow beside me, displaying the slightly shifting red and golden fluids of my body . . ..'

It's the human and ethical dimensions, though, not the blood and guts, that bring out the best life writing. Henry Marsh's *Do No Harm* is consumed by regret and even guilt at operations he performed that went wrong. As he says in his preface: 'Much of what happens in hospitals is a matter of luck, both good and bad; success and failure are often out of the doctor's control . . . You will inevitably make mistakes and you must learn to live with the occasionally awful consequences.' Neurosurgery isn't some calm and rational application of science, he argues, it's fraught and unpredictable. His descriptions of different brain calamities and procedures is wonderfully illuminating but it's this emphasis on error, on how mistakes are made when surgeons are 'insufficiently fearful', that makes his book compelling.

What's not in doubt is Marsh's capacity for truth-telling. With another celebrated neurologist, Oliver Sacks, it's a different picture. A recent piece by Rachel Aviv in the *New Yorker* identified embellishments he made to the medical case histories in books such as *Awakenings* and *The Man Who Mistook his Wife for a Hat*. Sacks's journals express remorse over 'lies' and 'falsification' and for projecting 'symbolic versions of myself' onto his patients. His empathy towards them isn't in doubt, nor his own vulnerability, but the extraordinary stories he tells sometimes border on fairy-tale. They fascinate but also fabricate. Even a good doctor can be guilty of white lies.

Memoir

What was once a geriatric, self-satisfied genre – politicians, generals and film stars looking back fondly on long careers – is now open to anyone with a story to tell. You don't have to be famous; since the 1990s, there has been a steep rise in so-called 'nobody memoirs'. Nor does your story have to be cradle-to-grave: a portion of life, or collage of fragments, may be enough.

There's no limit on how much you write, either: Diana Athill published *nine* memoirs. As Martin Amis says in his memoir *Experience*, 'We are all writing it or at any rate talking it: the memoir, the apologia, the CV, the cri de coeur.'

To write a memoir can be liberating: you get that stuff out of your system. Or it can feel suicidal, as if you've taken your life (and left behind only a Life). Memories aren't a solace, Joan Didion said, they're 'what you no longer want to remember'. Byron agonised when justifying his memoirs (later burned, though not by him): 'It is no great pleasure to have lived – and less to live over again the details of existence – but the last becomes sometimes a necessity and even a duty.' The necessity is telling the story; the duty, to tell it honestly.

Honesty is perilous but the best memoirs are transgressive because they offer alternative history – voices you don't expect to hear; candour that breaches the norms of polite society; episodes that seem shocking till you recognise their truthfulness. Memoirs allow self-assertion. But they aren't selfish. They have a unique story to tell – a story that resonates with everyone else's story. Even their anguish can be uplifting, making us aware that, as Charlotte Brontë said, 'there are countless afflictions in the world, each perhaps rivalling – some surpassing – the private pain over which we are too prone exclusively to sorrow.'

The director John Grierson called documentary films 'the creative treatment of actuality'. The same phrase holds for memoir. But how actual does it have to be? How creative? On one side you have the Prescriptors, who regard any departure from strict factual truth as an outrage. On the other are the Libertarians, as exemplified by Vivian Gornick ('I lie . . . I don't owe anyone the actuality. What is the actuality? I mean, whose business is it?') and Michael Chabon, whose book *Moonglow* poses as a memoir but admits that liberties have been taken 'with due abandon'.

To Nietzsche, memory was a truth-teller but pride a prissy censor: '"I have done that," says the memory. "I cannot have done that," says my pride and remains inexorable. Eventually memory yields.' A memoir shouldn't yield. It should admit the worst. And it should be trustworthy – even if life writers *construct* their reliability.

A would-be memoirist is bound to pause and ask: *why would my story interest anyone else? Won't readers think me exhibitionist, narcissistic, peacock-vain, an exponent of me-me-me self-regard?* But dissection of self can have a higher purpose. There's no fiercer impetus to life writing than the belief that what you've experienced is something others must have experienced too but about which little or nothing has been written. When someone is writing sensitively in a first-person memoir, the first person they're writing for is the reader.

Here Comes Everybody is a phrase used by James Joyce and the title of Anthony Burgess's book about Joyce. It's a good mantra for life writing. Open doors. Free admission. All welcome.

Memory

> *Miss Prism.* Memory, my dear Cecily, is the diary that we all carry about with us.
> *Cecily.* Yes, but it usually chronicles the things that have never happened and couldn't possibly have happened.
> (Oscar Wilde, *The Importance of Being Earnest*)

In your own mind, you're making a truthful-as-possible raid on the past. But memory is fallible. 'Memory is not false in the sense that it is wilfully bad,' Jenny Diski writes in *Skating to Antarctica*, 'but it is excitingly corrupt in its inclination to make a proper story of the past.' With key episodes, it's a useful check for a life writer to show drafts to friends and family, who can throw in details to add to the authenticity. But what readers value isn't factuality but psychological truth and emotional resonance. It's usually immaterial to them whether a certain episode in the book took place in 2001 or 2010, or whether the aunt was blonde or brunette. Believability rests on the narrative voice and the immediacy of the scenes described – matters that depend on writing skills rather than memory.

Virginia Woolf described her earliest memory as 'red and purple flowers on a black ground – my mother's dress' and claimed that memories can 'be more real than the present moment':

> I can reach a state where I seem to be watching things happen as if I were there. That is, I suppose, that my memory supplies what I had forgotten, so that it seems as if it were happening independently, though I am really making it happen with simple early memories. I am hardly aware of myself, but only of the sensation. I am only the container of the feeling of ecstasy, of the feeling of rapture.

She makes it sound mystical but it's something anyone will recognise – recall as time travel, where the past is more immediate than the present. In the best memoirs, recollection is eerily precise, as though a form of teleportation, with the author there, in the moment, not looking back from a writing desk or therapist's couch.

I don't have a great memory, but no one in the family has

taken issue with my account of the visit to Oulton Park racetrack that begins *And When Did You Last See Your Father?* I know we were stuck in a queue of cars and that my father jumped to the head of it (embarrassing us all) and bluffed his way into the paddock (embarrassing us again). I also have Oulton Park programmes that give the dates of the years we went there. But do I know for certain that the year of this episode was 1959? That our car at the time was an Alvis (we had several different makes over the years)? That people in other cars were eating sandwiches and drinking beer? That the tickets we had were brown and the ones we should have had for the paddock were red? No. The details are there to ground the story in time and place, not because my memory is phenomenal. The same with dialogue. Reproaching him for being so restless, Mum tells Dad, 'You're in and out of the car like a blue-tailed fly.' It's quite possible she used that simile. The phrase *blue-tailed fly* comes from a song made popular in the 1950s, thanks to a recording Burl Ives did with the Andrew Sisters in 1947. I didn't know that the song was originally a nineteenth-century slave song, and I'm sure my mother didn't either, but that wouldn't have stopped her using the phrase. Still, I can't swear, hand on heart, that she did. Does that make my book fiction? No, because I was remembering a real episode and attempting to recreate it authentically. 'Imagine your remembering,' Joan Didion says. Exactly. It isn't the same as making things up.

'Memory, I have come to understand, is everything, it's life itself,' Linda Grant writes in *Remind Me Who I Am Again*, a memoir prompted by her mother's multi-infarct dementia. 'She's here, with me, but her memory is on a boat that has had its moorings cut and is gone beyond the horizon.' This loss of memory stifles Grant's search to know more about her family's past in Poland and Russia: 'I don't know if it's a tragedy or blessing when Jews, who insist on forgiving and forgetting nothing, should end their lives remembering nothing.' All she has are bits and pieces, but she creates a powerful book from them, as well as writing both tenderly and exasperatedly about her mother's dementia.

Remembrance weakens with age. 'When I was younger I could remember anything, whether it happened or not,' Mark Twain joked, 'but my faculties are decaying now, and soon I shall be so I cannot remember any but the things that never happened.' If you're writing a memoir and you're not sure about the truth of a particular episode, own up to that. But don't agonise. Memory is unreliable and the reader knows it. As Julian Barnes puts it in his 2025 book *Changing My Mind*, 'the operation of memory is closer to an act of the imagination than it is to the clean and reliably detailed recuperation of an event in our past.' You just give it your best shot.

Misery

The phrase 'misery memoir' is always used sneeringly. It's understood that the genre is lamentable, inviting readers to be weepy voyeurs. The author sets down the worst and the audience gasps in pity and relief: pity for the unhappiness, relief that it isn't theirs. The narrator is a victim. Horribly put-upon. Unjustly treated but also (because a child, perhaps) weak. And the prose is cheaply agonised (*His words lit a fuse in my brain that detonated a bomb-blast in my chest. The walls around me crumbled and the ceiling fell in. I was lost in a cataclysmic nightmare of interminable, depthless suffering.*) It's one damn violation after another – not least violation of the reader, who eventually feels too pummelled to sympathise.

ON MEMOIR

Margo Jefferson wittily excoriates the genre in her memoir *Negroland*: 'I think it's too easy to recount unhappy memories when you write about yourself. You bask in your own innocence. Your revere your grief. You arrange your angers at their most becoming angles. I don't want this kind of indulgence to dominate my memories.' Her book is enjoyable rather than miserable because it's written from an unusual angle – that of a privileged, middle-class, highly educated Black girl, later a Pulitzer prize-winning theatre critic – and when documenting racial injustice it's level-headed, not vituperative. Even so, I'm not with Jefferson all the way. 'You don't tell your secrets to strangers,' she says, 'certainly not secrets that expose error, weakness, failure.' Really? Telling secrets can be a virtue, especially when you expose criminality or abuse. Error, weakness and failure can be engaging. And doing what you're taught to do as a child isn't necessarily a virtue, least of all when you've been told to keep your mouth shut.

Take Annie Ernaux's *Getting Lost*, her account of an affair with a Soviet diplomat. It's a classic tale of sexual infatuation: the man comes and goes as he pleases, while the woman yearns for his visits and phone calls; he's the powerhouse, she a woebegone lover. The reader-response (mine anyway) is exasperation: stop abasing yourself, Annie, he's a shit! But as the title implies, Ernaux is keenly aware of her haplessness. She lets it stand in all its shame. By publishing the book (in essence a series of diary entries) thirty-four years after the affair, she stands at a distance from it. There's misery but it's offset by humour and self-searching.

Salman Rushdie's memoir *Knife*, about the attack in 2022 that nearly killed him and blinded him in one eye, has every right to be miserable. But it's heart-warming as well as scary, a story of hate defeated by love. There's even room for a few jokes. Before the stabbing he was horribly overweight; after his time in hospital, he finds he has lost 55 pounds, though it's 'not a diet plan to be recommended'.

Mission

'My starting point,' George Orwell said, 'is always a feeling of partisanship, a sense of injustice.' Many life writers are on a mission: to change something that's morally bankrupt; to help victims who've suffered unjustly; to persuade law-makers or policy-makers to shift position; to alter how people think and feel. 'I will write to avenge my people,' Annie Ernaux wrote in her diary as a young woman, determined to speak for a provincial, working-class community whose experience wasn't being voiced. It took her years to learn how to do it.

In life writing, partisanship works better if it's not too repetitively declared. The writer's a *behalfer*, working for a cause, but the book isn't a megaphone – its job is to throw ideas in the air, not thump readers over the head. The narrative should be a journey of discovery, not a summary of long-arrived-at conclusions. In the process of the book both writer and reader will learn something. They know at the finish what they didn't know at the start.

Cathy Rentzenbrink's *The Last Act of Love* is a case in point. It tells of her teenage brother Matty's persistent vegetative state after he was knocked down by a car. The book didn't come out till twenty-five years after the accident, by which time Matty had been dead (after life-sustaining treatment was withdrawn) for over a decade. What Rentzenbrink had learned by then is that 'no human being should be made to linger on in a deteriorating body when the brain has gone'. But she keeps that message, with all it implies about current medical practice, in reserve and takes us back to the immediate aftermath of the accident, when the family, unaware that there are fates (or mental non-states) worse than death, are desperate to keep Matty alive. At the end Rentzenbrink sees herself as having 'opened up a conversation'. The intimacy of her narrative, as she works out what she thinks while she goes along, is more persuasive than a polemic could be.

Sometimes the mission is on a large political scale. Hisham Matar's father, an opponent of the Qaddafi regime, was kidnapped in 1990 and taken to a prison in Libya. In *The Return*, Matar attempts to find what happened to him after contact ceased in 1996. He knows his father may have been one of the 1,270 men executed in the prison that year. But he can't be sure ('I didn't believe Father to be dead . . . I didn't believe him to be alive either.'). No country cares to own up to its crimes. And neither the Libyans, nor the British Foreign Office, are willing to help Matar find out more. It's the same for Aminatta Forna in *The Devil That Danced on the Water*, when she sets out to discover the truth about the father she lost when she was ten – a doctor and later finance minister in Sierra Leone, he was executed for his alleged involvement in a coup. Unlike Matar, she knows her father is dead; like him, she is lied to and fobbed off. Both books are indictments of barbarous regimes and their denial of human rights. They're ferociously angry without having to preach.

They also record a fight for justice, as does William Wharton's *Wrongful Deaths* (1994), which tells how his daughter, her husband and their two children died in a traffic accident caused by farmers burning stubble in a field next to a highway in Oregon. All these books are written with passion and that's what carries their mission – they excoriate but they don't beat a drum. There's a vast chasm between a noble cause and a successful memoir, but these authors find a way across.

Mortality

There's death, which happens to others and there's mortality, which happens to us. One fills us with grief, the other with fear. One lies behind, and is coped with retrospectively, the other lies ahead and, for some people, can't be coped with at all. It's a fine distinction (the two words are usually conflated) but holds true in life writing, where the loss of those we love (death) is a staple of memoir whereas the imagined and perhaps imminent end of our own life (mortality) forms a no less significant sub-genre.

Larkin's poem 'Aubade', with its 'furnace-fear' of dying ('nothing more terrible, nothing more true'), is the great set-piece on the subject:

> Unresting death, a whole day nearer now,
> Making all thought impossible but how
> And where and when I shall myself die.
> Arid interrogation: yet the dread
> Of dying, and being dead,
> Flashes afresh to hold and horrify.

No poem about death is as definitive. But that hasn't daunted life writers from tackling the subject. 'Over the decades, my fear of death has become an essential part of me,' Julian Barnes writes in *Nothing To Be Frightened Of*, and his book is an attempt to 'get this death thing straight'. He pitches himself between his brother, who claims not to be worried by death, and Montaigne, who thought it important to keep death in mind at all times. 'For me, death is the one appalling fact which defines life,' Barnes says, while wondering which better prepares us for our own deaths, and which lets us live more contentedly, denial or awareness.

Barnes published the book nearly twenty years ago, in good health. More urgent reflections on mortality are by writers who know they don't have long, including Paul Kalanithi, whose memoir *When Breath Becomes Air* is the story of a brilliant neurosurgeon who died of lung cancer at the age of 37 – a man in a race against time to write about his experiences as both doctor and patient. He's used to death and recounts operations he carried out, not all successful, in compelling detail. Getting used to the idea of his own death is tougher but he ends the book with words for his eight-month-old daughter, who 'filled a dying man's days with a sated joy, a joy unknown to me in all my prior years'.

Like Kalanithi's book, Kate Gross's *Late Fragments* was written as she faced death from cancer (the Nuisance as she calls it) in her mid-thirties: 'I have fitted so much colour into my short life that I wonder if I lived on hyper-speed, as if, somehow, I knew my time was limited.' She was leaving behind a happy marriage, twin boys, loving parents and a stellar career: 'I can't shake this feeling that I'm letting them all down.' The book is written for her sons, as is Joe Hammond's *A Short History of Falling* (for his two boys) after he was diagnosed with motor-neurone disease in his forties. Both books are remarkably upbeat: 'Life is not worse than it was before. It doesn't have less value. It's not less interesting. Not at all . . . I've become adept at extracting pleasure from less.' (Hammond); 'I've had a great life. I still have a great life. What's the point in spending the last chapter of it being sad? . . . I am growing fat on the marrow of life.' (Gross). Both authors count their blessings.

In *I am I am I am*, Maggie O'Farrell does the same, recalling seventeen near-misses with mortality, the most terrifying of them an encounter with a man on a hillside who she knew wanted to kill her and who did indeed rape and murder another young woman on the same hillside shortly afterwards. The other brushes with death are scarcely less traumatic: three near-drownings, an almost plane crash, a mugging with a machete held to her throat, a post-partum haemorrhage, amoebic dysentery and cerebellar damage in childhood. Each chapter records a variant on 'having pulled my head, one more time, out of the noose'.

Larkin says that fear of mortality usually remains 'on the edge of vision, / A small unfocused blur,'. These authors face it close up. So do Simon Gray in *Coda* and Jane Miller in *Crazy Age: Thoughts on Being Old*, memoirs that explore senescence with humour and grace.

N

Names

Memoir writers often change the names of people who appear in their work – either to protect them, if identification would be embarrassing or incriminating, or to protect themselves from angry or legalistic reprisal. They sometimes also find that they write more freely when using an invented name: where saying Ben (his real name) about the friend who betrayed them was inhibiting, rechristening him Bernard allowed more candour. It's the kind of dilemma that can be tested out in a draft – with the real name, if need be, later restored.

With family members, it's more difficult. Your mum and dad are your mum and dad, and no disguising it. And changing your sister's name, because she asks you to, will only help up to a point – she'll still be identifiable as your sister. In my memoirs, I changed the names of my father's lover, along with her husband and daughter, because I didn't want to upset them. Which only worked up to a point – Aunty Beaty, as I called her, *was* upset, and when her daughter Josie read the book ten years after it came out she recognised herself, despite the disguise. At least I didn't expose them to others.

One thing to be wary of is over-naming. If there's a section describing someone, endless repetition of their name is horribly cumbersome. For instance:

> Imogen reached the end of the street and turned left. A car sped by. Imogen hated speeding cars – her brother had nearly died in one. They should put in speed bumps, Imogen believed. A man walking past nodded to Imogen. Imogen averted her eyes and headed on to the shop, where she bought a bottle of wine and some chocolate to go with the evening meal Imogen was planning to make.

It's an invented example but I've seen worse cases of writers avoiding 'he' or 'she' or 'they'. In this case, after the first 'Imogen', 'she' would have been fine. It's an obvious point (use the pronoun not the name!) that memoir writers, no less than novelists, too often ignore. (See PRONOUNS.)

Narcissism

Life writers are sometimes accused of it. The very word 'memoir' seems to embody self-absorption – me-*moi*. It's an unfair charge. In my experience those who write memoirs, far from being narcissists, need constant encouragement that their story is worth telling, that they're not being self-indulgent, that it's OK to use the word 'I'. Young writers are especially anxious: they worry their subject matter is millennial not perennial. For all life writers there's the anxiety, expressed by James Baldwin in *Notes of a Native Son*, that looking back on early years will be painful for oneself and tedious to others: 'The story of my childhood is the usual bleak fantasy, and we can dismiss it with the restrained observation that I certainly would not consider living it again.'

As with life drawing, so with life writing: we expect nakedness. But as a writer you don't have to reveal everything. And the self-revealing doesn't mean you're vain, it can also be a matter of survival: as Audre Lorde puts it, 'If I didn't define myself for myself, I would be crunched into other people's fantasies for me and eaten alive.' I would even make a case for memoir as the most self-sacrificial of forms, the author laying themselves open for the benefit of others, who feel less alone in the world once an experience they've been through is articulated by someone else. Writing in the *Guardian*, Leslie Jamison, the author of *The Empathy Exams* and *The Recovering*, notes the confessional memoir 'is often the opposite of solipsism. My confessions elicited responses. They coaxed chorus like a brushfire . . . the reader wants to confess something back, make a reciprocal exchange . . . whenever people talk about confessional writing as navel-gazing or self-involved, I think about those voices, and their offerings.'

Still, some courage is required to keep saying 'I'. And hitting the right tone is a challenge: to steer a path between self-regard and self-vilification (both ultimately exasperating to the reader) takes practice. Life writers ask themselves: *Do I come across as boastful or timid? Flushed with entitlement or self-abasing? Too up myself or too down on?* If the approach is wrong, tweaks will be needed. Or a bigger rewrite, to hit the right tone – an I-story that isn't I-enthralled or I-appalled.

'I study myself more than any other subject,' Montaigne said, but he's the most wide-ranging of writers. Exploring the self can be a means to understand the world beyond you. It doesn't make you Narcissus, let alone Boris Johnson or Donald Trump.

Nature

Nature writing has been a huge phenomenon over the last twenty years, with so many fine practitioners (among them Annie Dillard, Richard Mabey, Robert Macfarlane, Roger Deakin, Kathleen Jamie and Mark Cocker), that I'm tempted to omit it as a wholly separate genre from life writing. Certainly there are books by ornithologists, botanists, ecologists and so on that firmly belong to the realm of science. It's where an exploration of fauna or flora is combined with a personal story that the book becomes life writing. Even a taxonomic work, full of pie charts and statistics, can be personal, if the author is intimately invested in a threatened species or – as the Lake District farmer James Rebanks is in *English Pastoral* – in the future of farming. But what's striking is the number of nature books that are triggered by a human life crisis, where the authors are writing not so much to save birds, beasts and – in the case of Robert Macfarlane's *Is a River Alive?* – rivers, but to save themselves.

The worst of these books are stereotypical redemption narratives pitched at (and now saturating) the market, with *nature-as-cure* the message. You walk, you forage, you rewild yourself, you get over your lockdown blues: *that* – the rehabilitation trope – is the selling point. It has become too easy and predictable a publishing formula. As James Rebanks has said, nature is 'full of death and disease and failure and decline. It isn't all butterflies, sunshine and healing, is it?' The nature writers I admire allow for ambivalence and complication. And though their lives are central to the narrative, the natural world, in all its wonder and complexity, comes first.

In *H is for Hawk*, Helen Macdonald teaches us about goshawks, and about T. H. White, who wrote a famous book about goshawks, but she's also writing in the wake of bereavement ('It happens to everyone. But you feel it alone.'). As 'a protecting spirit', Mabel the goshawk doesn't distract her from thoughts of her deceased father, 'the quiet man in a suit with a camera on his shoulder'. But whereas in daily life she's depressed, angry, tearful and keeps having accidents, 'the world with the hawk was insulated from harm.' It's no easy ride to be a falconer, let alone to mend an emotional wound, and at one point Macdonald feels she has made a terrible mistake: 'I'd thought that to heal my great hurt, I should fly to the wild. It was what people did. The nature books I'd read told me so.' Wildness, she finds, isn't the answer; human company is essential, too, as is a drug to combat her depression.

In *Owl Sense,* Miriam Darlington's immersion in the 'mythology, kinship, otherness and mystery that wild owls offer' is interrupted by the seizures that afflict her teenage son, Benji. It's a struggle to conduct her owl-quest, for which she travels widely, while also looking after Benji. But his shared fascination with owls is a vital part of the story. Katharine Norbury's journey in *The Fish Ladder,* following a river from the sea to its source, is triggered by a miscarriage. The wild life she meets is beautifully observed (fox cubs like 'hot loaves knocked out of their tins') and the journey returns her to her own source, as she traces her birth family. There's similar voltage in *Soundings,* Doreen Cunningham's journey to see grey whales in the company of her two-year-old son, since the trip takes her back to the Alaskan town where she fell in love with the indigenous Billy some years before.

All these books honour a wildness that challenges humankind. How does the natural world affect us? What rights does it have? How can we address the climate crisis? Novels that ask these questions are cli-fi; memoirs bring a more personal perspective – cli-auto, perhaps. They're threaded with doubt and dread but unapologetically passionate about the creatures they extol.

New Journalism

For Tom Wolfe, the discovery that it was possible to write accurate non-fiction using techniques associated with novels and short stories was what defined the work of Hunter S. Thompson, Joan Didion and himself, samples of which he collected in his 1973 anthology *The New Journalism*. In their innovative prose and use of interior monologue, these writers subverted conventional reportage. They also, Wolfe claimed, walked through a door left open by contemporary American novelists, who had abandoned the realist tradition and turned to Neo-Fabulism 'like the engineer who decides to give up electricity because it has "been done".' The building blocks of the nineteenth-century novel – scene-by-scene construction, dialogue, third-person point of view and detailed attention to markers of social status (clothes, décor, food, etc.) – became the property of the Wolfe pack, who 'had the whole crazed obscene uproarious Mammon-faced drug-soaked mau-mau lust-oozing Sixties in America all to themselves.'

Wolfe's thesis is wildly exaggerated and self-serving. But it's worth looking at his redefinition of the non-fiction narrator. Till the arrival of New Journalism, he argues, 'Most non-fiction writers, without knowing it, wrote in a century-old British tradition in which it was understood that the narrator shall assume a calm, cultivated and, in fact, genteel voice . . . like the off-white or putty-coloured walls that Syrie Maugham popularized in interior decoration . . . *Understatement* was the thing.' Understatement still is a thing. Dramatic or traumatic scenes sometimes work best when described laconically. But Wolfe is right that if you adopt 'the standard announcer's voice', dull and neutral in tone, its drone will send readers to sleep.

He's right, too, that no author wants to be what he calls 'the Literary Gentleman in the Grandstand'. Life writers aren't above the fray. They need to be down there, among the crowd, at ground-level, in the shit. A memoir needn't be Wolfe's kind of firework but nor can it be bland. The narrator has to be visible and the prose energetic. By all means be deadpan, I used to tell students. But don't be beige.

O

Offence

Upsetting people is part of the business. 'How are you going to report life if you report it as a series of wonderful people?' Jonathan Raban asked. 'Some people are repulsive.' Novelists have the excuse that any resemblance between the imaginary X and the real-life Y is (ho-ho) pure coincidence. With memoir there are no get-outs. You can change names, places and dates but people in your circle will guess who's who and it'll be a miracle if none of them objects. The family of Alexandra Fuller were offended by her depiction of them in *Don't Let's Go to the Dogs Tonight*. As a memoir it was, she thought, 'mostly a love letter to my wild childhood starring my mother'. But her mother, portrayed as a drunk and depressive, hated it; her father and sister refused to read it, 'hating it on principle'; and her (later ex-) husband Charlie 'resented its success'.

Offence can be caused not only by unflattering characterisation but by the disclosure of secrets. 'I've despaired over sharing these darker parts of Molly, the parts she hated herself for and used against herself like cutting,' Blake Butler writes in *Molly*, a memoir about his wife, the poet Molly Brodak, who killed herself at the age of 39 and whose secret other life (and many affairs) he discovered only after her death. 'Should I be allowed to . . . bring to light a part of Molly's story she covered over at any cost?' he asks, worried about betraying and disrespecting her. In the end he feels he has no choice, 'given the way the story, bound up inside me, feels like frying in a slow electrocution, with nowhere else to set it down.'

For biographers rather than memoirists, the issue may be less personal but they too have a duty to be honest. If their subject, however distinguished, was a racist, thief, bully, sadist or worse, that should be made clear, not skipped or whitewashed. Widows, relatives and executors may resist, and when the subject of a Life has only recently died there'll be a pressure to soft-pedal. But as Hermione Lee puts it, apologising for the mixed metaphor, 'whatever the Elephant is, if you avoid it it will come back to bite you.' Not everyone enjoyed hearing the unpalatable truths about Philip Larkin in Andrew Motion's biography, published eight years after his death. But they'd have emerged anyway in due course and Motion was right not to shirk them.

Put it out there is my usual advice to students. *C'est la vie (et l'histoire de votre vie)*: you've a job to do and you want to do it honestly. In a letter to the *Guardian*, Hanif Kureishi's sister Yasmin accused him of selling her family 'down the line' with his depictions of them in his first novel and in his memoir *My Ear at His Heart*: 'My father was angry when *The Buddha of Suburbia* came out as he felt that Hanif had robbed him of his dignity.' After the novel came out, father and son did not speak for months. But Kureishi writes more warmly of him than Yasmin acknowledges, both in the memoir ('Father gave me what he wanted for himself, and it was a lot.') and in the more recent *Shattered*; he's every right to his interpretation of his dad's life and frustrated writing career.

'I feel a bit guilty about this Chapter,' Anthony Bourdain scrawls in the margins of *Kitchen Confidential*, because the man he was writing about was hurt by it, 'But that's the way it was.' Where authors are writing about hurt caused to them, there's all the more reason to tell it as it was. John le Carré puts it well, in a letter to his aunts, the sisters of his fraudster father Ronnie, about whom he'd written truthfully and disparagingly:

> The justification for what I have done, if one is needed, is surely in the comfort that I have given to people who are living, or have lived, in the shadow of their own Ronnie . . . In writing as I have done, I believe that I have not only alleviated my own pain, which has been prolonged and crippling, but lightened the burden of others who, in cloistered situations, are enduring similar miseries without being able to share them . . .. If a writer has any usefulness it is to say out loud what others perhaps feel but cannot say; and so add – we hope – to the sum of human compassion and understanding.

If friends or relatives think that the events the writer describes didn't happen that way, it's up to them to come back with their own versions, not to impose silence and censorship.

Omission

How much to put in? How much to leave out? *Less is more* goes the mantra, which is also a way of saying *more is less*. But it isn't necessarily true. An accumulation of detail can be telling. Even a writer as spare as Annie Ernaux eventually spread herself in *The Years*. Sometimes we're grateful for abundance.

John Ashbery: 'I tried each thing, only some were immortal and free.'

How much of *yourself* do you put in? The reason 'so many [memoirs] are failures', Virginia Woolf complained, is that 'They leave out the person to whom things happened.' Or as she puts it elsewhere: 'Confronted with the terrible spectre of themselves, the bravest are inclined to run away or shade their eyes. And thus, instead of the honest truth which we should all respect, we are given timid side-glances.' A memoirist may be instinctively self-effacing, as Primo Levi was: 'It was his nature to be clamped down,' Carole Angier reports in her biography, 'to leave himself out, to withhold expressions of feeling.' But when he made changes to the drafts of his first book, *If This Is a Man*, an opposite instinct took over which told him that he had eliminated himself too ruthlessly and which made him 'put himself and his feelings – just a little, just enough – back in'.

When Catherine Coldstream began the PhD at Goldsmiths that would become her memoir *Cloistered* she was unsure whether to write a memoir about her father, the painter William Coldstream, or about the twelve years after his death that she spent as a nun in a Carmelite monastery. Which should she write, she asked me? A book about growing up in a north London bohemian household? Or the story of a young woman who devotedly enters and unhappily leaves a closed religious community? I think you'd have said the same as I did: write the second! She took her time to find the right way, partly from worry that, however well she disguised the monastery and the women inside it, she'd cause offence, and partly from the struggle to out herself as a truth-telling, first-person narrator. It took courage not to omit stuff, out of discretion. But the book is all the better for her honesty.

Put it in. Own up. No disguises.

Omniscience

Writers don't have it. They're not all-seeing. Even the smartest can't offer celestial wisdom. For memoirists the perspective is always ground-level – kitchen-sink close-up, not heavenly overview; humble first-person, not God. Their impetus is to make sense of something they've been through. And that means writing intimately, in the first person.

Still, it's important to situate a personal account in a wider context – to rise above yourself, like a drone or an eagle looking down. Say you're writing a memoir about being abducted as a child – kidnapped by your father, who had never forgiven your mum for breaking up with him and who took you overseas to start a new life close to his parents. You were lied to, confused and, as a small child, unable to understand. The same, six months later, when you'd begun to settle, and were seized and taken home again to be with your mum. Years on, you're exploring all this. You don't have infinite knowledge but you're grown-up, you've talked to people about what happened and you're able to put events in perspective. The older you 1) recalls the experience of abduction through the sensations of the younger you and 2) stands back, as an adult, to explain what made both the abduction and the rescue inevitable. It's all there: past and present, inner feeling and outside world, autobiography and chronicle, with a range of different points of view.

Richard Beard drives himself towards omniscience in *The Day That Went Missing*, a book about the death of his younger brother Nicky in a childhood swimming accident. 'I want to find the missing emotional content in a lost true event,' he says, and determinedly recovers the circumstances of the fateful day, 18 August 1978, from psychic shutdown. At the same time, he 'conducts an inquest' into the epic denial that followed and the 'hardcore English repression' of his father, who didn't once talk about Nicky, even to his wife, in the remaining thirty-three years of his life. The family 'tried to diminish Nicky's death into an event that happened to him but not to any of the rest of us,' Beard decides. He wouldn't claim to be all-seeing but he transcends his limited point of view by speaking to everyone involved – which is as close to omniscience as a memoirist can get.

Orwell, George

In his essay 'Why I Write' Orwell gave four reasons for writing:

(i) Sheer egoism. Desire to seem clever, to be talked about, to be remembered after death, to get your own back on grown-ups who snubbed you in childhood, etc., etc. . . .
(ii) Aesthetic enthusiasm. Perception of beauty in the external world, or, on the other hand, in words and their right arrangement. . . .
(iii) Historical impulse. Desire to see things as they are, to find out true facts and store them up for the use of posterity.
(iv) Political purpose . . . Desire to push the world in a certain direction, to alter other people's idea of the kind of society that they should strive after . . .

He added: 'I write . . . because there is some lie I want to expose, some fact to which I want to draw attention . . . it is invariably where I lacked a *political* purpose that I wrote lifeless books and was betrayed into purple passages, sentences without meaning, decorative adjectives and humbug generally.'

Political purpose in Orwell always stems from personal experience. He is best known for his novels *Animal Farm* and *Nineteen Eighty-Four* but he's a key figure for life writers because of all the brilliant non-fiction he wrote – the essays and columns as well as *Homage to Catalonia* and *The Road to Wigan Pier*. Take his essay 'A Hanging', about an execution in Burma. Orwell told a friend it was 'just a story' and there's no factual evidence to prove that he was present at a hanging. But two key details suggest he must have been: the dog and the puddle. The dog appears out of nowhere, barking excitedly, 'wild with glee', as the prisoner is escorted to the gallows; innocent of what's going on, the dog destroys the solemn formality of the process. Till this point, Orwell's tone has been neutral: when he talks of a 'dreadful thing' happening, he means the dog's intrusion, not the impending execution. But when the condemned man steps aside to avoid a puddle, taking care to avoid getting his feet wet despite being about to die, Orwell realises 'the unspeakable wrongness of cutting a life short when it is in full tide'. It's likely that he already had firm views about capital punishment. But if so he hides them and affects to have this revelation only then. The dog and the puddle carry the moral burden of the piece more powerfully than if he'd set out to preach.

'A Hanging' isn't merely observational; Orwell is complicit in the process, holding the dog by putting his handkerchief through its collar and sharing the awkwardness everyone feels when the prisoner, with a noose round his neck, cries aloud to his god: 'the same thought was in all our minds: oh, kill him quickly, get it over!' Afterwards, there's a sense of 'enormous relief... One felt an impulse to sing, to break into a run, to snigger. All at once everyone began chattering gaily.' We think no less of Orwell for the gallows humour. He has already achieved what matters – to find the words for an 'unspeakable wrongness'. That the prisoner's offence is never mentioned makes the piece even more powerful. The man may be a murderer or he may be a petty thief. It doesn't matter. What does matter is the squalor and inhumanity of the execution: the hangman putting 'a small cotton bag like a flour bag' over the prisoner's face, the rope twisting as he hangs from the noose, the superintendent poking him with a stick to make sure he's dead.

P

Pace

Pace is tricky. What's the right speed for readers? Too quick and we won't be immersed. Too pedestrian and we'll get bored. The problem intensifies if a book is set over a long period.

The binary, as in fiction, is fast/slow. Fast means tension, car chases, page-turning suspense; slow means leisureliness and room to think. One gallops, the other ambles. One is John Grisham, the other is Marcel Proust. Life writing admits both modes. It aims for the same narrative pull as fiction. But it's a personal story, inescapably emotive, and what it discloses needs thinking about. Two sorts of pace then: a sprint and a saunter.

You can race through a human drama in a handful of words. A famous example, attributed to Hemingway, does it in six: 'For sale. Baby shoes. Never worn.' I once had a go at minimalism myself, cramming a life into seven rhymes: 'Womb. Bloom. Groom. Vroom. Rheum. Gloom. Tomb.' Time can be foreshortened. Many a novel is set over the span of a single day. A memoir could be too, if it makes room for back story.

What's crucial is to vary momentum – for the book to avoid being wildly episodic or a self-raptured meditative flow.

ON MEMOIR

In memoir a larger narrative should be unfolding. There's the author in the past, going through a drama, shell-shocked and inarticulate; and there's the author now, looking back and finding the words. There's event and there's contemplation.

Virginia Woolf writes of the importance of creating (or remembering) whole scenes: 'I find that scene-making is my natural way of marking the past. A scene always comes to the top; arranged; representative . . .'. Woolf shows how to avoid ducking out early; how to let a lunch feel as if it has taken an hour not five minutes. But she's also a writer who makes you think. There's the scene (then) and the philosophising (now). Life writing as perusal as well as event.

Lorna Sage has a multi-layered tale to tell in *Bad Blood*, involving her grandparents' marriage, her parents' marriage and her own. Splitting the book into three parts simplifies the narrative. But she still has the problem of accommodating four decades of family life. A device she hits on in part 3 of the book, with a nod to Wordsworth's phrase from *The Prelude*, 'spots of time', is to dwell on key moments, then speed through weeks, before pausing again over a single episode or image. Below is the way her paragraphs begin as she describes the period round the mysterious crisis of her adolescence – how she came to be pregnant without having penetrative sex. They shift between showing (slow) and telling (fast):

> I recall a flattened patch in the long grass going to seed on the bank of the towpath along the Shropshire Union Canal. It's a hot bright afternoon in summer . . .
>
> Spots of time. One day when my parents are out we're lying on the edge of the old tennis lawn at Sunnyside . . .
>
> Most days in the summer holiday merge into each other . . .

Charities didn't take you until you were six months pregnant . . .

Small scenes surface: Vic and I sitting together on the verge of the drive at Sunnyside . . .

As the dank, disgraced autumn of 1959 turned to winter, we reinvented marriage, for better and for worse.

In ten pages, she covers six months, from heavy petting to a shotgun marriage, but the pace doesn't feel rushed. She honours both romance and stigma.

The ending of Tobias Wolff's *This Boy's Life* alternates between a set of almost simultaneous events and a summary of the next few years. We go from 'One morning . . . that night . . . Several hours later' (*short*) to 'I did not do well at Hill [School] . . . Then I went into the army' (*long*) and back to a car journey to Seattle in a friend's car: 'It was a good night to sing and we sang for all we were worth' (*short*). I used to give students an exercise that meant them writing three or four sentences of a narrative sequence, as a lesson in how to vary pace: 'It happened in an instant . . .' (*scene*), 'But much has changed in the meantime . . .' (*summary*), 'Then last week this happened . . .' (*scene*), 'So here I am today . . .' (*summary – and maybe a scene as well*). Alternation between past and present is the commonest structure of memoirs, and variation in pace is vital to it.

Passion

Or should I say restraint? I'm talking about the tone that's adopted in scenes of high emotional intensity. 'In great fiction we are moved by what happens,' John Gardner believed, 'not by the whimpering and bawling of the writer's presentation of what happens.' Some authors are declarative, others laconic. The too-declarative writer, upping the ante because the scene is dramatic (a row, a stabbing, a hurricane), will resort to stylistic flourishes – tics that direct the reader's attention not to the scene but to the prose. The too-laconic writer will be no less self-defeating by draining the scene of emotional richness through flat-footed narration. Freaked by the challenge of an incendiary episode, both lose their way, either cranking up feeling or squashing it down.

If happiness writes white, passion writes red – and often requires a blue pencil. Byron thought passion best conveyed when it's spent. But that can result in self-protective irony, the lover mocking her infatuated self, the one-time wooer wondering why he ever wooed. That's why Annie Ernaux succeeds in her memoirs about her parents and upbringing: decades later she tells it, unashamedly, as it was. Her prose serves the truth, rather than over- or under-playing its hand. She leaves a scrupulous emotional record, without fireworks or a damp fizz.

Performance

Rousseau shows the way in his *Confessions*. His intention is to paint 'a portrait in every way true to nature', he says, one that will 'bare my secret soul.' But the metaphor then shifts from realistic portraiture to theatre or cabaret: 'Let the numberless legion of my fellow men gather round me and hear my confessions. Let them groan at my depravities, and blush for my misdeeds . . . And may any man who dares say "I was a better man than he."'

Rousseau doesn't actually shout *Roll up, roll up*, but the impression of a music-hall master of ceremonies is hard to miss. Honest or not, he's putting on a show. And what a show it is. He steals, he tells lies, he sends all five of his children to an orphanage, much to the despair of their mother, and that's not even to mention his sexual transgressions – flashing, sadomasochism, a long relationship with a woman twelve years his senior, a visit to a brothel, deep frustration when he fails to perform for a beautiful courtesan because she has a malformed nipple, taking turns with friends to have sex with a young girl . . .

Rousseau relishes being watched, even when he's misbehaving. There's the lesson for life writers, who will less feel awkward about exposing themselves (about invading their own privacy) if they think of the process as a drama they're acting in onstage. It's not plain first-person narration and yet it's honest: 'If I insist that there is a persona or a performativity at work,' Maggie Nelson writes in *The Argonauts*, 'I don't mean that I'm not myself in my writing, or that my writing somehow isn't me.' Life writers don't need to give the reader *all* of themselves, just the version that's relevant to the scene they're in. It's a play and they're performing. They profess as well as confess.

'I must remain incessantly beneath [the reader's] gaze, so that he may follow me in all the extravagances of my heart and into every least corner of my life,' Rousseau says. Self-dramatisation is integral to the genre. Writers have to keep their readership interested. The trick is to perform without overdoing the showmanship. Command of the prose, not a command performance of the self. Candour not exhibitionism.

Permissions

A friend emailed me a while back to ask for advice. She'd just finished a book that quoted some lines from famous pop songs and she wondered if I'd any tips for her. I had. Just one. *Don't ever quote lines from pop songs.*

ON MEMOIR

I wish someone had given me that advice when I was writing my novel *South of the River*, at the end of which there's a party, with music and dancing. The tracks I put on for my characters were a mix of sixties classics and more recent disco numbers, and because the songs echoed themes in the novel, I wanted to include the words, not just the titles. Of course I knew that when a novel quotes at length from a living writer, or even a less-than-seventy-years-dead one, you need permission. Such permissions come at a price and it's usually the author's duty, not the publisher's, to obtain and pay for them. But I'd restricted myself to just a line or two from a handful of songs and vaguely hoped that was OK and that no one would notice.

My editor was more cautious and at the last minute someone from the publishing house helpfully secured the permissions on my behalf. I still have the invoices. For one line of 'Jumping Jack Flash': £500. For one line of 'Wonderwall': £535. For one line of 'When I'm Sixty-Four': £735. For two lines of 'I Shot the Sheriff': £1,000. Plus several more, of which only George Michael's 'Fast Love' came in under £200. Plus VAT. Total outlay: £4,401.75. A typical advance for a literary novel by a first-time author wouldn't meet the cost. And doubtless permission fees are far more expensive these days – the novel came out in 2007.

For biographers and life writers, permission fees are even more of a nightmare than for novelists. Tracking down copyright holders and getting answers from them can be complex, laborious and extremely slow. But unless the subject has been dead for seven decades there's no getting round it – even if, as Michael Holroyd says, this means enriching the dead at the expense of the living. The Society of Authors and the Publishers Association have guidelines on what they call 'fair dealing': with prose, a single extract of up to 400 words or a series of extracts of up to 800 words shouldn't require permission; with poetry, up to 40 lines, provided that doesn't exceed a quarter of the poem's length. But these guidelines are for the purposes of critical commentary, not for an imaginative work.

The Internet is gradually changing this. Consumers expect owt for nowt. And, since literature is about breaking down barriers, who wants a paywall? But it's unfair if originators aren't acknowledged when someone quotes their words. David Shields ran into this problem with his book *Reality Hunger*. 'I am quite content to go down to posterity as a scissors-and-paste man,' he says at one point. Well actually he doesn't say it, James Joyce does. But there are no quotation marks to make that clear – deliberately so: the book's premise is that 'reality can't be copyrighted' and that all of us have (or ought to have) ownership of each other's words. Half the 618 soundbites in Shields's book are quotes from other writers. For copyright reasons, he was eventually forced to acknowledge his citations in small-print endnotes. But that wasn't his original plan and he invites readers to remove these with a razor blade. In the main text we can't tell whether he or someone else is doing the talking.

Breaching copyright is less of an offence than plagiarism, but both are a form of theft – a failure to credit others. If an author quotes someone at length in a novel or memoir, they must seek permission. Unless it's a pop lyric, the fee shouldn't be expensive. If it is, and they can't argue it down, the only option is to leave it out.

Persona

There's the 'I' you occupy in daily life, an 'I' who speaks, eats, drinks, sleeps, thinks and acts on your behalf. But when you *write* as an 'I', the voice may be different – go deeper, harden up, speak in another way. It isn't a straightforward process. A writer has to fashion a persona. Vivian Gornick writes about it well in *The Situation and the Story*, describing how for years she struggled to find a voice for her writing: 'The one I habitually lived with wouldn't do at all: it whined, it grated, it accused.' Her breakthrough was to tap into another self, 'a narrator who was me and at the same time not me . . . this other one telling the story that I alone – in my everyday person – would not have been able to tell. I could hardly believe my luck in having found her . . . she had become the instrument of my illumination.'

Gornick argues that it's the same for most gifted life writers – George Orwell, J. R. Ackerley, Joan Didion – that 'in each case a persona had been created to serve the insight'. In life writing, she says, 'we have to pull from ourselves the narrator who will shape better than we alone can the inchoate flow of event into which we are continually being plunged.' The event-I offers first-hand experience and the narrator-I frames and interprets it.

You can adopt a persona and still be writing from the heart. The troubles encountered by Henry, the persona of John Berryman's *Dream Songs*, are the poet's own: anxiety, unrequited love, ennui ('Life, friends, is boring. We must not say so.'), heavy drinking, self-hatred and suicidal depression. The jazz- or blues-inflected idiom of the poetry frees Berryman from a mode of 1950s politesse that had previously constrained him; even when he's down, the tone is upbeat, comic, vibrant. In worldly terms his persona doesn't resemble him ('I pay income tax; Henry pays no income tax.'), but emotionally he does. 'I took Henry in various directions', he said, 'the direction of despair, of lust, of memory, of patriotism, and various other things. To take him further than anything an ordinary life can take us to.' Further into himself, in fact, through a persona.

As with poetry, so with memoir. Alan Bennett, Simon Gray, Deborah Levy and Jenny Diski are great examples. All write personally, by using personas.

Photos

A picture is worth a thousand words, it's said. And modern technology has made it cheap and easy to add photographs to a text. Instead of a set of glossy plates inserted midway through a book, prints can be incorporated throughout. Many biographies adopt this method and an increasing number of memoirs do too. The question is, how much do photos contribute? If it's a family memoir, readers may appreciate seeing what the family looked like. Then again, they might prefer to create their own image. Family photos augment memoirs such as Sathnam Sanghera's *The Boy with the Topknot* and Lorna Sage's *Bad Blood*. And the mix of landscape photos and Renaissance paintings in Rachel Cusk's *The Last Supper* complements her travels in Italy. In many other memoirs, photos seem beside the point.

It's different if you've spent your life as a photographer, as Sally Mann has. In her memoir *Hold Still* the photos she chooses are integral to the story she tells, not least the photos showing her three small children, sometimes naked, at the family farm. When first exhibited, the photos got her in trouble; she was accused of being a Bad Mother and of encouraging paedophiles. But as she says, critics read a sexuality into the images that wasn't there: 'Yes, it was a physical desire, a parental carnality, even a kind of primal parental eroticism, but to confuse it with what we call sexuality, inter-adult sexual relations, is a category error.' Mann's genius as a photographer is her intimacy: she even took a shot of herself giving birth to her daughter Virginia. Her memoir is both a cogent self-defence and bold self-assertion; the photos help to make her case.

The photos in W. G. Sebald's books are there to add authenticity – here a real building, there a real person – so that we believe the story he's telling. But just as he fictionalised his 'true' stories, so he faked some of the photos. The cover jacket of *Austerlitz*, which also appears as a photo in the text, shows the eponymous hero as a pageboy in a white costume; Sebald claimed in interviews that it was a photo of the Czech architectural historian on whom *Austerlitz* is based. In fact he took the image from a 30p junkshop postcard. And the boy wasn't photographed in Czechoslovakia but in the north of England.

Does it matter? Not a lot. Sebald's photos are invariably poignant, adding to the melancholy of his prose. The only risk with photos, if they're not family photos, is copyright law. As with words (see PERMISSIONS), somebody else will own the rights and there'll be a reproduction fee.

Annie Ernaux's use of images in *The Use of Photography*, composed in collaboration with her then lover Marc Marie, is bold and inventive. She had the idea of taking photos of clothes that had been scattered on the floor during love-making; the shots, which both of them took, would preserve 'this arrangement born of desire and accident' which was otherwise 'doomed to disappear'; it was 'an attempt, in a way, to make them our *sacred ornaments*'. The photos (and the descriptions of the photos) are of limited interest. But the story around them, of an affair that began when Ernaux was having chemotherapy for breast cancer, is compelling, with many apercus about writing along the way ('I want words to be like stains you cannot tear yourself away from.').

It helps if the photo is more than a portrait – if some dynamic can be inferred. For the front cover of my memoir *Two Sisters*, the designer took a childhood photo of my sister Gill and me, giggling as we sat on a sunlit bench, and added the arm of a smaller child on my left to suggest that our half-sister Josie was with us. In reality no photo exists of us all sitting together but the jacket cover invents one – with Josie sidelined and half-effaced as she was in life.

In the end, reproduced images will do less for the authenticity of a narrative than the *photo-realism* of the prose. It's a term unjust to photos, which aren't necessarily striving for realism, but a useful reminder of what life writing is aiming at: the tough, inescapable truth.

Plagiarism

In Tobias Wolff's *Old School*, the teenage narrator, up against a deadline for a competition to be judged by Ernest Hemingway, copies a short story from a girls' school magazine, changing only the gender of the main character. He identifies so closely with the girl's tale of adolescent angst that he doesn't feel it to be cheating: it's *his* story; nothing he has written previously is as good – or as *true*. When his plagiarism comes to light, after Hemingway has chosen it as the winner, the Wolff narrator is expelled for bringing his school into disgrace. But copying has helped his development as a writer.

Young writers do often copy – literally. Jack London copied out extracts from Hemingway; so did Joan Didion, who said his sentences 'taught me how sentences worked'. Hunter S. Thompson typed out pages of Scott Fitzgerald's *The Great Gatsby* word-for-word, appropriating office supplies for the task; he also typed out Hemingway's *A Farewell to Arms* and some of Faulkner's stories. Robert Louis Stevenson did the same, picking a passage from a favourite author, reading it twice very carefully, then re-writing it from memory. Copywork was once a standard teaching exercise in schools. It's one of the ways people learn, through repetition and imitation.

I was once commissioned to write a book about plagiarism. On a month's sabbatical from my job, I did some useful research. Then life and other projects took over. (Eleven years later, when the publisher ran out of patience, I returned the modest advance.) In a few cases I came across, from fiction, the alleged offender seemed hard done by: they might have used a plot device previously used by another author but there were no verbal coincidences. Occasionally plagiarism can be inadvertent: I have a poem, 'Ties', which I like to think of as wholly original, but many years ago, on the book pages of a newspaper I was working for, I published a poem by Alan Jenkins called 'Ties', the theme of which is very similar. Other writers have used phrases they assumed were theirs, jotted down in a notebook, but which they took from something they were reading at the time. Jason Epstein did this in his first book, reproducing phrases from Martin Amis's novel *The Rachel Papers* word-for-word. Amis's exposure of the theft, in an *Observer* article, was gently reproachful rather than enraged, but for Epstein it was humiliating.

If an author knowingly copies out someone else's words and doesn't acknowledge it, that's all the worse in memoir, where the personal experiences described are meant to be authentic. All that's required for attribution is a name-check and a note with publication details (and perhaps a permission fee too). What's not acceptable is to behave like Joe Biden, who while bidding to be a presidential candidate in 1987 gave a speech about being the first person in his family to go to university – in the same words that Neil Kinnock had used in a speech a few months before. More recently there has been Melania Trump, who copied a speech by Michelle Obama. More to the point, since it's life writing, there's Alex Haley, whose bestselling *Roots* – which he called *faction* but was marketed as a non-fiction book enriched by extensive personal research – plagiarised up to eighty-one passages from a novel called *The African*, by Harold Courlander. The lawsuit against Haley resulted in a five-week trial and a settlement of $650,000 out of court. Let that be a warning.

Plain style

Explaining why he came to write a memoir, *Experience*, after years of writing fiction, Martin Amis said 'I want to set the record straight . . . and to speak, for once, without artifice.' It's what's expected of a life writer: to tell it as it was, no frills. Orwell argued that good prose is like a window pane. Transparency is the goal: *here I am*, the narrator says, *no flannel, no secrets, no tricks. Real life, plain as day.*

Hilary Mantel pretends to wrestle with plain style in her memoir *Giving Up the Ghost*, urging herself to 'just go for it' and cut all the 'persiflage'. It doesn't work:

> I stray away from the beaten path of plain words into the meadows of extravagant simile: angels, ogres, doughnut-shaped holes. And as for transparency – window-panes undressed are a sign of poverty, aren't they? How about some nice net curtains, so I can look out but you can't see in? How about shutters or a chaste

Roman blind? Besides, window-pane prose is no guarantee of truthfulness. Some deceptive sights are seen through glass, and the best liars tell lies in plain words.

Style is a choice. And the choice is limited by your character and capabilities: *Le style, c'est l'homme*. Or *la femme*. Your style is you and unless you're a chameleon it's not going to change. Still, an author needs to give it some thought. The meadows of extravagant simile might work for Mantel but few of us have her gifts. And no one wants a memoir with net curtains: we do want to see in.

Life writers who are too 'poetic' will be distrusted for having the wrong priorities – for putting style before content and tarting things up. I greatly admire Kathryn Harrison's memoir *The Kiss*, about the incestuous affair she had with her father: he'd abandoned her when she was a child, then came back into her life when she was a vulnerable young woman, with tumultuous consequences. The one scene I find less than convincing is when she walks into the kitchen one night, sees a cockroach and traps it under a glass tumbler: the description of it struggling to escape seems too pat a metaphor for her own entrapment. It may have happened exactly as she describes but the reader (this reader, anyway) takes against it. And with a memoir, doubt is fatal. As Annie Ernaux says, 'There can be no tampering with reality, with the *this-happened* element . . .'

It's a delicate balance. Too much artifice – flashy metaphors and decorative flourishes – and reader loses trust. But pedestrianism is no less debilitating. There needs to be a middle way. 'Language is a building site,' Deborah Levy has written. 'It is always in the process of being constructed and repaired.' To achieve the right style – plain but not too plain – is a labour of love.

Planning

Do writers plan ahead? It varies. The left-brainers schematise, jotting down chapter headings, laying out a structure, compiling notes for each character and completing the book in their head before writing a word of it. The right-brainers jump in, fumbling their way forward, unsure where the story is taking them, adding, discarding and eventually arriving where they hoped to be despite having no idea, at the start, where that was.

I'm in the latter category. I write to discover what it is I want to write. But everyone does it their own way, according to temperament and circumstances. In her diaries Helen Garner contrasts her method with that of her then husband, Murray Bail: 'Strange how differently we approach writing. I blunder in blindly and scrub-bash my way through a trackless forest, but he stays well back until he has laid out the route, created a fundamental map. He has an aim in mind.' *Scrub-bash* or *map*, intuit a path or mark out the territory: there's no right way to do it. And failure is possible either way.

The crime writer Sophie Hannah calls planning 'story architecture' and stoutly defends it: 'An architect wouldn't start a building project, slapping the cement onto the bricks, without first doing at least one drawing, and probably more, of the proposed house.' *Not* to plan, she says, would be 'like stripping the old wallpaper in your house and pulling up all the old carpets with literally no idea how you want the rooms to look at the end of the process.' A chapter-by-chapter synopsis does makes sense for anyone writing a thriller. And many memoirists will jot down a series of scenes-to-do in advance. But to start in the dark and feel your way towards the light makes more sense for those writers, myself included, who've little or no idea what the story is until they begin to write it. Jenn Ashworth puts it well in *The Parallel Path*: 'not knowing what happens next, being deeply tangled in a work that has not revealed its form to you, setting your hands to type before you know what you think: these are all essential practices for writing and involve a letting go of orientation to welcome in a more creative bewilderment.'

Plot

Do memoirs have plots? Not exactly. The plot is the life, or a portion of it. The plot is the truth a writer is uncovering. If you're writing a novel, you construct the plot – it's what you make up. But in non-fiction, the plot's a given – it's what happened. Life writers aren't inventing, they're documenting.

Still, it's a story and telling it isn't straightforward. There are the setting(s), themes, time-frame, structure, pace and characters. In effect, the life writer *is* building a plot much as novelists do.

Say the writer is you and it's the story of your relationship with your mother and of the day she left home – you were only seven and didn't witness what happened; all you remember are raised voices and slammed doors. Your dad refused to discuss it afterwards. Back in touch with you in your teens, your mum was more willing to talk but only up to a point. You don't have the full story. You will have to home in on key details she recounts, like the short black skirt she liked to wear and which he objected to, on the grounds that it made her look slutty. The skirt figures in the episode that (she does tell you this much) finally prompted her to leave him. They'd gone to a pub and were sitting in a corner when a friend of his came over and bought them both drinks. The friend wasn't especially flirtatious but when he moved off your dad was surly and a row began, first in whispers, then as they walked home past the gasworks in bawled insults ('Slut!') and comebacks ('I'm no slut') and – to cap it all – the smack of a fist on your mum's cheek. There's the climactic scene. It doesn't matter that you weren't present. You have all you need. The time (evening), setting (a pub), characters (a trio), theme (male possessiveness) and narrative (a life-changing row). It's real life but the stuff of fiction – the plot, or part of the plot.

Poetry

So much of poetry is life writing – joyous or mournful self-expression – that it's difficult to know who to recommend as a model. (Memoirists can learn from poets.) Donne, Wyatt, Keats, Wordsworth, Auden, Plath, Larkin, Sharon Olds . . . the list is long even without including the 1960s American confessionals. Some poets are resistant to intimacy: T. S. Eliot, for example, wrote that 'poetry is not a turning loose of emotion but an escape from emotion, it is not the expression of personality but an escape from personality'. And yet *The Waste Land*, we know, is highly personal.

The life writing of Tony Harrison has a special place in my heart. His elegies for his parents work brilliantly as one-offs as well as in sequence. The poems are tear-jerking but they also, as in 'Marked with D', make us think:

> When the chilled dough of his flesh went in an oven
> not unlike those he fuelled all his life,
> I thought of his cataracts ablaze with Heaven
> and radiant with the sight of his dead wife,
> light streaming from his mouth to shape her name,

'not Florence and not Flo but always Florrie'.
I thought how his cold tongue burst into flame
but only literally, which makes me sorry,
sorry for his sake there's no Heaven to reach.
I get it all from Earth my daily bread
but he hungered for release from mortal speech
that kept him down, the tongue that weighed like lead.
The baker's man that no one will see rise
and England made to feel like some dull oaf
is smoke, enough to sting one person's eyes
and ash (not unlike flour) for one small loaf.

The title alludes to the nursery rhyme 'Pat a Cake, Pat a Cake, baker's man', and the phrase 'baker's man' turns up four lines from the end, to underline the theme of servitude – to be someone's man is to be at the beck and call of a master. The 'D' in the title could be the 'D' on a dunce's cap, Harrison's father (who worked as a baker) having been made to feel thick by his social betters. The 'D' also stands for death and dad. Yet it's not the father's death that's being mourned so much as his life: 'kept down', he dreamed a life hereafter where he'd be reunited with his wife. Hence those cataracts, a standard Romantic or pantheistic trope – the Glory of God as embodied in the mighty rush of a waterfall. Except that here the cataracts are an eye condition that results in blurred sight and magical thinking about an afterlife. The poet doesn't undercut that faith, or deprecate it, so much as register disappointment that he can't share it, using an image from the Lord's Prayer (daily bread) to convey his atheism. When his father's tongue bursts into flame, it doesn't do so metaphorically, allowing a man of few words to become articulate, 'but only literally', a pedantic expression that in the context (cremation) becomes heartbreaking.

'I try to make connections where I can,' Harrison writes elsewhere, and in this poem he makes connections between flesh and dough; between a bakery and a crematorium; between ash and flour; between bread rising, and people rising in society, and the soul rising, or maybe not, after the body dies. A reader coming to that word 'smoke' in the penultimate line might find it hard to suppress the thought of Auschwitz, with its ovens, and of lives even more brutally curtailed than Harrison's father's was, but the poem doesn't invite it. On the contrary, the smoke is sufficient only to 'sting one person's eyes', that of the bereaved son. Private grief then, but grief fuelled by anger that any man should be made to feel 'like some dull oaf' – a perfect rhyme with loaf. *Use your loaf,* people say, meaning *wise up*, and that's what the poet is doing, on behalf of his father who worked so hard earning his bread (by making bread) that he'd no opportunity for the getting of wisdom.

In sixteen lines Harrison packs a book-length piece of life writing that's sociological, political and religious as well as intimate, angry and moving. The poem is a memoir in its own right, a passionate piece of family history.

Point of view

In memoir, the author writes from personal experience. But just as biographers set out to access the minds and hearts of their subjects, so memoirists strain to inhabit other perspectives. It may be that of a parent, sibling, colleague or lover. More likely, though, it will be their own mind and heart at a time from which they're removed but which they now want to recover.

Often the point of view will be that of a child. To represent a child convincingly isn't easy. 'I wanted Pop to tell me that

America was unbeatable not only in science and technology, but as a moral force,' sounds daft coming from a five-year-old; put a full stop after 'unbeatable', though, and the writer would get away with it. Granted, vocabulary doesn't need to be that of a five-year old; what a dull read that would be, though James Joyce does it brilliantly, for half a page, in *A Portrait of the Artist as a Young Man* ('When you wet the bed first it is warm then it gets cold. His mother put on the oilsheet. That had the queer smell.'). With early years, life writers need to go carefully. They were once a child. They spoke, thought and felt as a child. To put away childish things defeats the object. But their readers are adults, who won't want babytalk, and they can't be ignored.

Seamus Deane solves the problem brilliantly in his autofictional *Reading in the Dark*. In one chapter he writes as a child hiding under the kitchen table while a traumatic scene unfolds, the removal of his dying sister Una to hospital: she has meningitis, a word 'with a fright and hiss in it' (unlike rubella or influenza, which make him think 'of Italian football players or racing drivers and opera singers'). From where he's sitting, at floor level, all the young Deane can see is feet. But the feet are markers of social class and profession: the redness of the stretcher the ambulance men are carrying is reflected in their shiny black shoes, and his uncles' shoes are 'rimed with mud and cement' from the building site where they've been working. In the case of his parents – her shoes with 'low heels that needed mending', his work-boots 'with laces thonged round the back' – the movement of feet denotes intimacy and grief:

> My father's boots moved towards her until they were very close. He was saying something. Then he moved yet closer, almost stood on her shoes, which moved

apart. One of his boots was between her feet. There was her shoe, then his boot, then her shoe, then his boot. I looked at Smoky [the family dog], who licked my face. He was kissing her. She was still crying. Their feet shifted and I thought she was going to fall, for one shoe came off the ground for a second. Then they steadied and just stood there . . .
That was my first death.

We don't see or get to know Una. And there's no dialogue. But by limiting his point of view and highlighting sensory impressions Deane makes her loss – 'a life rinsed out and gone' – powerfully moving. He does it all through shoes.

Politics

Barack Obama wrote his memoir *Dreams from My Father* at the age of 33, after graduating from law school at Harvard, where he'd become the first African-American president of the *Harvard Law Review*; this was fourteen years before he became US president. J. D. Vance published his memoir, *Hillbilly Elegy* at 32, after graduating from Yale law school, where he'd been an editor of the *Yale Law Journal*; this was eight years before Donald Trump chose him as vice-president. Of the two books, the latter caused more of a stir, not because it was better written (and later became a film starring Amy Adams and Glenn Close), but because its portrayal of the Rust Belt, the disaffected white working-class of small-town America, was seen as an 'explanation' of how Trump became president (first time round) the year it was published.

The two memoirs could hardly be more different: Obama's

explores racial division, a fractured identity and what he owes to a father he never really knew; Vance's, which describes 'a ragtag band of hillbillies struggling to find their way', is a story of violence, poverty and addiction. Obama's is nuanced, Vance's in-your-face (if less objectionably so than he now is as US vice-president). Both are more memorable for what they show of their author's childhood than for laying down markers of a future career in politics. And it's this that sets them apart from most political memoirs, which are self-exonerations *after* a career in high office.

Tony Blair's *A Journey* was published in 2010, three years after he'd ceased to be prime minister. Though I'm not especially anti-Blair, much of the book leaves me cold, not so much because it's self-aggrandizing (to win three successive elections for the Labour Party is no mean feat) or because it's short on humour, but because of its obstinacy in proving himself right, not least over Iraq, which takes up 100 pages ('I can't regret the decision to go to war', 'The military campaign of conquest was a brilliant success.'). Though he agonises over the questions that have been raised about his warmongering, his conclusions are unrepentant. Still the book is worth having for his account of tensions with Gordon Brown. And his obstinacy isn't as woeful as Boris Johnson's, whose wilfully self-deluding *Unleashed* refuses to apologise for any of his many mistakes (Brexit, Covid, the Downing Street parties, etc.). Johnson takes refuge in linguistic jauntiness and mixed metaphors instead, as when he likens Donald Trump to 'an orange-hued dirigible exuberantly buoyed aloft by the inexhaustible Primus stove of his own ego'.

It helps a memoir if the politician hasn't risen to the top: Rory Stewart's *Politics on the Edge*, Alan Clark's diaries and Alan Johnson's *This Boy* all suggest as much. Reach the highest office and, when you look back, you'll have catastrophes to explain away, and there's nothing worse than a whitewash memoir.

Prizes

To win a prize is good for a writer's profile and ego; it's also usually a boost for sales. And the cash, when there is cash, comes in handy. But for most practitioners the competition is with themselves, not fellow authors: the contest is to write as best you can. Longlists and shortlists are a distraction. So is the envy or resentment at missing out. The most worthwhile prize I've heard of is the Hubert Church Memorial Award, which in 1952 was given to Janet Frame, in New Zealand. She was in a psychiatric hospital at the time, facing a lobotomy. The £25 prize persuaded the superintendent to remove her from the ward and discharge her: 'My writing saved me.'

Life writing has no prize as noisy or prestigious as the Man Booker for fiction. At present the biggest non-fiction prize in the UK is the Baillie Gifford, named after its sponsor (an investment management company) and with the motto 'All the best stories are true'. Established in 2015 and now worth £50,000, the Baillie Gifford succeeded the Samuel Johnson Prize, itself a successor to the NCR Award (short for National Cash Register), which was launched in 1987 and disbanded ten years later after it was revealed that the judges had used 'professional readers', summaries and book reviews instead of reading all the entries. That's the catch with big prizes: to increase their profile, they use celebrity judges, who don't have the time to read books cover to cover or, worse, who're unused to reading at all.

There's no such problem with the Ackerley Prize for autobiography, founded by the author's sister Nancy in 1982 and now tied in with the *Times Literary Supplement* – it's worth a modest £4,000 and you can be sure the judges will read all the entries. The new £10,000 Unwin Award is for non-fiction writers at an early stage of their career, as are the £2,500 Hatchards & Biographers' Club First Biography Prize and the three Giles St Aubyn awards (£10,000, £5,000 and £2,500) for a first commissioned work of non-fiction. Older writers can look to the Christopher Bland Prize, for a novel or work of non-fiction by someone over 50. Other prizes for non-fiction have fallen by the wayside, including the Waterstones/Esquire/Volvo Prize, which was gloriously if briefly around in the 1990s – one of its winners, Tobias Wolff, received a new Volvo. Still, the Duff Cooper and James Tait Black prizes are well-established, and there are more specialist awards for works of history, travel, sport, nature and crime non-fiction. Better still, the £30,000 Women's Prize for Non-Fiction was created in 2024 – and given in its inaugural year to Naomi Klein.

To win a prize is a boost. But many great books have won no prizes at all. What a committee decides is not the ultimate judgement.

Pronouns

A line from a poem by one of my students sticks with me decades later: 'daring to say I'. Poets and memoirists are sometimes accused of being self-absorbed, but most of them feel as my student did: nervous about speaking up. Anyone who had an academic education back in the 1960s and 70s will remember being trained to avoid saying 'I' in their scholarly writing; you were supposed to sound impersonal rather than expressing what Virginia Woolf called 'the damned egotistical self'.

Using the first-person pronoun doesn't come easy. In life, yes. On paper, no. The effrontery of it makes the writer hesitate: *what can I offer that's worth listening to? why would anyone be interested?* But in memoir the 'I' is essential. The personal can be universal. (See NARCISSISM.)

The personal is more emotive too. Given a name or individual identity to connect with, people feel more involved. In one notable psychological experiment, research subjects were handed money to donate towards alleviating world hunger and were offered the choice of giving it to Rokia, a girl in Mali aged seven, or to 21 million Africans. Most chose Rokia. In another study, people were asked to give $300,000 to fight cancer. One group was told the money would save the life of a single child, another that it would save eight children. People gave almost twice as much to save one child. Individualism is the key.

'I' stands for self-expression. But as Chris Kraus describes in *I Love Dick*, using the pronoun can be a struggle: 'I don't think I was able, ever, to write any of those notebooks then in the 1st Person. I had to find these ciphers for myself because whenever I tried writing in the 1st Person it sounded like some other person, or else the tritest most neurotic parts of myself.' In the end she got there: 'writing "I" was the last chance I'll ever have to figure some of this stuff out.' Deborah Levy found it a struggle too but succeeded in the wake of her marriage break-up, when working in a friend's borrowed shed: 'It was there that I would begin to write in the first person, using an *I* that is close to myself and yet is not myself.' Close to herself but not herself: the 'I' as persona. She doesn't entirely give herself away.

Esther Summerson in Dickens's *Bleak House* feels 'vexed' that she's 'always writing about myself. I mean all the time to write about other people, and I try to think about myself as little as possible . . . but it is all of no use. I . . . can't be kept out.' For the 'I' to be kept out in memoir is rare. But there is sometimes a case for other pronouns. bell hooks uses *she* and *we* as well as *I* in her memoir *Bone Black*. As one of six children, five of them girls growing up together, she has chapters written in a collective 'we' voice: 'We cannot believe we must believe our beloved Crispus Attucks and go to schools in white neighbourhoods.' An 'I' is there too, because hooks feels self-assertively at odds with her family: queer, defiant, immersed in books. But in key emotive episodes, she also presents herself, at a distance, as 'she'. There's the time she's beaten, for instance:

> Jumping from his chair the father began to hit her – not wanting to damage his hands since he needed them for work, he tore a piece of wood from the screen door that kept flies out. As he hit her with the wood he kept saying Didn't I tell you to leave those marbles alone? Didn't I tell you? The mama stood watching, afraid of his anger, afraid of what it might do, but afraid to stop it.

The distancing is further enforced by those prepositions – *th*e father, *the* mama – as if her parents were generic, anybody's as much as her own. Third-person also frees hooks to dwell on moments she would otherwise feel shy to describe, such as masturbation: 'When she finds pleasure touching her body, she knows that they [her family] will think it wrong; that it is something to keep hidden, to do in secret.' Here the hidden self is outed with a 'she', which also registers bewildered retrospection, as if she were looking at another person, the self that hasn't yet grown up to be bell hooks.

When Salman Rushdie published a memoir about his experience of the fatwa, he called it *Joseph Anton*, the name he gave himself when asked by the police to choose a pseudonym: he was honouring Joseph Conrad and Anton Chekhov, though his minders called him Joe. Throughout the book, he refers to himself as 'he' not 'I' – an expression of his weird displacement, of having become someone he doesn't recognise, a religious hate figure rather than a novelist. J. M. Coetzee similarly uses 'he' in his memoir *Boyhood*. In a section about his school years, he describes how 'Cape Town is not making him cleverer, it is making him stupider. The realisation causes panic to well up in him. Whoever he truly is, whoever the true "I" is that ought to be rising out the ashes of his childhood, is not being allowed to be born, is being kept puny and stunted.' Coetzee's 'I' has yet to be born and in *Youth*, the sequel to *Boyhood*, he is still 'he'. It's a distancing device – *autre*biography – with the author an everyman called 'John'.

'You' is another option. (See YOU.) Pronouns offer multiple possibilities. But in intimate non-fiction, anything other than first-person will look odd. If a life writer doesn't use 'I' there has to be a reason. It can't be mere evasion.

Q

Questions

Life writing often begins with a question. Or several questions. Or adopts a tone that's interrogative, not declamatory. *What's your book about?* writers are asked and it's a question they invariably ask of themselves. They might frame it as a single question (it's a childhood memoir that asks *Why did Dad leave us?*) or as a series of questions (it's a childhood memoir that asks *Did Dad leave us because he'd stopped loving Mum? Because he had a breakdown? Because he hated children? Because of his work? Or because he'd developed a drink problem?*). The book may go off in other directions but having a question to address creates a strand to pull everything together. My memoir *And When Did You Last See Your Father?* owes its title to a famous Victorian painting. The question kept thrumming in my head and gave the book its structure, as I searched back in time to find the last moment when my father was truly, inescapably *him*.

Catherine Taylor's memoir *Stirrings*, set in Sheffield, follows the author from her infancy to her early twenties. Why her dad walked out on the family is a central question for her, but along with it come related questions about masculinity, violence, class, fear, work, war, the Yorkshire Ripper murders and what it is to be a young woman in a misogynistic culture. Darker still are Hisham Matar's *The Return* and Aminatta Forna's *The Devil that Danced on the Water*, memoirs which try to solve the mysteries of their fathers' imprisonments and deaths. All these books ask big questions, of others and of themselves. If they don't entirely answer them, that's fine too. There are always mysteries in a life – gaps, contradictions, muddles and secrets – and life writing should embrace that, not deny it.

R

Rape

Moral values change and life writing is one way to measure that. At one point in his *Confessions,* Rousseau describes how a religious minister called Klupfel invites him and a friend called Grimm to have sex with a 'little girl': 'The excellent Klupfel did not want to do the honours by halves, and we all three went in turn into the next room with the little girl, who did not know whether to laugh or to cry.' Rousseau confesses to 'shame' at his actions but the passage is shocking. So too with Langston Hughes, describing an episode during his time as a ship-hand. When 'two little African girls' row out to his moored boat, the bo'sun grabs one of them, leaving the other to the crew:

> Someone threw the other girl down on the floor on a blanket in the middle of the sailors' quarters and stripped her of her flowered cloth. She lay there naked . . . Thirty men crowded around, mostly in their underwear, sat up on bunks to watch, smoked, yelled and joked, and waited for their turn. Each time a man would rise, the little African girl on the floor would say 'Mon-nee! Mon-nee!' But nobody had a cent, yet they wouldn't let her get

up. Finally I couldn't bear to hear her crying 'Mon-nee!' any more, so I went to bed. But the festival went on all night.

Hughes, whose sexuality was elusive, didn't join the abhorrent 'festival' – the gang rape of a minor. But what makes him 'finally' leave the scene is less disgust at the violence than distress at that unrewarded cry for money. The passage provoked no reaction at the time it appeared, in 1940. Today an editor would want it cut or rewritten or wouldn't publish the book at all.

Alice Sebold's *Lucky* describes her rape while a student at Syracuse University. It's an ugly and immensely detailed account. By chance, five months after the rape, she spotted (or thought she spotted) her attacker. And though she misidentified him in a police line-up, Anthony Broadwater (to use his real name) was tried and sentenced to imprisonment, serving sixteen years. He always denied the crime and in 2021 he was exonerated thanks to the investigative efforts of an executive film producer working on an adaptation of the book who became convinced of Broadwater's innocence. The publisher withdrew the paperback and the film adaptation was cancelled. But Sebold's memoir isn't disqualified because the wrong man was convicted. The rape still took place; so did the emotional damage to Sebold.

Kathryn Harrison doesn't name her father's sexual grooming of her when she was 19 as rape. But if a man has sex with someone who's asleep that *is* rape. And as she records, the trauma of incest expressed itself as sleep:

The sight of him naked: at that point I fall completely asleep . . . In years to come, I won't be able to remember even one instance of our lying together . . . I sleep because I'm shocked and because I'm frightened. I want to avoid contemplating the enormity.

Harrison was victim-shamed by male critics when her book came out for complicity with an incestuous relationship. But she didn't consent so much as submit, overwhelmed by 'the exhaustion of withstanding his desire'. She shut down from shame and fear. Sleep as refuge and denial.

Many of us (men as well as women) have had the experience of a sexual assault or molestation; mine was being fondled next to some bookshelves by a university librarian. Your experience may not have been as traumatising as Sebold's. But it may be something to write about, if only in private – to speak of what (it seemed) couldn't be spoken is healing. To read books by survivors of sexual abuse (there are many available, a couple of which I mention in the ME TOO section) can be consoling too. Virginia Roberts Giuffre certainly thought as much. Her posthumously published *Nobody's Girl* describes her years in Jeffrey Epstein's entourage after being recruited by Ghislaine Maxwell to have sex with (among others) the then Prince Andrew. 'I was groomed to be complicit in my own devastation,' she writes, 'I believed that I might die a sex slave.' She apologises for the ugliness of what she recounts but believes that by publishing the book she can help others who have been sexually abused.

Readers

The Modernists patronised them. 'Damn their eyes,' Ezra Pound said. 'No art ever yet grew by looking into the eyes of the public.' That's *de haut en bas*. Readers aren't necessarily idiots. Then again, a good writer won't want to suck up to them. Arrogance won't do and nor will spoon-feeding. The secret is a balance between giving readers a steer and allowing them to wander. Writers can't control what will be made of their work. But unless it's a secret activity, under wraps, for no eyes other than their own, they do have to care about the audience. 'All writing depends on the generosity of the reader,' Alberto Manguel has said.

To start with, your first reader is you. But others need to be engaged and drawn in. And this means standing outside yourself and asking: *Is it honest, immersive and thought-provoking? What would I feel if someone else had written it? Does it work?*

Some authors have a clear picture of who they're writing for, whether a good friend or a tutor/mentor. For others, readers are a faceless mass – they can't envisage them. Neither approach is altogether helpful: the first risks cosiness, the second means writing into a void. Better than thinking of many readers or just a few, T. S. Eliot said, is 'to address the one hypothetical Intelligent Man who does not exist and who is the audience of the artist.' But this Ideal Reader isn't much good either; they will 'get' every allusion, however obscure, and confirm the writer's idealised image of themselves as brilliantly clever. More useful is to think about where the reader sits in relation to you. If they're behind you, peering over your shoulder, you'll be inhibited; and if they're out front, in the stalls or upper circle, you'll be oracular. Why not think about them sitting next to you – as though on a train, taking the same journey? They'll see things you don't (you can't stop them spotting things you're unaware of) but they're beside you, as an equal. You might even want to address them directly. You're neither crowding nor snubbing them. You're treating them as a companion you respect.

Reading

Writers read a lot, or ought to. Wasn't it reading that got them interested in writing in the first place? And reading other authors, dead or alive, is more than a matter of pleasure or curiosity – it's a way to learn what to do (and what not to do) in your own work. To start with, you're a sponge, unfailingly absorptive, and your voice a cacophonous impersonation. But in time the demons of influence are cast out. You have your own style.

Some authors say they can't read when they're immersed in writing. They've a book to finish; they don't want the distraction. More commonly, reading is a later-in-the-day pursuit: they do their writing in the morning (and perhaps beyond), then unwind with a book when they're free. It doesn't matter what kind of book. The poet reads science fiction, the historical novelist reads crime. Escapism is fine. And may have lessons to impart.

Then again, ignorance sometimes works to a writer's advantage. To feel everything worth saying has already been said; that you can't compete with the greats; that there are already too many books in the world – all that's discouraging. It may be an illusion to think there are gaps to fill but thinking it can be an inspiration. The main reason I had for writing about my father in the year after his death was lack of choice: his death felt so huge – what else would I write about? But I was also driven by ignorance. I'd not read the filial classics by Edmund Gosse and J. R. Ackerley. I'd not watched John Mortimer's play *A Voyage Round My Father*. I'd not seen *Hamlet* more than twice. I thought I was breaking new ground. Which was idiotic but empowering – a failure in reading transformed into a reason to write.

For good books about reading and what it can contribute to childhood and beyond, I'd recommend Lucy Mangan's *Bookworm: A Memoir of Childhood Reading* and Patricia Craig's book of the same title, along with Francis Spufford's *The Child That Books Built*.

Reading aloud

It's crucial to the writing process. Authors can't see their failings – the clunky expressions, verbal repetitions and missed beats – until they hear them. As Samuel Butler put it, 'I feel weak places at once when I read aloud where I thought, as long as I read to myself only, that the passage was all right.' Reading aloud exposes disharmony – and makes writers pay closer attention to the rhythm of their prose (or poetry). Silent editing only goes so far; vocal readjustments are needed too. The tongue finds flaws: stilted dialogue, stunted pace and strident phrasing. Pleasure lies in sound as well as meaning. Sound *is* meaning. For life writers whose work is deeply personal, reading aloud is all the more crucial: a way of bodying forth the story, of owning it, of making it theirs.

Reality hunger

Sometimes you go through an experience so consuming that you've no room in your head for imaginative literature. The novelist Andrey Kurkov says that this happened to him after the Russian invasion of Ukraine: he abandoned the novel he was working on and wrote diaries and think-pieces instead. Hanif Kureishi said something similar after an accident left him disabled (that writing about what had happened to him was more interesting than writing fiction) and so did Salman Rushdie when recovering from a knife attack in 2022: 'However much I wanted to focus on fiction, something immense and non-fictional had happened to me . . . Until I dealt with the attack, I wouldn't be able to write anything else.' It's sometimes the same for readers too. Why waste time on made-up stories and characters when you (and the world) are in crisis? Only the real consumes you and only non-fiction can serve it: reportage, memoir, blogs, essays, confessional poetry.

The American critic David Shields coined a term for this condition, Reality Hunger, which is more than just a response to trauma. His book of that title argues that every artistic movement is a bid to get closer to reality, and that Reality Hunger is the defining spirit of our age. He issues a spirited polemic on behalf of non-fiction, arguing that it's in lyric essays, prose poems and collage novels (as well as in performance art, stand-up comedy, documentary film, hip-hop, rap and graffiti) that such impetus is to be found today. A loosely defined genre, then: in fact, a genre committed to genre-busting. A too-obvious pattern in writing (triumph against the odds, say) is mechanical and manipulative, he says. By contrast, the lyric essay mirrors the contingency of life.

Shields's book is full of instructive quotes and maxims. He's an enjoyable provocateur and in his hunger for reality he's a great mentor. He reminds life writers that their mission is to Make It Real.

Recognition

Memoir is as powerful as poetry and fiction in prompting

those moments when a reader thinks *Wow, someone else has been through things I've been through*, or *Incredible, I thought such feelings or ideas were exclusive to me*. bell hooks had such a moment when she read Toni Morrison's *The Bluest Eye* in her teens: the novel spoke to 'us girls confronting issues of class, race, identity'. In her memoir *Firstborn Girls* the novelist Bernice L. McFadden reports having the same experience with Alice Walker's *The Color Purple*: 'Over a span of 245 pages, I had been cracked wide open. Here finally was a story about my people – my messy, beautiful, dangerous, loving, grieving, curious, joyful Black people. Black people like the family who raised me.' For George Eliot, recognition was the sole purpose of authorship: 'the only effect I ardently long to produce by my writings is that those who read them should be able to *imagine* and to *feel* the pains and joys of those who differ from themselves in everything but the broad fact of being struggling erring creatures.' Anne Brontë speaks similarly in *Agnes Grey*, describing how 'the effusions of others [can] seem to harmonise with our existing case'. And then there's Horace: 'Mutato nomine, de te fabula narratur.' (*Change the name and the story is about you.*)

A writer can't plan for recognition. But if there's candour and honesty, not least in owning up to shameful thoughts, feelings and actions, readers will make connections. Justin Webb's memoir *The Gift of a Radio* begins with a childhood memory of his stepfather, Charles, swimming at Lulworth and going so far out that he disappears from view, lost among currents and riptides:

And then he comes back.
   Many decades have passed but I remember the feeling I had at that moment with vividness undimmed. I was disappointed. There's no other word. It wasn't hatred

or anger or petulance. I was too young to think about the consequences, good or bad, of the actual body being dragged out of the waves and worked on and declared dead. But I formed in that instant the considered opinion that it would have been better if he had drowned. Better for me. Better for her [Webb's mother]. Better for us.

I've not had that experience or anything like. But Justin Webb's animosity towards his stepfather invites recognition nevertheless.

It's the same when John Burnside thinks about killing his dad in *A Lie about My Father*. We're warmed up for it at the start of the memoir when a friend asks him what his father is like: 'I could have talked about the violence, the drinking, the shameful, maudlin theatre of his penitences . . . the gambling, and the fits of manic destruction . . . his cruelty, his pettiness.' By the time a teenage John is standing there ready to do the job – in an alley, with a knife, late at night, as his dad walks home drunk from the pub – we've seen enough of his father to feel he deserves what's coming to him. From common sense or cowardice, John holds back. But the murderous intent is real. And it hasn't abated when his father dies of a heart attack: 'I buried my father with gratitude.'

If a story is told powerfully enough, as Burnside's is, readers will identify with the author. As Robert Douglas-Fairhurst says in *Metamorphosis*, 'It's one of the definitions of a good book that it can seem to speak for us as well as to us. When we open such a book, it's as if we have discovered our innermost thoughts assembled in language by someone else.' If there's recognition, we also accept the worst – and take the author's side. And there'll be the pleasure of noticing something we might otherwise have missed, as Robert Browning puts it in his poem 'Fra Lippo Lippi':

> we're made so that we love
> First when we see them painted, things we have passed
> Perhaps a hundred times nor cared to see;
> And so they are better, painted – better to us,
> Which is the same thing. . . .

Rejection

It happens a lot. Think of William Golding's *Lord of the Flies* (rejected at least seven times, maybe as many as 20), J. K. Rowling's first Harry Potter book (12 times), Beckett's *Murphy* (at least 40 times) or Robert Pirsig's *Zen and the Art of Motorcycle Maintenance* (121 times). Think of the brush-offs given to Louisa May Alcott for *Little Women* ('Stick to your teaching, Miss Alcott. You can't write.') or to Stephen King for *Carrie* ('We are not interested in science fiction which deals with negative utopias.') or to the agent who submitted *The Spy Who Came in from the Cold* and was told that John Le Carré had no future. Or think of the readers' reports for the US publisher Alfred A. Knopf, advising rejection of Jorge Luis Borges ('utterly untranslatable'), Joyce Carol Oates ('incomprehensible'), James Baldwin's *Giovanni's Room* ('repellent', 'bleak', 'hopelessly bad'), Vladimir Nabokov's *Lolita* ('impossible for us'), Milan Kundera's *The Joke* ('a long sentimental wail') and Sylvia Plath's *The Bell Jar* ('ill conceived, poorly written, occasionally atrocious'). Many great books have been serially rejected before finding a home. A distressing number must also have fallen altogether by the wayside.

Life writers suffer too. Anne Frank didn't herself struggle to publish the diary she kept before dying but her father Otto did. A Dutch version came out in 1947 but publishers further afield were less receptive, including the reader for Alfred Knopf in the US, whose report was damning: 'The style, occasionally effusive, never compelling, is not at all distinguished. The perceptions, naturally childish, are never sparked by originality. It is not in any way a literary achievement, and would not add prestige to a publisher's list. Even if the work had come to light five years ago, when the subject was timely, I don't see that there would have been a chance for it.' Luckily not everyone agreed. The book was later picked up by Doubleday and finally came out in the US and UK in 1952.

Closer to home, among the students I worked with at Goldsmiths was Yvonne Craig Inskip, who wrote a beautiful memoir about growing up under the care of two women, Tyna and Bigga, uninformed about which of them was her mother. The book describes her belated search to find the truth and to discover the identity of her father. She's much else to narrate too, and the book is ingeniously constructed; I didn't mind that the title she chose for it, *Things My Mothers Never Told Me*, cheekily echoed a book of my own. Commercial publishers balked at it; she had to bring it out herself. You can find a Kindle version of the book on Amazon, along with five-star reviews ('poignant', 'enthralling', 'very moving and extremely well written') one of which rightly says that it's 'a book that publishers should have accepted'.

These days, brush-offs from publishers are polite – indeed, so full of praise the author will wonder why they haven't been taken on. Sometimes there's useful feedback. More often, there are vacuous compliments and a *Sorry, not for us*. The rejection

Gertrude Stein received from a publisher A. C. Fifield, which parodied her prose style, is unusual in its brutality:

> Being only one, having only one pair of eyes, having only one time, having only one life, I cannot read your MS three or four times. Not even one time. Only one look, only one look is enough. Hardly one copy would sell here. Hardly one. Hardly one. Many thanks. I am returning your MS by registered post. Only one MS by one post.

In the early 2000s the publisher Black Lace listed a set of reasons for rejecting an erotic novel. However unerotic your book, if you're a life writer guilty of any of the following you'd better start revising:

> The prose lacks fluency.
> The central characters are unsympathetic/unattractive.
> The tone is flowery/romantic.
> The writing suffers from:
> > Repetitive sentence structure
> > Limited vocabulary
> > Overlong, overcomplicated sentences.
> > Blatant exposition
> > Excessive adjectives, adverbs, etc.
> > Lack of coherence/focus
> > Obsessive attention to details of genital anatomy at the expense of thought/dialogue/action.

OK, a life writer might not be especially fixated on *genital* anatomy, but even that advice is worth heeding: excessive attention to someone's physical appearance at the expense of thought/dialogue/action can be debilitating.

Rejection is hard to take but as Stephen Marche writes in his comically dejected book *On Writing and Failure*, 'You have to relish the rejection. Rejection is the evidence of your hustle. Rejection is the sign that you are throwing yourself against the door.' More to the point, rejection is a sign that something more might need doing to your work-in-progress. 'The gap between my feelings and my skill / was so immense, I wonder I went on,' John Betjeman writes in *Summoned by Bells*. But he did go on. And improved his skills. As persistent writers do.

Reliability

There was once a view that what separated life writing from fiction was trustworthiness. As Vivian Gornick puts it in *The Situation and the Story*, 'In fiction a narrator may be – and often famously is – unreliable (as in *The Good Soldier*, *The Great Gatsby*, Philip Roth's Zuckerman novels). In nonfiction never. In nonfiction the reader must believe that the narrator is speaking truth.' Times change. Readers are less trustful. They know life writers don't speak the whole truth, only a subjective version, 'based on' rather than definitive. But where the truth has been badly bent out of shape they feel cheated.

Few life writers want to come across as unreliable narrators. The term's a tricky one, anyway. What does it mean? A narrator who's naïve? Wayward? Ethically compromised? Self-deluding? Knowingly deceitful or unknowingly incorrect? Unreliability can take many forms and writers need to be aware of the impression they're making. Moral judgement goes with the territory. As Philip Roth said, 'we judge the author of a novel by how well he or she tells the story. But we judge morally the author of an autobiography, whose governing motive is primarily ethical as against aesthetic.' He's overstating the case. But it's true that life writers are always judged as *people*.

The liveliest guidance on reliability comes in Dave Eggers's preface to *A Heartbreaking Work of Staggering Genius*. What makes a work of non-fiction believable, he says, involves a degree of fictionalising, 'to round the truth up or down'. He confesses to liberties taken with dialogue ('though all essentially true . . . [it] has been written from memory, and reflects both the author's memory's limitations and his imagination's nudgings.'), characters ('The author, though he was loath to do it, had to change a few names.'), locations ('There have been a few instances of location-switching.'), omissions ('Some really great sex scenes were omitted, at the request of those who are now married or involved.') and accuracy ('The author would also like to acknowledge his propensity to exaggerate.'). He even adds an appendix called 'Mistakes We Knew We Were Making', which includes extensive corrections and apologies. By admitting his unreliability, he comes across as *more* reliable. And he offsets a tragic tale about the early death of his parents with wacky amendments.

By contrast, there's Binjamin Wilkomirski's prizewinning 1995 memoir, *Fragments: Memories of a Wartime Childhood*, which was taken to be reliable when it first appeared, and received glowing reviews ('achingly beautiful', 'an unforgettable tribute'), until investigations by the Swiss journalist Daniel Ganzfried, then analysis in greater depth by the historian Stefan Machler, showed that Wilkomirski (b. 1941, real name Bruno Dossekker) had fabricated the truth about his early years and couldn't have directly experienced the horrors of Hitler and the Holocaust. Other writers took up the case, mostly agreeing that Wilkomirski had lied and that his hitherto acclaimed masterpiece was 'kitsch'. Whether he wrote with knowing dishonesty or from false memory syndrome isn't clear. But it's odd that no one smelled a rat. 'My earliest memories are a rubble field of isolated images,' he writes. The images that follow are ones that anybody might come up with if asked to imagine the brutalities of Nazism:

> The feeling of deathly terror in my chest and throat, the heavy tramp of boots, a fist that yanks me out of my hiding place . . . Uniforms, boots, screaming . . . A cry of terror echoing down the staircase . . . Uproar everywhere, lots of people milling round . . . faces of terrible rage.

The tramp of boots, the screams, the rage: it's predictably B-movie – clichéd, false testimony at its worst.

At the end, Wilkomirski recalls how he was encouraged to discount his memories of 'the camps, the barracks, the bodies, the starving, the uniforms'. Put it behind you, his foster parents tell him, 'It was all a dream', and when he confides in others they respond 'You're making it up.' Indeed so. The life he recalls wasn't his. And the paucity of the writing proves it. Compare it with the authenticating detail that Primo Levi offers when, for example, he describes the importance, in the camps, of taking soup from the bottom of the vat, because there it's thicker and more nourishing.

Repetition

If a life writer records a 'traumatising' episode that took place, once is enough. Tell us again and the effect is diluted. Tell us four or five times and we'll be frustrated. If you were beaten by your father, in a string of violent childhood scenes, we'll sympathise. But as the blows come down, with little variation, in episode after episode, or other versions of the same episode, we'll feel battered and numbed. What you've gone through is terrible but in recounting it with little variation you're doing to the reader what was done to you; it's a recurrent, samey pummelling.

John Burnside illustrates the point in his memoir *A Lie About My Father*. His 'frightening' dad would often 'hit out at random', with his son a victim. But rather than describe his own experience, Burnside saves the worst for an episode he *witnessed*, when his father laid into his best friend Bill, stamping on him, 'the expression on his face cold and ugly . . . like a man performing a routine action, a man at work, doing something he did every day.' In Burnside's hands a single episode does the job.

Creative writing tutors often cite the Rule of Three. Something that happens once could be random; three times makes a pattern; a triad is more memorable for the reader. I take the point: omne trium perfectum. But unless it's varied, repetition is a turnoff. Tell it properly and once is enough.

Research

Sometimes a brief acknowledgement of the when, where, who and how of a writer's research discoveries is enough. But the unpicking of sources can also make a fascinating story in its own right. Where an author is immersed in decoding ciphers and joining dots, as Edmund de Waal is in *The Hare with Amber Eyes*, it's exhilarating for the reader: the thrill of the chase.

In *The Cut Out Girl* Bart van Es tells the story of Hesseline (Lien for short) who, after being smuggled away from The

Hague during the Second World War, was raised by foster parents – Bart's grandparents – with whom she later fell out. The book is as much about his pursuit of the facts as about her wartime past. We see him rootle through photo albums and cardboard boxes, travel to the places she lived in, be reproached for snooping, go for a jog, type on his laptop, read material that connects with his own life (not least with his daughter Josie) and spend many hours interviewing Lien, by then a woman of over eighty. This front story isn't intrusive. Without the friendship he forms with Lien, he'd be unable to tell the back story. To him the book is 'a work of partnership' and the warmth of that partnership offsets the ugliness that Lien recalls, which includes her being raped as a 10-year-old in another house (not her grandparents') that was meant to be a refuge.

In *The Rooster House*, Victoria Belim returns to the Ukraine of her childhood to spend time with her grandmother but also to solve the mystery of a great-uncle, Nikodim, who disappeared in the 1930s while fighting for a free Ukraine. The book is as much a sleuth story as a memoir, documenting Belim's gradual access to information hidden in archives. As it turns out, Nikodim is only part of the mystery: in the final pages, Belim is forced to examine the truth behind her father's suicide while also searching for 'pieces of myself'. Joe Dunthorne's *Children of Radium* is no less emotive, albeit told in a winningly amiable and sometimes humorous voice. His Jewish great-grandfather Siegfried ran a secret chemical weapons laboratory in 1930s Berlin, and Dunthorne sets out to discover how far he was implicated in Nazism, and in the carbon-monoxide poisoning of Jews. It's a quest that takes him to Germany and has him poring through archives, psychiatric records and Siegfried's 2,000-page unpublished memoir in search of clues. There are no simple answers, but that's part of the point: it's a buried inheritance which can't be fully unearthed.

These three books make a virtue of the sleuthing. But the inclusion of your research must always be selective. Say your grandfather was an RAF pilot in the Second World War. Or your great-aunt was a pioneer of hospices. You know about them through your family. And that knowledge has been enormously added to by your work in archives, museums, history books, memoirs, websites and friendship groups. You've discovered a great deal about the RAF and hospices. And it's fascinating. But only a little of it is relevant to the story you're telling. Cruel, heartbreaking even, but you have to let the bulk of it go. Save it for another book. And credit the relevant stuff in your acknowledgements.

Research should never be Wiki-ish or Googly, something worked up to give an impression of substance. A personal investment is what counts – the writer as investigator.

Resolution

Should memoirs provide a decisive ending? Many practitioners say not. Since life for the writer goes on after the book has been finished, a big-bang finale is bogus. Better, they argue, to keep things hanging. Besides which, loose ends are truer to the transitory nature of existence. Helen Garner: 'I am learning not to round a scene off. I like to leave the reader with one leg hanging over the edge.'

It's a seductive argument which John Irving disparages: 'Reading a [book] that ends up nowhere – no win, no loss; life as a treadmill – is like discovering, after we have run our hearts out against the timekeeper's clock, that the timekeeper forgot to switch the clock on.' If readers are engaged through hundreds of pages, then left in the dark at the end – not knowing how things worked out – they'll feel cheated or, worse, the victims of a scammer or sadist. They don't need the full works but they do need to be given *something*.

A resolution doesn't mean a happy ending – nor an unhappy one. In fact, it doesn't mean an ending at all, only a drawing together of strands. And it can take various forms: a scene that stands as an epilogue, subtly linked to scenes before; a circling back to the start, with qualifications; a reassurance to readers that the story, for now, has gone as far as it can go. 'Reader, I married him' (*Jane Eyre*) is maybe too overt – a full stop rather than a comma. 'Joe [Simpson] continues to climb to this day' is the ending to Kevin Macdonald's 2003 film *Touching the Void*, a conclusion that's equally upbeat but less of a grand finale. Readers want a send-off. The gesture of a few words or paragraphs. Not to be left high and dry.

Revision

> If you hope to deserve a second reading you must often use
> The rubber at the end of your pencil. (Horace, *Satires*, 1.10)

In a piece for the *Guardian* James Fenton described the different phases of writing a poem. You start with an idea and as you write 'begin to see the shape of your aimed-for poem, but at the same time you also see all these appalling faults cropping up all over the place.' You revise the poem and move towards completing it but 'intractable faults' remain, including 'slackly chosen words, effects lifted consciously or unconsciously from other people's work, moments of portentousness, surprisingly obvious grammatical errors and fundamental lapses of taste'. You revise again till 'all the gaps have been filled in', but when you read through the latest draft you find that 'the bits you have fixed have by now, through over-reading, ceased to mean anything. All you can see are the glaring errors. And so you put your poem away and let time do its work.'

His account applies as much to life writing as poetry. You slave away through many drafts then time must do its work. You want to get the thing off your hands but it can't go till it's ready. You need a break. *It* needs a break. When you go back to it, after a decent gap, new things will happen that you'd not anticipated. Without an openness to the unwilled and subconscious, writing suffers. Without the exercise of choice and deliberation, it suffers too. 'Things occur to me at a keyboard that do not occur anywhere else,' Graham Caveney writes in *The Body in the Library* (a book about his cancer diagnosis and much besides). 'Writing means letting the language take over, allowing it to discover what it wants to say. Writing is editing, hearing the rhythms that are trapped within the sentence. To write is to re-write.'

I once had a student who derided revision. If what he'd written seemed weak, he said, it was not because he'd chosen the wrong words but because there was a deeper significance, a symbolic undercurrent, and bugger readers if they couldn't see what it was. But some of his word choices *were* wrong – inept, crass or confusing. To trust entirely (as he did) to immediacy and spontaneity, with no second look, no pause to rethink, is self-defeating. He was the kind of student described by Helen Garner who 'will cling and cling to [a] thin first draft . . . and will strike out into the ocean only under extreme duress'.

With another student I was in the habit of suggesting so many cuts and word changes it was as if I was revising my own work, not hers. One day she'd had enough, left my office in tears and said she was quitting the course. We both mishandled things. I overdid the negative feedback, frustrated that after so many sessions together she still hadn't learned to revise. And she was over-sensitive to criticism because the material was so intimate and first-hand. Within a few days she relented and was back on the course. And she went on to complete her book. We're still friends. But revision, or the lack of it, briefly made us enemies.

'Beyond talent lie all the usual words,' James Baldwin said, 'Discipline, love, luck, but most of all endurance.' Virtue isn't always rewarded but without endurance and a willingness to revise, the writer doesn't have a chance. I love Seamus Heaney's poem 'Keeping Going', written to his brother Hugh, with its celebration of persistence – an attribute which writers need as badly as farmers:

> I see you at the end of your tether sometimes,
> In the milking parlour, holding yourself up
> Between two cows until your turn goes past,
> Then coming to to the smell of dung again
> And wondering, is this all? As it was
> In the beginning, is now and shall be?
> Then rubbing your eyes and seeing our old brush
> Up on the byre door, and keeping going.

Roth, Philip

Roth is best known for the novels he wrote over a long career that stretched from *Goodbye, Columbus* and the controversial *Portnoy's Complaint* through *American Pastoral* and *The Plot*

Against America to the slimmer fictions of his later years, many of them based in his native Newark, New Jersey. But he also wrote non-fiction, and what he calls his 'novelist's autobiography', *The Facts*, has a brilliant, thought-provoking debate on the memoir versus the novel, as conducted between Roth and his fictional alter ego Nathan Zuckerman.

Roth tells Zuckerman in a preface that he's sick of using 'masks, disguises, distortions, and lies', and that after a health crisis, period of depression and the death of his mother he needed to recover his sense of self – hence a book of undisguised autobiographical remembering: 'In its uncompelling, unferocious way, the nonfictional approach has brought me closer to how experience actually *felt* than has turning the flame up under my life and smelting stories out of all I've known.'

It's a great rationale for life writing. But Zuckerman's reply, in an afterword five times as long as Roth's preface, is no less persuasive. He accuses him of '*de*-imagining' – of misrepresenting facts as solidly dependable when they're actually 'refractory and unmanageable and inconclusive'. Worse still, 'I just cannot trust you as a memoirist the way I trust you as a novelist.' Zuckerman has an agenda: to keep his place as doppelganger in Roth's work and, as he sees it, to help him fulfil his potential: 'Your medium for genuine self-confrontation is me.' Still, biased or not, he makes a serious point about the limits of Roth's life writing: in the guise of Philip rather than Zuckerman, he's too decorous, too self-censoring, too nice.

As Zuckerman rightly says, inhibition is fatal in life writing. You don't have to tell all but you need to be honest – pitiless even – in what you do tell. Roth's two major contributions to life writing, *The Facts* and *Patrimony*, are tremendous achievements nonetheless, and far less compromised than Zuckerman suggests.

Rousseau, Jean-Jacques

As I discuss elsewhere (see PERFORMANCE) his *Confessions*, completed in 1765 and published in 1781, is the most notable autobiography after St Augustine's, over a millennium earlier. 'I have resolved on an enterprise which has no precedent,' he begins, which is inaccurate as well as boastful. Still it's true that St Augustine addressed himself to God, whereas Rousseau's audience is his 'fellow man' (and woman). Moreover, the sins he owns up to aren't religious transgressions so much as ordinary human failings. He doesn't claim to have perfect recall but nor will he allow himself to fictionalise: 'if by any chance I have used some immaterial embellishment it has been only to fill a void due to defect of memory. I may have taken for fact what was no more than probability, but I have never put down as true what I knew to be false.' No autofiction, then. But a good deal of performance. That's what makes him a model for memoirists. It's not enough to be emotionally truthful, he thinks. There has to be self-dramatisation too – the opera of the ego.

Rules

In his essay 'Politics and the English Language' Orwell lists just six writing rules. They're worth considering if not (as the last admits) necessarily following:

i. Never use a metaphor, simile or other figure of speech which you are used to seeing in print.
ii. Never use a long word where a short one will do.
iii. If it is possible to cut a word out, always cut it out.
iv. Never use the passive where you can use the active.

v. Never use a foreign phrase, a scientific word or a jargon word if you can think of an English equivalent.

vi. Break any of these rules sooner than say anything outright barbarous.

The crime writer Elmore Leonard ups Orwell's six rules to ten. His, too, are usefully provocative:

1. Never open a book with weather.
2. Avoid prologues.
3. Never use a verb other than 'said' to carry dialogue.
4. Never use an adverb to modify the verb 'said'.
5. Keep your exclamation marks under control.
6. Never use the word 'suddenly'.
7. Use regional dialect, patois, sparingly.
8. Avoid detailed descriptions of characters.
9. Ditto places and things.
10. Try to leave out the part that readers tend to skip.

Rules should be distrusted. One writer's meat is another's poison. Still, to take just one of Leonard's commands: lavish use of exclamation marks *is* invariably the sign of an unaccomplished writer, who'll use them to convey a sense of surprise, drama or excitement (*Then he kissed me!*) that can be better conveyed without. Good prose is its own exclamation mark.

S

Salt Path

Unless they're categorised as autofiction, which allows for some mucking about, memoirs are expected to tell the truth. Raynor Winn has said that her bestselling book *The Salt Path* is a true account of the 630-mile walk she and her seriously ill husband, Moth, did together after losing their home. But behind the loss of their home lay a story she obfuscated, which, after the *Observer* exposed it, seeded doubts in readers' minds about how much else she might have fabricated.

The problem is the set-up to her book. Bailiffs arrive and the Winns lose the home they've built up over twenty years because a friend, Cooper (not his real name, any more than Raynor Winn is the author's real name), a man who moves in 'financial circles few of us understood', has diddled them. They're innocent souls, 'just a number amongst the unrepresented masses', with no right to free legal representation. And though they have 'written evidence that would convince the judge of the truth', without a barrister they're 'constantly outmanoeuvred'. Crucially the judge won't allow them to submit the 'true' new evidence, because they haven't followed the correct procedure. As a result they're made homeless. A few days later Moth is diagnosed with CBD, Corticobasal degeneration, a rare degenerative brain disease.

All very powerful. And I'm not so partial (as some have been) as to question the CBD diagnosis, even if Moth has survived much longer than predicted and it's mysterious why trekking for hundreds of miles and camping in sometimes grim conditions should have eased his symptoms. I don't mind the comic exaggeration in the book, either; it's enjoyable light relief; Robert Graves in *Goodbye to All That* and Gerald Durrell in *My Family and Other Animals* set a precedent for hamming things up in non-fiction. But the underlying story is that the Winns are victims, betrayed and made homeless by a sleazy friend and a pernickety judge, and only redeemed by their long walk. In reality, the Winns' difficulties date back to an episode she conceals, her alleged embezzlement of tens of thousands of pounds from a family for whom she was working as a bookkeeper. Nor was she altogether honest to call herself homeless, given that she and Moth owned property in France. In short, her salvation narrative is far less simple and heartwarming than she makes out.

'You see the point,' Joan Didion wrote, 'I want to tell you the truth.' Raynor Winn said something similar to an interviewer from *The Times* in 2022: 'If you're going to write about something, and you don't write about it honestly, you're not giving the full texture of what you're writing about.' *The full texture.* It's not there in *The Salt Path*. What Winn did, to put it at its mildest, was to tidy up the truth so that she and Moth came across as victims and underdogs. Her apology, after the *Observer* exposé, for 'any mistakes I made' while feeling under 'pressure' was feeble; the readers who'd bought into her tale of resilience deserved more.

Honesty is perilous, but in memoir there isn't much wriggle room. Mislead us about one thing, and we may well disbelieve the lot. 'When you tell a story,' Raynor Winn writes in *The Salt Path*, 'the first person you must convince is yourself; if you can make yourself believe it's true then everyone else will follow.' Indeed, I'm reminded of Toad in *Wind in the Willows*:

> 'O, Ratty!' he cried. 'I've been through such times since I saw you last, you can't think! Such trials, such sufferings, and all so nobly borne! . . . and all so cleverly planned and carried out! . . . Humbugged everybody – made 'em all do exactly what I wanted! Oh, I AM a smart Toad, and no mistake!'

Schedules

It's fascinating to read how writers carve out a particular time of day or spend weeks cloistered away: whatever it takes to be unimpeded. Getting up early is one solution, before the kids do, if you're a parent or even when, like Graham Swift, you're not: 'I can be at work as early as five thirty,' he says, 'when I have the feeling that the rest of the world is asleep, but I am alert and not going to be interrupted. If you get going in those early hours you are launched and safe.' By contrast there's the Norwegian Jon Fosse, who wrote his massive 800-page novel *Septology* at night, in stints that ran from four or five in the afternoon till nine next morning: 'When I'm writing well, I have this very clear and distinct feeling that what I'm writing on is already written . . . I just have to write it down before it disappears.'

Mornings were the time when Hemingway wrote ('as soon after first light as possible') but he also emphasised the need to shut down and forget about the work-in-progress till next day, so it didn't go backwards: 'If you kept thinking about it you would lose the thing that you were writing before you could go on with it . . . I had learned already never to empty the well of my writing, but always to stop when there was still something there in the deep part of the well, and let it refill at night from the springs that fed it.' Other writers set themselves a word-limit. Graham Greene did so, breaking off once he'd reached it: 'Over twenty years I have probably averaged five hundred words a day for five days a week . . . I have always been very methodical, and when my quota of work is done I break off, even in the middle of a scene. Every now and then during the morning's work I count what I have done and mark off the hundred on my manuscript.' Stephen King's target was 2,000 words a day (which he sometimes achieved by 11.30 a.m.) but 500 words, five days a week is a decent average, meaning a book-length draft will be finished in nine months. The book won't yet be born. But the worst of the labour will be over.

I'm inconsistent: a couple of books have been written in a year, others have taken six or seven. A regular schedule helps, a minimum word target too. But so does a blissful state of forgetfulness, when you're hardly aware of writing at all (as can also happen when you're reading). John McGahern describes it perfectly in *Memoir*: 'It's a strange and complete happiness when all sense of time is lost, of looking up from the pages and thinking it is still nine or ten in the morning, to discover it is well past lunchtime.'

Sebald, W. G.

By the time he died in a car accident in 2001 at the age of fifty-seven, Sebald was internationally renowned. His reputation rested on four books, the last of them *Austerlitz* and the most intriguing of them *The Rings of Saturn*, which described a walk through East Anglia, to which he'd moved from his native Germany thirty years before. Can we call him a life writer? I think so. His books are usually classed as novels but he said he wasn't a novelist. He straddles several different genres – history, travel writing, biography, essay – with photos and documents to create an impression of authenticity even when he's making things up. The narrator is him but also not-him: a real person and an invented persona, with all he observes filtered through a funereal lens. The weather is bleak and wintry. The places he visits are deserted. The people he passes look like ghosts or zombies – or prisoners who've just received death sentences. He has panic attacks, hallucinations and fainting fits. He'd like to offer hope but life's too bleak for it. His gloom is affecting, almost comic: always look on the blight side of life. And for all his isolation, he's forever meeting people and hearing their stories. As he listens, he seems to *become* them – the 'I' isn't him any more, it's them.

The Sebaldian is as unmistakeable (and pastiche-able) as the Dickensian or the Pinteresque. Yet he draws on innumerable sources. The basis is collage, or bricolage, but the fluency of the prose, with its long sentences, is seamless. There's no dialogue, only reported speech. There are no paragraphs either, the nearest equivalent being his occasional use of a dash:

> . . . [the swallows] moving their outspread wings only occasionally, until they came back down to us at break of day. – Austerlitz had been so deeply immersed in his Welsh tale, and I in listening to him, that we did not notice how late it had grown.

Reported speech, long sentences, unattributed photos, paragraph-lessness, a fluid first-person pronoun, writing that's fictive but true: they're tools available to any writer but when they're used all together, the author will be Sebald or one of his imitators.

Self-expression

Many books, novels especially, are an escape from self – a denial, renunciation or dust cloud (John Fosse: 'to me writing is not to express myself, it's to get rid of myself.') But in life writing you're talking about yourself and/or about people, places and stories that matter to you. Some critics think it's immodest for authors to write personally. But we're on earth for just a mini-second and sometimes there's stuff that only a memoir can say.

Self-expression is never straightforward, though. You're not just being you; you're being you on the page – as bereaved child, rape victim, uprooted migrant, betrayed friend, cancer survivor, etc. The book-you doesn't encompass all the attributes of the real-life-you. It's selective, excising the selves that sit outside the story. And it's reflective, which your core self, immersed in the moment, doesn't have room to be. The pledge you make is to realism. (Don't bother otherwise – write fantasy instead.) Not everyone will like what you write. Fine: not everyone likes you in life, either. And not everyone likes life writing. No matter: if you've been true to yourself, or to the persona integral to the story you're telling, that's what counts.

There's still a prejudice that self-expression is the mark of a novice, second-string or narcissistic author. 'As we develop as writers and learn to distance ourselves from our personal material,' I read in one creative writing handbook, 'self-expression is likely to give way to other concerns, such as the desire to create writing that embodies experience and ideas in ways that have a broader appeal than the purely personal.' But private experience does have broad appeal. Self-expression is the basis of many great books. And 'purely personal' material can be universal: if it works, readers will connect.

Self-publishing

It used to be called 'vanity' publishing. Now the terms 'independent' and 'autonomous' are preferred, which remove the stigma. It would be great to see the stigma permanently stigmatised – for no shame to be attached when people fund their own publications. Not every book is commercial. And with a piece of family history, say, written so that a younger generation or wider clan can learn about their predecessors, self-publishing is the obvious choice. Many companies now offer that service. Costs will vary, and though bookshops, even friendly neighbourhood bookshops, might decline to stock them, self-published books can be sold online, where more can be earned per copy than the 10 or 15 per cent royalty on a commercially published book. With good marketing skills and stamina, a writer can cover costs, though cost is rarely the chief consideration.

Many self-published books have later been taken up by a commercial publisher. An online fan base or serial blog can pave the way. E. L. James self-published *Fifty Shades of Grey* and connected with readers through Facebook; as the book's popularity spread, Century bought the rights. Other examples include *Still Alice* by Lisa Genova (later adapted as a film starring Julianne Moore), *The Martian* by Andy Weir (ditto, Matt Damon), *Legally Blonde* by Amanda Brown (ditto, Reese Witherspoon) and *milk and honey* by the poet Rupi Kaur. Further back came Beatrix Potter's *The Tale of Peter Rabbit*, privately printed in an edition of 250 copies for friends and family until she agreed to have colour illustrations and was published by Frederick Warne. If publication by subscription (the equivalent of crowdfunding) is included, Milton's *Paradise Lost* is there too – as are books which Jane Austen, Marcel Proust, Ezra Pound, Margaret Atwood, e. e. cummings, Walt Whitman and Mark Twain part-funded or brought out under their own imprint. Not a bad list to join.

Most of the authors above are novelists and poets. With self-published memoirs, commercial publishers are less likely to bite. Still, the priority is for the book to be out there in the world. And if dreams of bestselling stardom are set aside, doing it yourself – with greater say about cover design, format, distribution, etc. – may be the answer.

Sex

If authors are going to write honestly about their lives or the lives of others, can they afford not to talk about sex? Sometimes sex might play little part in the story. Then again, it's hard to imagine a story in which sex doesn't play *some* part; even its absence or suppression may be significant. There's little difficulty in generalising about sex – *our relationship stayed passionate to the end; she was a determined polyamorist; we lost our virginity together*, etc. It's trickier when you come to detail. You might be someone who has never discussed your sex life with friends. So why do it with strangers? Then again you might find it easier with strangers: readers aren't in the room with you; you won't blush when they react.

How to come clean but not overshare? In Katherine Angel's *Unmastered: A Book on Desire, Most Difficult to Tell*, the difficulty owned up to in the subtitle isn't candour per se but the complications for a feminist with a love of submission: 'I long to be weighed down by the Man's body.' 'I ask him if he would tie me up.' 'I want him to do something like hitting.' The Man is never identified or named, only capitalised; he remains abstract. But she's respectful of his manhood ('I lock him into his masculinity. I am anxious to protect it.') and at a talk given by Shere Hite she feels at odds with the audience in their disparagement of men as sexual partners. It's the same when she's at a seminar on pornography and takes on the speaker for not recognising the distinction between violent sex and 'consensual play with domination'. She's made to feel that her 'problematical' desires would disappear if she knew about feminism. But she does know about feminism. What's brave about her book isn't just its exploration of sensuality but its format: ideas and experiences offered as prose-poem fragments, among acres of white space.

Tabitha Lasley's *Sea State,* based on 103 interviews with men who work on oil rigs in the North Sea, has a more conventional narrative structure. 'What do you want to write a book about oil rigs for?' her editor asks. 'I want to see what men are like with no women around,' she replies. It's a self-contradictory mission: since she's there with them, onshore, asking them questions, the men aren't behaving as they do on the rigs with no women around. Moreover, she complicates her research by falling in love with the first of her interviewees, Caden, who's married with children but promises to leave his wife for her. She's bold in documenting their first time: 'I took his hand, guided it under the elastic of my knickers (ugly, threadbare, high-waisted things) and between the lips of my cunt . . . "You're not going in there," I said in what I judged to be a reasonably accurate approximation of his accent. "It's *too* wet." Long before Caden lets her down and she despairs ('I went on a few dates, but it was like trying to treat a heroin addiction with Calpol.') it's clear this is a meeting of un-equals; even the sex between them isn't that great. But her infatuation is real enough and she conveys that in a quietly vengeful but humorous book.

Julia Blackburn's *The Three of Us* is similarly adept in evoking infatuation and intimacy. The book is, in part, about her sexual awakening as a teenager, in defiance of her mother, who fears she'll steal one of the lodgers who double as her mother's lovers. Which indeed she does, going off with the much older Geoffrey. Before the relationship ends in tragedy, she's torn between three different men.

> The day arrived on which Herman and I were setting off to Corfu. He had stayed with me overnight . . . Just after he left, my first lover, Rowland, dropped by to say hello and we made love. Then a couple of hours later Geoffrey telephoned and said he needed to see me, so he turned up at the flat and I made love with him as well. I remember imagining the sperm from three different men swimming around in my body and mingling together.

There's nothing unseemly about Blackburn's torn loyalties and desires. Nor should Angel be reproached for exploring domination fantasies or Lasley be insulted (as she was by one rigger) as a 'slut'. All three are candid about the complications of love and sex. But they don't sensationalise or, as happened with *The Sexual Life of Catherine M* ('the most explicit book about sex ever written by a woman': Edmund White), get marketed as a libidinous blabber.

There are gay, trans and non-binary perspectives to consider, too, but it's perhaps no coincidence that in the examples above I've mentioned only women writers. In the current climate a heterosexual male writer may well back off from writing candidly about sex because he fears being accused of phallocentrism, and because it has been done so often before, not just in fiction (John Updike! Henry Miller!) but in the long history of pornographic memoirs. It surely *can* still be done by men, or at any rate by a gay man such as Edmund White was or by authors outside the hetero-normative majority, but for now the genre feels tired. It's hard to imagine a twenty-first-century man documenting a six-year journey of erotic exploration (phone sex, tantric sex, group sex, etc.) as Monique Roffey did in *With the Kisses of His Mouth*. Where he would look self-vaunting, she's engagingly vulnerable.

Shock

Sometimes the facts are shocking, without embroidery. Thomas Blackburn's memoir *A Clip of Steel* takes its title from the mechanical device sent to him at boarding school by his father, in order to discourage involuntary ejaculation or masturbation: 'the instrument had an outer clip of thin firm steel whose inner edge was serrated with spiked teeth . . . if you had an erection then your expanding penis pressed into the sharp teeth of the firm outer clip.' Ouch.

It's said that today's memoirs keep upping the ante, with shock piled on shock, and explicitness reaching new levels. 'The words *I love you* come tumbling out of my mouth in an incantation the first time you fuck me in the ass, my face smashed against the concrete floor' appears in the first paragraph of Maggie Nelson's *The Argonauts* in 2015. But Thomas Blackburn's book came out over half a century ago, as did J. R. Ackerley's two memoirs *My Dog Tulip* and *My Father and Myself*, which are frank not only about his homosexuality and his father's secret second family but describe canine love (his sensual arousal when touching his pet Alsatian) in astonishing physical detail. Life writers who worry that their story may be OTT should take heart – others have paved the way. And sometimes shocks are playful, such as the one Seamus Heaney pulls off at the end of his poem 'The Skunk', his delight in the sight of a skunk ('snuffing the boards five feet beyond me') prompting a love song for his wife Marie: 'the sootfall of your things at bedtime, / Your head down, tail-up hunt in a bottom drawer / For the black plunge-line nightdress.'

Siblings

Siblit isn't a crowded genre. There's a long tradition of 'vertical' memoirs (grown-up children writing about parents) but very few horizontal ones (brothers and sisters writing about brothers and sisters). In most life writing, siblings get marginal roles. But they may be crucial to the story and to a relationship that involves the eternal sibling verities – love, hate, rivalry, envy, protectiveness, disparagement, separation and loss.

Tara Westover's *Educated* tells of a large, violently dysfunctional Mormon family in Idaho, with parents who're suspicious of hospitals, schools, the state and more or less anything outside their private domain. Most of her hostility is reserved for her brother Shawn – not his real name – who bullied and threatened to kill her; when she complained about him to the family, he persuaded them that she'd been possessed by the Devil. Shawn is a terrifying figure. The personality change that followed a serious brain injury may be part of the reason, so her siblings suggest. She allows them their say. Truth in families is complicated.

'A brother behind bars, my own flesh and blood, raised in the same houses by the same mother and father': John Edgar Wideman's *Brothers and Keepers* asks why two siblings from the same background should take such diverse paths. While John enjoys a successful academic and writing career, his younger brother Robert is given a life sentence for homicide. The book seeks out the parallels between the brothers as well as the difference. Other notable recent examples of siblit are Richard Beard's *The Day That Went Missing*, about the death of his brother Nicky (aged 9) who drowned while swimming in the sea off Cornwall; John Niven's *O Brother*, which commemorates his troubled younger brother Gary, who died – shockingly, by hanging himself in a room off an A&E ward – in his early forties; Miriam Toews's *A Truce That is Not Peace*, which grapples with her sister Marjorie's suicide; Annie Ernaux's *The Other Girl*, on the older sister her parents never told her about, who died of diphtheria at six; Arifa Akbar's *Consumed: In Search of My Sister*; Martha Baillie's *There Is No Blue*, which is largely about her older sister Christina, also a suicide victim; and *Brother & Sister* by Diane Keaton, which explores why her brother Randy's life took a direction so unlike her own, into solitude, alcoholism and self-loathing.

Though they shared the same parents and upbringing why were she and her sibling so different, Keaton asks herself, much as Wideman does and much as I do, in a similar search for answers, in *Two Sisters,* about my sister Gill.

Similes and metaphors

Similes connect. They find in a person or object or situation a surprising likeness to something else. And unless they're old hat, they astonish with their freshness. It's a mode of doubling up, of turning singles into couples: look how this resembles that.

Here are a few I remember from students I've worked with or pieces I've read (apologies if I've got them slightly wrong).

> Needlemarks on an arm like a tiny red-mouthed chorus.
> Happiness slapped out of a child, like dust out of a carpet.
> A penis hanging unused like an umbrella in July.
> A waving arm like a dislocated windscreen wiper.
> Commuters heading to work like a procession of clouds.
> A deer's eyes clouded like boiled sweets.
> A car cigarette lighter like an organ stop.
> A weak smile like someone pleasing a photographer on a rainy day at the seaside.
> A Citroën rising like a waking beast lifting its haunches, ready to chase its next meal.
> Shaving foam expanding like a hissing meringue.
> A gurgle in the throat like a glug of batter on a hot griddle.
> Shops brightly lit like open fridges.
> The hushed prayers of a woman in church like grass rustling in the wind.
> Mackerel like convulsing truncheons.
> The clatter of a heartbeat like soil on the lid of a coffin.

Metaphors drop the 'like' (or 'as') in order to unify rather than compare. They're faster and more incisive. There's no pause to weigh up the parallel; it's complete; the singles have moved in together. Here are a few more I remember.

Herons in a park in rogue grey suits trailing thin addicts' legs.
The dog's tail a barometer of excitement.
Liver-spots the colour of dark tea.
The weak suck of linoleum.
The lacquered flanks of bulls.
A trampoline of dizziness.
A man climbing back into his own daylight.
The open stove of a village.
The static-fizz of cow parsley.

Life writing fails if it's fussily 'poetic' but not if it's poetry.

Sport

I'm fairly sporty: play tennis (never that well and now creakily), used to play football (schoolboy trial with others in my team for Preston North End) and have run three marathons. And I like watching sport, everything from Wimbledon to the Olympics. The sports pages are the first thing I turn to when reading a newspaper (Samuel Beckett did the same, I was told). But I hardly ever read sports memoirs. Why? Because of their too-predictable *how-I-did-it*, *rags-to-riches* arcs? Partly. Because they're written by or co-written with ghosts? That too, though credit to Andre Agassi, whose memoir *Open* is astonishing in its approach (he *hates* tennis), disarmingly un-starry and generous in acknowledging the help he had from J. R. Moehringer in transforming taped interviews into a book. Chiefly, though, the appeal of sport is its present-tense unpredictability; it's live; you're immersed, mid-action; you don't know the outcome. Whereas a sports memoir is unexcitingly retrospective.

Still, I have read a few sports memoirs, the sort that reach non-initiates as well as fans. 'I don't know anything about surfing but I was gripped,' Olivia Laing says of William Finnegan's Pulitzer-winning *Barbarian Days*, a dream endorsement. And it is a compelling book, the story of a search for the perfect wave (Tavarua in Fiji comes closest), to be kept secret from other surfers when found, as well as the story of a lifelong obsession as Finnegan moves from his days as an acid-dropping flower-child in California, through sojourns round the globe, into his frailer but still wave-addicted sixties. The varieties of wave (rights, lefts, barrels, a 'run-and-gun with a glorious tube', 'a roaring blue freight train all down the reef'); the difference between longboards and shortboards; the fear and ecstasy of riding monsters – he makes you care, even if like me you've never surfed. 'Nearly all of what happens in the water is ineffable,' he says, 'language is no help', but he finds the words.

Haruki Murakami's *What I Talk About When I Talk About Running* is as much about writing as running. Note the title: he doesn't *think* about anything when he runs ('I run in a void') but the book allows him to talk about what novel-writing and long-distance running have in common (concentration and endurance) and what divides them (novel-writing is unhealthy, he says, because the writer works with toxic material, whereas running improves wellbeing). Still, the best parts of the memoir are the accounts of him running his first marathon in Greece, a triathlon in Japan, and a 62-mile ultra-marathon ('at the end I hardly knew who I was or what I was doing').

Murakami's is an insider memoir: the account of a doer, not a watcher. And there are many of these, including Conor Nilan's *The Racket*, about the highs and lows of his years as a tennis professional, and Helen Mort's *A Line Above the Sky*, about her passion for climbing and the additional difficulties mothers face when they're mountaineers. But fan memoirs are no less important. The novelist Tim Parks's *A Season with Verona* is a classic (his *Teach Us to Sit Still: A Sceptic's Search for Health and Healing* is well worth reading too). A long-time Verona supporter since moving to Italy in his twenties, Parks resolves to attend every fixture in a season and write about it. He's in luck: from the first chaotic away trip to the final game (a play-off to escape relegation), there's no shortage of drama. It's a story about racism, policing, violence, corruption and Italy as a nation as well as a story about football. The best sports memoirs do range wide, into worlds outside the arena. The Jamaican bowler Michael Holding's *Why We Kneel, How We Rise*, put together after the murder of George Floyd, in conjunction with other Black sports professionals (Naomi Osaka, Usain Bolt, Hope Powell, Thierry Henry), is a notable example.

When I first mingled with writers, I concealed my love of sport for fear I'd be thought a nerd. How daft was that? Murakami on running, Updike on golf, David Foster Wallace and Geoff Dyer on tennis, Tim Parks and Nick Hornby on football, C. L. R James on cricket, Norman Mailer and Joyce Carol Oates on boxing . . . many writers are sports nuts.

Structure

Sentence by sentence the writing may be fine, but if a story doesn't hang together the structure is wrong. Common symptoms of a lousy structure include: a self-defeating narrative line (e.g., too much given away too soon so there's no impetus to keep going); intrusive back story; muddled chronology; inconsistent tenses; emphasis thrown on the wrong character or episodes; a self-satisfied narrator. However complex, stories need to be shaped. Chapters can't be jumbled up or 'reveals' located in the wrong place. The time-frame is a particular challenge: where to begin and end?

The life writer sets limits, as novelists do, imposing a frame on the narrative. Most memoirs are broken down into chapters (numbered, titled or both) and often into larger segments as well (Part 1, Part 2, etc.). Sam Miller's *Fathers* is nicely minimalist, with 215 numbered sections, bracketed by a prologue and epilogue; Geoff Dyer's *The Last Days of Roger Federer* has three parts, each with sixty sections, plus a postscript. A diaristic dateline can also work, for part of a book if not all. Breaks of some sort mirror the writing process. When a writer is on song, it flows – but not uninterruptedly for 80,000 words.

The challenge is: what should come where? The risk with a dramatic revelation at the start is that what follows will be anticlimactic. Equally, a memoir can't hold back too much. Unless the text is private, never to be shown to anyone else, there'll need to be signposts and markers. A book's a building and the layout has to be intelligible: here's the reception room, there the stairs to the next stor(e)y, here the hotspot (bedroom), there the scary cellar, here the sunny backyard. Now readers can find their way.

Surprise

Because of the title, blurb or front cover, readers will come to a text with expectations. The canniest life writers defy them. They surprise.

Maxime Gorky's *My Childhood* begins with a death, though we don't know that at first, since Gogol is inhabiting his infant self; you might think from his description in the opening sentence – 'In a narrow, darkened room, my father, dressed in a white and unusually long garment, lay on the floor under the window.' – that his father could be having a nap. Afterwards, Gorky recalls the funeral:

> I am standing by a slippery mound of sticky earth and looking into the pit wherein they have thrown the coffin of my father. At the bottom there is a quantity of water, and there are also frogs, two of which have even jumped on to the yellow lid of the coffin . . . The gravediggers, bending nearly double, began to fling the lumps of earth on the coffin rapidly, striking the frogs, which were leaping against the sides of the pit.

The frogs bother the boy more than the corpse inside the coffin does. When he cries it isn't for his father but for those poor creatures. Will they be able to escape? The perspective is fresh and the psychology convincing. There's comedy as well as loss.

Gorky kills off his dad on the first page and so does Andrea Ashworth in *Once in a House on Fire*, which begins, 'My father drowned when I was five years old. A picture of me, framed in gold plastic, was fished from his pocket and returned to my mother with a soggy wallet and a bunch of keys. The keys were to our new terraced house, which could now be paid for with his life insurance.' The tone is direct, brisk, unsentimental: a child has lost her father and a wife her husband; Ashworth simply sets this out, leaving the reader to supply the emotion. She even risks a little comedy (that life insurance policy) and adds to it when she describes the banality of her father's death: he had 'stopped to take a pee' by a stream, 'slipped, landed on a rock and drowned in four inches of water'.

Two parental deaths, recalled without a display of strong feeling and yet authentic; death as tragi-comedy. It's not that the authors are trying to shock; on the contrary, they're staying true to what they recall of themselves at the time, as children, in a tone as much playful as mournful. Patricia Lockwood is playful too in 'Rape Joke', a paradoxical title for a prose-poem that explores why rape can't be a joke:

> Can rape jokes be funny at all, is the question.
> Can any part of the rape joke be funny. The part where it ends – haha, just kidding! Though you did dream of killing the rape joke for years, spilling all of its blood out, and telling it that way.
> The rape joke cries out for the right to be told.
> The rape joke is that this is just how it happened.
> The rape joke is that the next day he gave you Pet Sounds. No really. Pet Sounds. He said he was sorry and then he gave you Pet Sounds. Come on, that's a little bit funny. Admit it.

Surprise is a useful weapon. But with a last-chapter volte-face (e.g., it was actually Mum who fired a gun at the neighbour, not Dad as implied all along) the reader may feel cheated, the victim of a trick rather than the beneficiary of a bold structural device. In other words, surprise shouldn't be a *deus ex machina*: we need to be startled but then to look back and see the clues we missed – the writer dropped hints she was pregnant, or that her Polish father changed his birth-name, so why didn't we see it coming?

T

Telling

Show don't tell, goes the mantra. At worst, it's silly advice. It's impossible, or at any rate unwise, to write a book consisting entirely of scenes. And as Graham Swift argues in *Making an Elephant*, the word 'tell' is more nuanced and versatile than creative writing tutors allow: *I can tell* 'suggests knowing and understanding, a seeing into a situation'; it's not 'a mere matter of informing'. For life writers, that need to *see into a situation* is vital: the making sense of an experience as well as the account of it.

'The temptation to explain should almost always be resisted,' John Gardner writes in *The Art of Fiction*. 'A good writer can get anything at all across through action and dialogue . . . Set beside the complex thought achieved by drama, explanation is thin gruel, hence boring.' He's right. But I've worked with writers who make such a fetish of not telling that they fail even to show: from a fear of being obvious, or an obsession with beguiling the reader, they hide all the cards. Overtness isn't a sin; occasional passages demand it. Writers don't want to ram meaning down our throats, but nor can they be too elusive. To be in*tell*igible they have to tell, at least a little.

The danger comes when they're moralising – about the damage childhood abuse does, the evils of misogyny, global warming, religious persecution, whatever. Then it's better to trust the reader to get the message than to preach. Stick to the details of the story and contextualise it, and the meaning will be inferred. Tell it like it is but don't tell the reader what to think.

Tense

The use of the present tense creates immediacy but can inhibit measured reflection. The past tense is a more obvious choice for memoirs but can seem sedate and over-tidy. Often you'll get both in the course of a book, which is fine as long as the writer stays consistent within sections so that the *now* isn't muddled with the *then*.

Google 'hatred of present-tense narratives' and you'll get a lot of results, including Philip Pullman, who as a Booker Prize judge in 2010 wrote:

> What I dislike about the present-tense narrative is its limited range of expressiveness. I feel claustrophobic, always pressed up against the immediate . . . There's a close parallel here with the increasing use of the hand-held camera in cinema. Just like the present tense, the hand-held camera is an expressive device whose expressive power is being drained away by making it the only way of shooting a film.

Ian Jack, at the time he was editing *Granta*, attributed the popularity of present-tense narratives to the speech habits of a younger generation: it's how kids talk (*So she's wearing this denim thing, and I'm, like, wow, cool...*). He didn't approve:

> A step into the dramatic (or false) present is nearly always a mistake; it tends to break our belief in the reality that the writer is trying to describe. The past tense is simply the more truthful tense, and in in this way it conveys a precision and conviction that the present tense lacks.

Like Ian Jack, I sometimes get irritated by the present tense, for instance when historians in television documentaries use it to talk about centuries-old events. But in life writing it doesn't destroy belief in the events described; if anything the opposite – see how vividly the author remembers what happened! Besides, where tense is handled well you barely notice. Past tense or present? Ask yourself which is used in a favourite book and chances are you won't remember.

Which might imply that tense doesn't much matter. But it's a choice the life writer will have to make. And if the book is confessional, the present tense may be the right choice (at least for parts of the narrative) so that readers, immersed in the moment, don't know what's coming – which was true for the writer at the time. 'The present is forever and forever is always shifting, flowing, melting,' Sylvia Plath wrote in her journals at 17. 'This second is life. And when it is gone it is dead.'

The Earl of Shaftesbury (1671–1713) is eloquent about this in his letters, highlighting the importance of now-ness as against memory:

> The metaphysicians . . . affirm that if memory be taken away, the self is lost. [But] what matter for memory? What have I to do with that part? If, *whilst I am*, I am as

I should be, what do I care more? . . . – The *now*; the *now*. Mind this: in this is all.

It's a great slogan for a life writer: the *now*, the *now*. Though with room for some *then* as well.

Ten(tative) commandments

I've never handed rules to students but I do have a list of suggestions (plus a PS).

1 **Grab the reader's attention from the off.** You can't hit us with everything at once. You don't even need to start with a major episode from the central narrative. But you have to draw us in, establish a voice and hint at what lies ahead.

2 **Put us there.** Make us see, hear, smell, taste and touch. In general use dialogue rather than reported speech. Whatever the episode, it's vivid to you (or you wouldn't have chosen to write about it), so make it vivid to us.

3 **Dramatise yourself as the narrator.** This is your story (or a story to do with your family, or a story about someone you think important), and as our guide you can neither be a blank sheet nor too prim and perfect (if you are we'll hate you for it). Don't go missing at intense emotional moments of the narrative. It's not compulsory to be confessional (you might be shy or reticent by nature) but you should let us get to know you a little.

4 **Be strict about point a view.** If you're writing from the vantage point of a child, create a voice that sounds like a child (in tone if not vocabulary). When dealing with moments of pain, panic or crisis, use an idiom that conveys that. You can't be too calm or retrospectively all-knowing or we won't be engaged or convinced.

5 **Choose your tense**. The present tense creates immediacy but inhibits reflection. The past tense is the more obvious choice for memoirs but lacks bite at dramatic moments. There may well be a case for your using both in the course of a book, but through any single episode or sequence you should be consistent.

6 **Remember God is in the detail**. For your story to speak to others, it has to be specific. The details that mark an episode as unique (and which you may fear are too personal and idiosyncratic) will be the ones that make it universal. The stronger our impression of something happening to a particular person at a particular time in a particular place, the greater our sense of recognition. Small can be beautiful. You don't need big events to create a compelling story. You do need particularity.

7 **Use the same story-telling devices that novelists use** – plot, character, voice, motif and structure. You're telling a story with a beginning, middle and end (though not necessarily in that order) or composing a lyric essay. Either way there has to be development, momentum, a reason to read on. A sense of style, too: just because it's non-fiction doesn't mean you can't be 'literary'. (But be wary of being too 'poetic' or decorative – we'll lose trust if the effects seem forced.)

8 **Give signposts**. Find ways to help the reader along, especially if you have a complex plot and/or large cast list. If you don't feel like a reliable narrator, because you're recalling events of decades ago or incidents you weren't present at, you can signal that to the reader – to do so will make you doubly reliable.

9 **Be surprising**. Work against the material. Readers will bring their own experience to it, so you should allow for that and avoid being predictable – don't be afraid to find humour round a deathbed, say, or tenderness amid abuse. Vary the tone. Avoid cosiness and hagiography when describing happier times

or loved relations. If you're dealing with traumatic material, make sure it doesn't become relentlessly grim.

10 **Pace the story**. It can't be all showing and no telling. You may need to spend thirty pages on the events of an hour – then speed through twenty-five years in two pages. Be bold with chronology. Find ways to keep us interested. We're in your hands.

PS: *Rules and commandments are there to be broken.*

Therapy

Authors are generally sniffy about writing as therapy. I used to be sniffy myself until a poet in a workshop I ran brought along a poem which, he said, had saved his life: he'd planned to kill himself, had run a bath and had a razor sitting on the side, then left the bathroom and wrote a poem instead. After that it was hard to discuss his poem objectively, as an aesthetic construct: had any poem ever been more important?

'If you're doing it for therapy,' Mary Karr says, 'go hire somebody to talk to. Your psychic health should matter more than your literary production.' Maybe – but I'm not in her camp. And nor, really, is Karr, who sees honest self-examination, through writing, as a way to heal ancient wounds: 'For the more haunted among us, only looking back at the past can permit it finally to become past.' Isn't that writing as therapy? And isn't there a similarity between a therapist (who listens to a patient) and a reader (who 'listens' to an author's voice)?

Catharsis is an ancient concept, first used by Aristotle in the *Poetics* and pointing to the power of tragedy to purge emotions: exposed to the worst, you feel sad but also cleansed, purified, appeased. What's true for a reader or member of an audience can also hold true for the author: words as remedy. Some things I've written have made me feel better: cured me of grief, helped me cope with a setback or upset, given me a new perspective. Letters and emails I've had from readers say they've been helped too – that no matter how fumbling and inelegant what I'd written, it articulated what they too had felt, thought or experienced.

The memoirist will always be asked, sometimes with a hint of disapproval: was writing the book therapeutic? To Katherine Angel, in *Daddy Issues*, 'it's the wrong question. The more accurate formulation, for me, is that writing is how I experience my experience. Until writing, in mere living, everything is out of focus.' I'm with her on that.

The prejudice against writing as therapy is that it's a logorrheic and self-indulgent pouring out of emotion. On the contrary, the therapy comes, not in an overflow of powerful feeling, but in finding the right words, the right form, the right structure – in shape, not a stream of consciousness. 'You can write your way out of this' is a note the memoirist Alexandra Fuller stuck on her computer. Tennyson says it well, too, owning up to the shame of self-revelation – 'I sometimes hold it half a sin / To put in words the grief I feel' – then correcting himself:

> But, for the unquiet heart and brain,
> A use in measured language lies;
> The sad mechanic exercise,
> Like dull narcotics, numbing pain.

To find a measured language for disorder; to numb pain by expressing it – there's the challenge. And if the writer rises to it, the reader will be lifted too. 'One sheds one's sicknesses in books,' D. H. Lawrence said, 'repeats and presents again one's emotions, in order to be master of them.' I once interviewed Ted Hughes some years before the publication of the *Birthday Letters*, his collection of poems about Sylvia Plath, whose death he had famously shied away from writing about. Or so we all thought; in reality he'd been writing about her, in private, for years. Sitting in his garden in Devon, Hughes talked about the risks of *not* writing autobiographically:

> It's like not mourning someone; if you don't it becomes damaging. It's better to try to get control of it . . . if you don't, it drifts away and takes a whole piece of yourself with it, like an amputation. To attack it and attack it and get it under control – it's like taking possession of your own life.

When he finally published his *Birthday Letters*, Hughes told friends a great weight had been lifted by getting the book out into the world.

Among life writers, Annie Ernaux has been especially adept at using words to take possession of her own life. 'If I don't write things down,' she says in the epigraph to her book *The Young Man*, 'they haven't been carried through to completion, they have only been lived.'

Trauma

Trauma is often the trigger for a memoir: an abusive childhood, a family death, a public calamity. It may be decades before the experience is written about, as happened with Lemn Sissay, whose book *My Name is Why* recalls his years in the care system between the late sixties and early eighties but didn't come out till 2019. Then again, some books *are* composed in the immediate aftermath of an emotional upheaval. I wrote *And When Did You Last See Your Father?* in the eleven months after Dad's death and drew on diaries I'd kept while he was dying: whatever the book's flaws, it benefited from heat-of-the-moment composition. I was acting like the bereaved in Shakespeare's plays, who are encouraged to 'give sorrow words'. With public traumas, as Ford Madox Ford writes in *The Good Soldier*, it's the same process:

> It is not unusual in human beings who have witnessed the sack of a city or the falling to pieces of a people to desire to set down what they have witnessed for the benefit of unknown heirs or of generations infinitely remote, or, if you please, just to get the sight out of their heads.

Impassioned witness-bearing helps both writer and reader. No holding back. No protective ironies. Get the experience out of your head and on to the page.

Freud talked of how a traumatised patient 'is obliged to repeat the repressed material as a contemporary event instead of . . . *remembering* it as something belonging to the past.' With luck, writers of memoirs who revisit a traumatic moment will, by finding the right words, consign it to the past. Tobias Wolff does this in his memoir of his time as a soldier in Vietnam, *In Pharaoh's Army*. He counts himself lucky to have survived the war. But there were near-misses and several men he knew died there, including a close friend: 'I'd carried a little bit of Vietnam home with me in the form of something like malaria, ulcers, colitis, insomnia, and persistent terrors when I did sleep.' Angry and alienated, he felt adrift. The only appeasement came through writing: 'It takes stamina and self-mastery and faith . . . It toughens you up and clears your head. I could feel it happening. I was saving my life with every word I wrote, and I knew it.'

The most full-on memoir about trauma I've read is Jessica Stern's *Denial*. In 1973 she and her sister were raped at the age of 14 and 15 by a man who entered the house one evening when they were doing homework, made them put on their younger half-sisters' dresses, and had sex with them at gunpoint. Stern went on to make a career interviewing terrorists and men of violence; she learned a lot about PTSD but wouldn't own up to her own: 'Something got cut out of me in that hour – my capacity for pain and fear were removed . . . A soft blanket of numbness descended.' More than three decades after the rape, an intrepid policeman helped her find the identity of her assailant, who in two years had raped as many as forty-four girls (aged between 9 and 19) in Massachusetts – always at night and near private girls' schools. The man later killed himself; she didn't get to meet him. But she met friends of his as well as victims. She also saw that her father's impulse to 'forget about' and 'move on' from traumatic events (as well as the rape of his daughters, his childhood in Nazi Germany, his first wife's death from irradiation at 28 and the break-up of his second marriage) was misconceived. 'The impact of the violation drips lazily down,' she says, 'like that clock in Dali's painting, pooling in the form of shame.' She will never be 'cured' but by facing up to the past she's stronger, more self-aware, no longer in denial.

A writer confronting trauma has to go deep. It's as if a huge wave is crashing towards you; stand still and it'll knock you over; dive through it and you come out safe on the other side.

Travel

Bill Buford has talked of the 'armchair emancipation' of reading about travel when you can't travel yourself, and Jenny Diski said her ideal method for writing a travel book would be to stay at home with the phone off the hook (she nonetheless ended up writing two travel books, *Skating to Antarctica* and *Stranger on a Train*). More than most genres, travel writing has become suspect of late, as a white saviour genre, with practitioners open to accusations of neo-colonialist patronising or western-outsider ignorance. It's a fair objection to lazily researched or hastily assembled travel books. Unless you get to know a place intimately, or send yourself up as a hapless ingenue, you're not doing the job.

Diski's solution, in *Skating to Antarctica*, is subversive. 'I have not always longed to go to Antarctica,' she says, 'or even wanted to especially, but the thought was as powerful as if it had been a lifelong dream.' The impulse came from an addiction to 'boundless expanses of white' which began when she was a patient in a psychiatric hospital. Though she does go to Antarctica, the real journey is back to childhood and to her parents' confrontations – a journey more revealing than the 'real' journey. 'I am not a travel writer in any reasonable sense of the word,' she says, 'I don't feel compelled to bring the world to people . . . I just want to drift in the actual landscapes of my daydreams.'

Of many rewarding travel writers in past decades – Paul Theroux, Bruce Chatwin, Jonathan Raban, Jan Morris, Colin Thubron, Bill Bryson and Sara Wheeler among them – several also wrote novels and allowed fictive elements to infiltrate their non-fiction. When *Songlines* was shortlisted for the Thomas Cook Travel award, Chatwin withdrew it on the grounds that the journey had been 'invented' – 'made up in order to make a story real'. He disliked the label travel writer, as did Raban, who rejected it as facile ('I see a travel writer as someone who's sampling other people's holidays and writing a bright little piece about the glories of Weston-Super-Mare.') and who defined his work as a 'mixture of memoir and travelling – not going to get anywhere, but going for the going's sake'. To him travel is 'a miniature scale-model life'.

There'll often have been a cataclysm in an author's life – divorce, loss of employment, the death of a loved one – with travel a search to replace what has been lost or to find a new way of living. *The Parallel Path* by Jenn Ashworth describes the 192-mile coast-to-coast walk, from St Bees in the west to Robin Hood's Bay in the east, that she took after Covid had left her with cabin fever, itchy to be elsewhere after the long months of caring for her family and students ('a one-woman battle against entropy'). What's captivating about her book is all the thinking she does mid- or post-trek: on writing, friendship, welfare, illness, Charles Atlas, climate change, protest marches, knitting, and why it is that in popular mythology 'walking women' are either models on a catwalk or sex workers. As she wanders, her mind wanders. *Solvitur ambulando*: she's not sure what exactly it is she's trying to solve by walking, but the book's as much an invigorating mental workout as it is a hard physical trudge. Like the best travel books, hers is an inner journey, not a set of touristic notes. And it's honest. Hers, unlike some, is a path you can trust.

Truth

'You must write according to your feelings, be sure those feelings are true, and let everything else go hang.' So Gustave

ON MEMOIR

Flaubert felt, about fiction, and with life writing the pressure to be truthful is paramount. Siri Hustvedt puts it well in her 'catalogue of thoughts' about non-fiction:

> 1. Because the characters inside a work of non-fiction also exist or once existed outside the pages of the book you are writing, you have a responsibility to them or their legacy.
>
> 2. You are not supposed to lie . . .
>
> 5. Even though there may be no truth with a capital T, there are some facts that can be verified – birth and death dates, places where particular events took place, etc. As a writer of non-fiction, you must do your best not to garble documentary facts.

She's right. It might be tempting to present your abusive father as monstrously tall and muscled when in reality he was a scrawny 5 foot 5 inches. But he was still an abuser. And staying with the facts rather than altering them for 'colour' gives the story an extra kick, as well as honouring the truth.

After all, one of the virtues of memoir is the inclusion of material which, if you put it in a novel, readers would find laughably implausible. In *Two Sisters* I recount how when my sister Gill divorced her husband Wynn he used the money from the legal settlement to buy a camper van, which he then parked in her drive. His motive, far from malicious or vengeful, was to keep an eye on her, since her heavy drinking and increasing blindness made her vulnerable. To help the process he attached a long blue rope from her front door to the door of his van, so she could feel her way along it if she needed him. If I'd put that in a novel no one would have believed it, any more than they'd believe that my mum delivered the baby that her friend Beaty had as the result of an affair with my dad – or that Beaty was her closest friend after his death. In life writing the plain truth can be fantastical and the more compelling for that.

Whatever the counter-appeal of autofiction, where the author can play around, I'm with John Edgar Wideman in believing that memoir, unlike fiction, requires serious truth-telling. 'In stories I made up,' he writes, 'a large part of the fun derived from playing fast and loose with the so-called facts of my life', whereas in his memoir, *Brothers and Keepers,* those same facts 'forced me to be accountable to readers and myself for certain kinds of information I didn't make up, couldn't alter or ignore. I was answerable to the story.' A novel may create sympathy for a fictional brother whose fictional crime has landed him in a fictional prison. But a memoir by an author whose real brother is in a real prison after committing a real murder will be read in a different way.

Truth doesn't necessarily mean a single truth – yours and no one else's. You can allow for multiple versions. 'More often than not you stumble upon the truth in the dark,' Harold Pinter said in his Nobel Prize lecture,

> But the real truth is that there never is any such thing as one truth to be found in dramatic art. There are many. These truths challenge each other, recoil from each other, reflect each other, ignore each other, tease each other, are blind to each other. Sometimes you feel you have the truth of a moment in your hand, then it slips through your fingers and is lost.

The truth may be slippery but searching for it isn't futile. It's the basis of the best non-fiction. 'An Autobiography is the truest of all books,' Mark Twain thought, 'for while it inevitably consists mainly of extinctions of the truth, shirkings of the truth, partial revealments of the truth, with hardly an instance of plain straight truth, the remorseless truth *is* there, between the lines.'

Typeface

Works of life writing often divide into two strands, with a pair of storylines running in tandem or a separation between past and present. A common way to denote the difference is typographically, with one strand in roman and the other in italics. But italics are hard on the eye. They succeed in small stretches, over a sentence or paragraph or even a page. But over a dozen or more pages they're a liability and readers will skip (as word of mouth suggests many readers did when reading the italicised sections in A. S. Byatt's *Possession* and Monica Ali's *Brick Lane*). Using different fonts is another option. Section breaks work best, though. They're enough to indicate a change of voice or perspective. And they're easier to take.

U

Ugliness

There's an idea that certain bodily topics – piss, shit, haemorrhoids, cystitis, swollen testicles, urinary tract infections, gonorrhoea, herpes – are best avoided, to spare the blushes of the sensitive reader. But if they're integral to the story they ought to be there. Would you be offended if you came across them in a memoir? Only if the writing is bad. Great works of art, Azar Nafisi says in *Reading Lolita in Tehran*, are 'an act of insubordination against the betrayals, horrors and infidelities of life. The perfection and beauty of form rebels against the ugliness and shabbiness of the subject matter.'

I wouldn't say that there's beauty of form in Constance Briscoe's *Ugly: The True Story of a Loveless Childhood*. It's overlong and unrelentingly combative. But there's plenty for her to feel combative about given the treatment she gets from her mother, Carmen, and to a lesser extent her stepfather, Eastman. Beaten with a stick for bed-wetting, she's scapegoated as 'Miss piss-a-bed', a 'dirty little whore'. And she's repeatedly mocked for being ugly, worst of all when she brings photos home from school as a small child, in the vain hope her mother will buy them:

'I'll say one thing, you sure is fucking ugly . . . Carmen, you ever see a child so ugly?'
'Jesus Christ, me give birth to that? . . . Lord, sweet Lord, how come she so ugly? Ugly. Ugly . . . Heavenly Jesus, sweet and kind, why have You given me a swine?' . . .
'But Carmen, you forget them rubber lips . . . [and] potato skin.'
'Ah yes, Eastman, I see it now. Is not just too much mouth she have, she have too much nose.'

Much of the book consists of dialogue and though Briscoe's protracted recall of conversations from thirty years ago strains belief you can see why the derision here would be unforgettable. The book's title plays on that, though what's ugly isn't the little girl's face but the violence her mother metes out with sticks, belts, knives, fists and knees. Not content with physical abuse, Carmen also tears up the form she's supposed to fill in so that Constance can study Law as a degree ('only clever people go to university').

It's bold of Briscoe to describe the bed-wetting, a condition that persisted into her teens. Craig Raine's poem 'Arsehole' is no less bold. It honours a bodily part not often attended to in literature: 'It is shy as a gathered eyelet / neatly worked in shrinking violet; / it is the dilating iris, tucked / away, a tightening throb when fucked.' The poem caused a fuss when first published (with Mary Whitehouse calling for it to be banned) but it's a beautifully worked sonnet in immaculate taste.

Art that's candid about the body isn't ugly. The ugliness would be in censoring it.

V

Vengeance

When life writing is vengeful there are consequences: not just from friends or family, who feel betrayed, but from readers, who take against a malicious tone or get bored by a list of resentments or start to feel there must be another side to the story. Grudges don't make pretty reading. And retribution-by-memoir is, on one level, a doomed pursuit since it won't banish the past or kill the offenders. In *Coming Undone,* when Terri White thinks of killing the stepfather who forced her into oral sex as a child, the thought of murder remains a fantasy, gruellingly entertained and oddly entertaining; it's the same in John Burnside's *A Lie About My Father*; vengeance isn't taken in life; the score is settled by life writing instead. Wit is more incisive than a knife.

A fascinating sub-genre of the vengeance memoir is that of the *daughter of a famous woman getting even.* Christina Crawford started the trend with *Mommie Dearest,* about her mother Joan, in 1978, and Maria Riva continued it in 1992 with *Marlene Dietrich: The Life* (*New York Times*: 'leaves no sequin unturned'). The daughters portray beloved movie stars as selfish monsters. More recently, in *How to Lose Your Mother,* Molly

Jong-Fast demythologises the *Fear of Flying* icon Erica Jong, whom she describes as a terrible parent who resented spending even an hour with her small daughter: 'I always wondered if she would have been better off with a dog.'

I'd not call James Rhodes's *Instrumental* vengeful though it is a retaliation. He's a talented concert pianist and celebrates music for helping him stay alive at times when he felt like ending it all. But as he admits, he 'all too frequently blame[s] everyone and everything' for his suffering. Specifically, with good reason, he blames Peter Lee, the gym teacher at the prep school Rhodes attended, who repeatedly raped him. The 'Everest of trauma' Rhodes endured led to 'multiple surgeries, scars (inside and out), tics, OCDs, depression, suicidal ideation, vigorous self-harm, alcoholism drug addiction . . . sexuality confusion, paranoia, mistrust, compulsive lying, eating disorders, PTSD' and more besides. Some of Rhodes's anger is directed at his school, where his plight as a six-year-old boy with blood on his legs, begging to be let off gym, somehow failed to register. (It was only many years later, after a former head of the prep school read an interview the adult Rhodes gave and then contacted the police, that Lee was tracked down to Margate, where he was working as a boxing coach with boys under ten.)

Rhodes failed to bring his rapist to justice – Lee died before standing trial – and then faced a trial himself: his ex-wife had an injunction slapped on the book, on the grounds that their son, who had Asperger's, dyspraxia and ADHD, would be distressed if he ever read it. The injunction was eventually lifted by the Supreme Court ('There can be no justification for keeping secret the information contained in this book.') but only after great effort and expense. It's a miracle the book got written and only thanks to the Supreme Court that it was published.

Was this a case of a vengeful memoir temporarily blocked by a vengeful ex-wife? Not really, since Rhodes had every right to his *J'accuse* – unlike John Osborne, whose venom towards the women in his life (mother, lovers and ex-wives) is simply malicious. 'A year in which my mother died can't be all bad,' he wrote, and when his fourth ex-wife, Jill Bennett, killed herself, he said: 'I have only one regret now in this matter of Adolf [his nickname for her]. It is simply that I was unable to look down upon her open coffin, and, like the bird in the Book of Tobit, drop a good, large mess in her eye.' Wittily vengeful? No, pathetic.

Vignettes

If a book doesn't lend itself to a long unfolding narrative then vignettes offer an alternative: story-shards or impressionistic fragments; flash non-fiction from which a bigger picture emerges. It's the style that Leila Berg adopts in her memoir *Flickerbook*, set in the 1920s and 30s, which recounts her life from the age of 3 to 21. A flicker book is a set of pictures in sequence on pieces of paper, which you flip through at speed to give the illusion of a moving picture. And that's the effect Berg's text aims for as it moves from a small-child's observations ('Daddy never speaks to me. He is just in the same house.') through a teenager's struggles at school ('They always make me play at school concerts. The sweat runs down the inside of my legs, and my legs shake.') to a young woman's love life ('I have had ten offers of marriage in as many weeks. How conventional and idiotic the Communist Party is. I sleep with a boy and immediately he asks me to marry him.'). Berg's brief is brevity. Levity, too, and an aspiration to poetry: 'I am so tired. I feel drained, like a teapot emptied of tea, and turned on its side on the slopstone to dry.'

The vignette method works especially well when evoking the texture of early childhood. Hilary Mantel adopts it, to comic effect, in her memoir *Giving Up the Ghost*, preferring episodic fragments to 'the smooth dishonesty of narrative connection'. She takes care not to be coy. Shortness is her selling point but she doesn't sell herself short.

Violence

There has always been violence in literature (from Homer and Shakespeare to Anthony Burgess and Brett Easton Ellis) and there have always been critics who object to it – who accuse authors of glorifying violence or getting off on it or generating vicious tastes in the reading public. But if it's part of their experience, life writers have every right to describe violence, however horrific. It's a way of shedding light in dark places.

If you take it on, you have to be incisive – sharp, flexible, imaginative in the way that war generals or murderers rarely are. Homer in the *Iliad* understood that:

> Patroclus coming close up to him stabbed with a spear-thrust at the right side of the jaw and drove it on through the teeth, then hooked and dragged him with the spear over the rail, as a fisherman who sits out on the jut of a rock with line and glittering bronze hook drags a fish, who is thus doomed, out of the water.

It's a great image. The only risk in describing violence lies in creating luxuriant beauty out of terror – in making something horrendous into self-pleased 'high art'. If writers are paring their fingernails in the face of atrocity, that's suspect.

The worst atrocities occur in wartime. And though there haven't been many war memoirs in the UK in recent times there have been several memoirs from the Troubles, including Kevin Myers's *Watching the Door: A Memoir 1971–78*, Malachi O'Doherty's *The Telling Year: Belfast 1972*, Martin Doyle's *Dirty Linen: The Troubles in My Home Place*, and *Here's the Story* by Mary McAleese. Seamus Heaney's poems are also invaluable in exploring the sources of the conflict.

I've twice got into trouble for writing about violent crime, once with a long poem, *The Ballad of the Yorkshire Ripper*, and once with a book about the Bulger case, *As If*. Both were notorious cases, much discussed in the media, but journalists don't like it when a different kind of reportage moves in on territory they've colonized. What interested me was what had caused those acts of violence, not the violence itself. Still, I could hardly leave the violence out. Nor do Truman Capote or Gordon Burn underplay it in their accounts of murders. (See CRIME.)

Here's one area of writing where we don't want to hear that the author has carried out his own research, as a perpetrator (William Burroughs and Louis Althusser killed their wives). But if you've been a victim of violence, the reader will side with you, especially if you tell it as it was. 'Graphic' is a word used pejoratively when a writer includes scenes of sex and violence. But graphic detail is what we *want* from literature. If words don't make us see and aren't precise enough to make us think, then they fail.

Voice

Creative writing programmes emphasise the importance of would-be authors *finding their own voice*. But as novices they can't help but adopt other writers' voices – the one they're currently enthralled by and, when the addiction passes, the one after that. And so on, through many a derivative draft, till something of their own voice breaks through. The process is less about finding than nurturing, as with a parent raising a child. It takes time. It takes work. It takes false starts and horrible failures. In his essay 'Feeling into Words' Seamus Heaney compared the process to dropping a bucket in a well: to begin with you don't go deep enough and all the bucket brings up is air, but eventually, when you reach water, 'You'll have broken the skin on the pool of yourself.'

To have a distinctive voice in a book doesn't stem from being eloquent in life, let alone from being vocal. On the contrary, writers are often people who mumble, mispronounce, stammer and hedge – or even stay dumb. Famous writer-stutterers include Arnold Bennett, Elizabeth Bowen, Lewis Carroll, Henry James, Somerset Maugham and John Updike. The last writes about it in his memoir, *Self-Consciousness*: 'Stuttering, perhaps, is a kind of recoil at the thrust of your own voice, an expression of alarm and shame at sounding like yourself, at being yourself, at taking up space and air.'

You can be shy in person but commanding in print. Shyness may be the reason you've taken to writing in the first place – a stab at the self-assertion you're incapable of in company. At home, with a notebook or laptop, you've the comfort of privacy and alone-ness, and that can build confidence. Your words, you now realise, don't have to stop with you. Writing is your speech therapist, allowing your voice to break through.

What you know

Write what you know, aspiring authors are advised, especially if they're life writers. Novelists invent plots, characters and epochs that have nothing to do with them; life writers inhabit home truths. I'm wary of the mantra even so. Rather than write what I know, I write what I'd like to find out. I suspect it's the same for most memoirists. There may be a cataclysmic episode from childhood that resists their comprehension. The time, place and cast list are clear but the episode feels fuzzy. Why? Because, although they're scribes, it hasn't yet been *in*scribed; because they've not yet made it theirs. There's stuff still to uncover – stuff they won't know until they know it through the written word (and which then makes it knowable to others).

'Nothing can be more limiting to the imagination,' John Gardner says in *The Art of Fiction*, 'nothing is quicker to turn on the psyche's censoring devices and distortion systems, than trying to write truthfully and interestingly about one's home town, one's Episcopalian mother, one's crippled younger sister.' He has a point: I've worked with students who find it impossible to write honestly about people they grew up with and towns where they've lived. But if Gardner were right, we'd not have James Joyce's *Ulysses* or Jeanette Winterson's *Oranges Are Not the Only Fruit*. And we'd not have the memoirs in which home towns, fundamentalist parents or disabled siblings are central to the narrative.

For myself, though I've written three memoirs about family and several poems in which they feature, I've never felt to be writing what I know – I've been writing to discover what I need to understand. As Joan Didion puts it: 'I write entirely to find out what I'm thinking, what I'm looking at, what I see and what it means.' Or, more starkly, in Helen Garner's words: 'writing about my life is the only thing that makes it possible for me to live it.'

Why I write

George Orwell's 1946 essay of that title gave four reasons: sheer egoism, aesthetic enthusiasm, historical impulse and political purpose. The last was the most important to him: a mission to engage with readers and make the world a better place. George Eliot believed the same, that literature should offer an 'extension of our sympathies . . . a mode of amplifying experience and extending our contact with our fellow-men beyond the bounds of our personal lot.' Others say they write by staying *within* the bounds of the personal. 'I rhyme / To see myself, to set the darkness echoing' Seamus Heaney wrote, and Kafka – in a strikingly violent metaphor - felt similarly: 'A book must be the axe for the frozen sea within us.' Larkin said his aim was to save things from oblivion:

> I write . . . to preserve things I have seen/thought/felt . . . both for myself and for others, though I feel my prime

responsibility is to the experience itself, which I am trying to keep from oblivion for its own sake. I think the impulse to preserve lies at the bottom of all art.

The impulse to preserve may take the form of commemorating someone who isn't well-known. As Horace put it, 'Many brave men lived before Agamemnon's time; but they are all, unmourned and unknown, covered by the long night, because they lack their sacred poet.' If a writer is that poet, however un-sacred, however iconoclastic and irreverent, they're doing a worthwhile job. Their words keep the dead alive.

In *A Truce That is Not Peace*, Miriam Toews is invited by the organiser of a literary conference in Mexico City to address the question 'Why do I write?' She offers an answer he doesn't understand and is disinvited from the conference. Over the 180 pages of her memoir she explains it better. 'Why do I write? Because she asked me to,' *she* being her sister Marj, who suffered from depression; that was the deal they made: 'You live. And I'll write.' Miriam's letters, written with clownish humour, helped keep Marj alive for twenty-odd years before she committed suicide just as their father had done.

I think most people, Toews included, write because they've no choice. Life has such urgency and peril that confronting it is unavoidable. 'Do not hunt for subjects,' Samuel Butler says in his Notebooks, 'let them choose you, not you them. Only do that which insists upon being done and runs right up against you, hitting you in the eye until you do it. This calls you and you had better attend to it, and do it as well as you can.' He elaborates on this in relation to his own books:

> I never make them: they grow; they come to me and insist on being written, and on being such and such. I

did not want to write *Erewhon*, I wanted to go on painting and found it an abominable nuisance being dragged willy-nilly into writing it. So with all my books – the subjects were never of my own choosing; they pressed themselves upon me with more force than I could resist. If I had not liked the subjects I should have kicked, and nothing would have got me to do them at all. As I did like the subjects and the books came and said they were to be written, I grumbled a little and wrote them.

Sometimes writers would rather be doing something else. But it's a must-do. They don't light on a subject; it lights on them.

Wolfe, Tom

It's ironic that Wolfe, late on in his career, wrote two mega-selling novels, *The Bonfire of the Vanities* and *A Man in Full*, since the premise of his earlier career as a New Journalist was that, with fiction falling into neo-fabulism, non-fiction was the way to embrace the real world. John Updike dismissed Wolfe's novels as 'entertainment, not literature', and some of Wolfe's non-fiction is no better: show-off high jinks from the man in a white suit. But the best of his New Journalism is invigorating, not least his account of Ken Kesey and the Merry Pranksters in *The Electric Kool-Aid Acid Test*.

More impressive still was his book on US test pilots and astronauts, *The Right Stuff*, the result of seven years' 'saturation' research and interviews. Where his New Journalism is satirical, with a scoffing tone he wildly exaggerated in his attack on modern art and modern art theorists in *The Painted Word*, *The Right Stuff* is more sober and almost reverential in its admiration for the courage and heroism it takes for people to go into space. At his best Wolfe renewed the realist mode and life writers can learn from him.

Wolff, Tobias

Born in Alabama in 1945, Wolff is highly rated for his short stories ('the greatest living exponent of the form') but nothing can compete with his two memoirs, *This Boy's Life* and *In Pharaoh's Army,* or with his novel *Old School*. The last of these is strongly autobiographical but over his career he has been scrupulous in drawing a line between writing loosely based on personal experience (fiction) and writing that aspires to be wholly truthful (memoir). His older brother Geoffrey has also worked in both forms, and it's fascinating to compare their Gatsby-ish father as portrayed by Tobias (sparingly) in *This Boy's Life* and by Geoffrey (with an extensive account of his slipperiness) in *The Duke of Deception*.

A recurrent theme in Tobias Wolff's work is duplicity, yet his tone is painstakingly honest: the two are beautifully conjoined towards the end of *This Boy's Life* when Wolff describes the scam – his forging of letters of recommendation from his lowly school in the West – that will get him into a prestigious private school in the East: 'The coach wrote a fine letter for me, and so did my teachers and the principal. They didn't gush. They wrote plainly about a gifted, upright boy.' Wolff had been getting Cs for his schoolwork but his fabrications of excellence didn't seem dishonest to him:

> I felt full of things that had to be said, full of stifled truth. That was what I thought I was writing – the truth. It was

truth known only to me, but I believed in it more than I believed in the facts arrayed against it. I believed that in some sense not factually verifiable I was a straight-A student. In the same way, I believed that I was an Eagle Scout, and a powerful swimmer, and a boy of integrity...

I made no claims that seemed false to me ... I wrote without heat or hyperbole, in the words my teachers would have used if they had known me as I knew myself. These were their letters. And on the boy who lived in their letters, the splendid phantom who carried all my hopes, it seemed to me that I saw, at last, my own face.

It's a great passage about the complexities of truth and the glamour of self-deception.

Woolf, Virginia

To complete the trio of Wolves, here's the greatest of them, primarily a novelist but also an indefatigable diarist and the author of one of the great twentieth-century essays, *A Room of One's Own*. Woolf is stalwart in her affirmation of life writing. 'I sometimes think only autobiography is literature,' she wrote, 'novels are what we peel off, and come at last to the core, which is only you or me.' She's also lucid about the benefits of writing as therapy, describing (in her essay 'A Sketch of the Past') the 'horror' that comes when buried memories are recovered but how 'the sledge-hammer force of the blow' can be blunted through words – to the point where the blow becomes 'welcome':

> the shock-receiving capacity is what makes me a writer ... I feel that I have had a blow; but it is not, as I

thought as a child, simply a blow from an enemy hidden behind the cotton wool of daily life; it is or will become a revelation of some order; it is a token of some real thing behind appearances; and I make it real by putting it into words. It is only by putting it into words that I make it whole; this wholeness means that it has lost its power to hurt me; it gives me, perhaps because by doing so I take away the pain, a great delight to put the severed parts together. Perhaps this is the strongest pleasure known to me. It is the rapture I get when in writing I seem to be discovering what belongs to what . . .

Put it in words and it loses the power to hurt you: that's what life writing can do.

Workplace

A room of one's own in which to write? Ideally yes – an office, attic, spare bedroom, conservatory, garden shed or, if you're David Cameron, a £25,000 'shepherd's hut' with a sofa bed and sheep's wool insulation. But a kitchen table when no one is around will serve as well. Silence is good for concentration but some writers work with music playing – they don't hear it as they would if actively listening; the sound is a balm or buzz. Shutting down the Internet is advisable, though websites are helpful for research or when you have brain freeze (e.g., for finding synonyms). Many writers keep favourite possessions or lucky mascots close by; I don't know if having Dad's pacemaker by my desk has helped me write a word but it's there as a good-luck charm. Historical novelists have been known to kit out their workplace with the paraphernalia of the period they're writing about – or even to dress in period costume, as Lucy Worsley does in history documentaries on television.

'One cannot think and write except when sitting,' Flaubert said. But Hemingway wrote standing up, with his typewriter on a chest-high shelf, Thomas Wolfe used a fridge as his desk, and according to Quentin Bell the young Virginia Woolf worked at 'a desk standing about three feet six inches high with a sloping top; it was so high that she had to stand to her work.' Lewis Carroll also stood, while Proust and Truman Capote ('a completely horizontal writer') wrote lying down, and Mark Twain did so in bed. If you've a good memory or a handy notebook, there's nothing to stop you writing while moving about: Wordsworth composed poems while walking outside, his sister Dorothy picking up his gems as he strode back and forth.

If it matters enough, writing gets done anyhow and anywhere, with the workplace a train carriage, park bench or (as in J. K. Rowling's case) a cafe. 'I wrote most everything I wrote and read most everything I read in public,' Maggie Nelson says in *The Argonauts*, 'just as I am writing this in public now.' The more secluded or defended a spot, the better. A writer's self-interruptions (coffees, cigarettes, texting and googling) are bad enough – you don't want other people's intrusions on top.

Workshops

Despite their long history (Iowa offered a course on Verse-Making as far back as 1897), many people regard creative writing programmes with suspicion – workshops most of all. According to Louis Menand in the *New Yorker*, workshops are based on the theory that 'students who have never published a poem can teach other students who have never published a poem to write a publishable poem. The fruit of the theory is the writing workshop, a combination of ritual scarring and twelve-on-one group therapy where aspiring writers offer their view of the efforts of other aspiring writers.' There is, he concedes, 'one person in the room, the instructor, who has (usually) published a poem', but this instructor will be 'either a product of the same process – a person with an academic degree in creative writing – or a successful writer who has had no training as a teacher of anything and who is grimly or jovially sceptical of the premise on which the whole enterprise is based: that creative writing is something that can be taught.'

Menand ends up admitting that, 'in spite of all the reasons that they shouldn't, workshops work'. But the question he raises – *can you really teach creative writing?* – hasn't gone away. If ever I'm asked, I reply that well, yes, skills can be passed on, just as they are to trainee musicians, painters, potters and dancers – then I add that a better question would be *Can you help writers to rewrite?* To which my answer is an unqualified yes.

Invariably, to start with, aspiring writers don't revise their own work as eagerly as they edit the work of others. But over time they get tougher. Walk in on a good creative writing class and you'll hear the kind of babble you might have heard from Edward Garnett with D. H. Lawrence, or Ezra Pound with T. S. Eliot, or Max Perkins with Scott Fitzgerald: *Why not think of losing that or moving this there? Stop bombarding us with so many characters. Don't parade your research, integrate it. Get in and out of the scene more quickly. Is that simile really working?* And so on.

Given his scepticism, Menand might not be surprised to hear that I set up a poetry workshop at Goldsmiths before I'd published a word. I put myself forward to the two men who ran what was then called (it now sounds pornographic) the Adult Studies department and to my amazement they agreed. Beyond writing and studying poetry, I'd no credentials. But I was lucky in the people who came along to the class over the next couple of years, among them Wendy Cope, Alan Jenkins, Vicki Feaver and Fred D'Aguiar. We learned together: I got as much from them (or more) as they did from me. And I saw how workshop feedback can help writers move their work along when it reaches an impasse. That's where sympathetic readers help, less in congratulating you on what you're doing right than in pointing out what's wrong. The flaw can be something glaringly obvious that you repress all knowledge of until someone else identifies it, at which point you think *Yes, of course, Eureka*, and you go back and fix it.

Not all the eight, ten or twelve members of a workshop will have useful advice when someone's stuck. But even in the least inspired of groups one of them will – and never mind if it's not the tutor (who may be as callow as I was when I first ran that workshop). Sharing your work is what makes the difference. In Beckett's *Waiting for Godot* when the two main characters, Vladimir and Estragon, exchange insults – 'vermin', 'moron', 'sewer-rat', 'cretin' – the ultimate vanquishing insult, worse than all the others, is 'crritic'. But a workshop group with critics, rather than *crritics*, can be a great help.

Of course when it's memoir under discussion, workshop participants need to be especially sensitive in their feedback, since the material will be highly personal and often distressing. In one of my year-groups there were two parents who'd lost grown-up sons, a woman who'd been orphaned at eight, a man whose mother disappeared when he was six, an ex-alcoholic whose mother was also alcoholic, and a young woman who was parenting her schizophrenic father. The final member of the group, a man in his eighties writing about his modest upbringing, must have felt like the straight man on a stage full of tragedians. Tears weren't unknown. More often the students under scrutiny felt relief to have the reassurance of an audience: no, they weren't just wanking; no, their stuff wasn't too boring or weird.

There remains a suspicion that writing can't be institutionally taught, and insofar as my work with students hasn't been teaching but mentoring and editing I've some sympathy with that argument. Many authors in the past did their learning alone. Even workshop students do most of their learning alone. But they also learn from other people sitting round them in the same room.

Writer's block

Say *writer's block* and people picture a distraught author stalled over a blank page and/or hurling scrunched-up false starts into a wastebin. Samuel Johnson was impatient with the concept: 'A man may write at any time, if he will set himself *doggedly* to it.' I don't agree and nor did Johnson: 'No man is always in a disposition to write,' he said on another occasion, 'nor has any man at all times something to say.' Even if you do have something to say, you may be blocked. Blockage comes in many different forms. You can be blocked in the morning (or in early adulthood) but fluent in the afternoon (or in middle age); you can be blocked in one genre (essay) but fluent in another (fiction); you can get three-quarters of the way with a poem or memoir but lack the vision or command to complete it; you can be going along nicely then be foiled by a person from

Porlock. Whatever the impediment, every writer knows the phenomenon: you're *choked, paralysed, stuck in a rut*, your creative powers are *frozen*, you've *dried up*, you feel *totally fucked*.

First there's the inability to write *anything*, as expressed by Joseph Conrad: 'I sit down for eight hours every day – and the sitting down is all. In the course of that working day of eight hours I write three sentences which I erase before leaving the table in despair.' There's the story, possibly apocryphal, of James Joyce slumped in despondency after writing only seven words in a day. 'But James . . . that's good, at least for you,' a friend consoles him. 'Yes,' Joyce says, 'but I don't know what order the words go in.'

There's also the block of having written at inordinate length but without a shape. Something's wrong, but you don't know what, and that can make you desperate, so that if a casual acquaintance rashly expresses an interest in taking a look at what you've written, as happens to the Californian wine buff and would-be published author Miles in Alexander Payne's film *Sideways*, you foist your typescript on them, which in Miles's case means retrieving from the back seat of his car not one whacking heap of pages but two, and even though he knows this might a) place the recipient in an awkward situation b) sprain her back and c) ruin a beautiful friendship, still, he does it anyway . . .

To which the short answer is: don't impose a vast unfinished typescript on a stranger or even a best friend.

How does an author overcome blockage? The usual recommendations – making a coffee, going for a walk, sticking the manuscript in a drawer for a while – sound bland and may not work. The key is not to panic. Rather than despair at your uselessness, remind yourself the block is for a reason: you're being held up by your text because your text expects better, knows you're not yet ready to do better but also trusts you'll do better in the end. No breakthrough ever comes without a preliminary obstruction.

Writer's block is a minor illness. The writer has to bear the pain and trust that the illness will eventually be cured.

X

X-rated

Nothing is. Or nothing should be. 'Homo sum, humani nihil a me alienum puto' goes a line in a play by the ancient Roman playwright Terence: *I am human, and nothing human can be alien to me.* Life writers have to write fearlessly. To say what needs saying. To face rather than dodge difficult subjects.

They should also prepare to be damned – to be unsurprised if their subject matter (*My Life as a Drug Baron, The Joys of Stalking, Confessions of a Copro-, Zoo-, Formico-, Stygio-* or *Necro-philiac*) proves a turn-off. Every age has its taboos. Abortion, homosexuality, masturbation, mental illness, babies born out of wedlock – all were difficult for a memoir writer to broach as late as the mid-twentieth century, when things that we now find offensive (racism, sexism, homophobia, transphobia, child-beating) were acceptable. Once writers were censored; now they're cancelled. It's not just libel writs that publishers fear, it's the flak they'll get for bringing out books by authors with disreputable private lives or outrageous opinions. I know of a prize for which a writer was shortlisted then removed before the shortlist was announced because charges of impropriety, true or otherwise, had been made against him;

the subject of his book had nothing whatsoever to do with the charges but to shortlist him risked a social media storm and the organisers feared trouble. This was cowardice, not integrity. Sally Mann says it well in her memoir *Hold Still*:

> Do we deny the power of *For Whom the Bell Tolls* because its author was unspeakably cruel to his wives? Should we vilify Ezra Pound's *Cantos* because of its author's nutty political views? . . . If we only revere works made by those with whom we'd happily have our granny share a train compartment, we will have a paucity of art.

Life writers can't afford to ignore the moral climate of the times. But they don't have to abide by it. Someone on X might X-rate them. But if they're writing truthfully, someone else will give them A-stars.

Y

'You'

To write a personal story as a 'you', in the second person, rather than 'I', is a means to shy away from self-exposure and to make readers complicit, as if they were going through the same experience. But when I come across a narrator using that pronoun I often resist the coercion and find myself muttering (or even scrawling in the margin) 'Speak for yourself! Don't affect to know how I think and behave! Leave me out of it!' Morven Crumlish wrote a hilarious attack on the 'overused and irritating' you-mode for the *Guardian*:

> You are having ideas, actions and habits attributed to you, with the understanding that you are in the same clique as the writer . . . .. While it is beguiling to be drawn so far into a narrative that you are assumed to have experienced it, there is usually a point when the sound of a needle being ripped off a record should be inserted, as the reader takes a step back and holds up her hands: "Oh, no, sister, you're on your own here."

At best, the intimacy and openness of 'you' do allow for

inclusion. Even Crumlish admits that 'When it works, a "you" story hijacks the reader's thought process, so that every shameful twist is achingly familiar.' But a 'you' full-length memoir will struggle not to seem mannered.

Another option is to address one's story (whether angrily or mournfully) *to* a 'you' – violent father, loathed ex, beloved sibling, lost child. Or the 'you' can be a stranger, like the American in a Lahore cafe addressed by Mohsin Hamid in *The Reluctant Fundamentalist*. The risk, over a full-length memoir, is that the reader – the first 'you' for an author – may feel ousted by this other 'you'. But the focus gained by framing a memoir as a conversation, with the author talking to someone, can energise the prose.

Z

Zzz

Unless it's a guidebook for insomniacs, no writer wants to send people to sleep. Still, it's an effect that books can have, especially when read late at night, so it's important to write wide-awake prose. And sleep, unlike dreams, which usually make for dull reading (even the inestimable Annie Ernaux recounts too many of them), can be a good subject – and rewardingly unpredictable.

Samantha Harvey writes about sleep-not-come-by in her memoir *The Shapeless Unease*. Her insomnia is rooted in grief at the death of her cousin. Other factors add to it: childhood traumas, traffic noise outside her window, anger over Brexit, sadness that her sister and partner have broken up and, as the insomnia worsens, isolation from friends. There's something like comedy in all the curative measures she takes, none of which works: Buddhist mantras, visits to a CBT sleep clinic, acupuncture, dietary supplements, French lessons, jigsaws, games of solitaire, Sanskrit chanting, podcasts and 'counting backwards from one hundred in French or German'. But the panic and feral behaviour are no joke, and though she stages a recovery at the end, through wild swimming, what remains is the depiction of her suffering. 'Sleep. Like money, you only think about it when you have too little. Then you think about it all the time, and the less you have the more you think about it. It becomes the prism through which you see the world.'

Arifa Akbar also has 'a fraught relationship with sleep'. Her memoir *Wolf Moon* recounts her fear of, and thrilled fascination with, darkness. As the *Guardian*'s theatre critic, on duty most evenings, she's a night owl but not to the same extent as others she meets – nurses, carers, sex workers, clubbers, security guards, merchants at New Spitalfields Market. Her quest is to find 'peace within the waking world of the night', and in the end, on Sark, she does: 'this darkness feels like it is opening something up inside. It is as serene as a sunset or sunrise. I want more of it . . . I am as exhilarated as I am scared.'

The definitive memoir on insomnia is *Sleepless* (*Pas Dormir* in the original French), in which Marie Darrieussecq offers an exhaustive and exhausting history of her own and others' struggle to sleep. She seems to have read everyone on the subject: 'Gide! Pavese! Plath! Sontag! Dostoevksy!', not to forget Proust and Kafka. As for herself, 'I've tried everything', she says, and lists all the attempted remedies, from herbal teas and cranial osteopathy to fasting, meditation and hypnosis. No joy: she still wakes at 4.04 a.m. every day. *The world is divided into those who can sleep and those who can't* is the message, with insomniacs deemed noble spirits and sleepers dull idiots. Unrelenting wakefulness is a nightmare but her book has comic verve: it's a brilliant compendium of ideas and apercus, with photos to help it along.

So . . . insomnia can be written about. And, like everything in life writing at its truest, the shame, wonder and weirdness of it can be shared. Reviewing Marie Darrieussecq's book in the *Guardian*, Samantha Harvey wrote that 'For all its turmoil, at its core there's a kind of rest.' That's true of all the best memoirs: they put us through the mill, but we come out feeling better for it, enlightened, rewarded, safer, at peace.

Bibliography

I regret that this list of memoirs is so long but I've aimed to include all those I've quoted from, plus a few books I admire and haven't had room to discuss; I also regret that the list couldn't be longer because I've excluded other titles I've read and enjoyed. The dates and publication details are mostly for my own copies of these books, often in paperback – where the original publication was significantly earlier I've indicated that.

CLASSICS
St Augustine, *Confessions, 397–400*, Penguin 1961
Teresa of Avila, *Autobiography, the Book of Her Life, 1562–65*, Penguin 1987
Michel de Montaigne, *The Complete Essays*, 1595, Penguin 1991
Samuel Pepys, *Diaries*, 1665, Penguin 2003
Jean-Jacques Rousseau, *The Confessions*, 1781, Penguin 1953
Thomas De Quincey, *Confessions of an Opium-Eater, 1822*, OUP 1985
Edmund Gosse, *Father and Son*, 1907, Penguin 1986
W. N. P. Barbellion, *The Journal of a Disappointed Man*, 1919, Penguin 2017
Virginia Woolf, *Selected Diaries*, Vintage 2008

James Agee, *Let Us Now Praise Famous Men*, 1941, Penguin 2006
George Orwell, *Collected Essays* (4 volumes, 1920–50), Penguin 1970
Simone de Beauvoir, *Memoirs of a Dutiful Daughter*, 1958, Penguin 2001
Primo Levi, *If This is a Man*, 1958, Penguin 1979
Truman Capote, *In Cold Blood*, 1966, Penguin 2012
J. R. Ackerley, *My Father and Myself*, 1968, Pimlico 1992
Nadezhda Mandelstam, *Hope Against Hope*, 1970, Harvill 1999

MODERN CLASSICS
Martin Amis, *Experience*, Cape 2000
Andrea Ashworth, *Once in a House on Fire*, Picador 1998
Julia Blackburn, *The Three of Us*, Cape 2008
Joan Didion, *The Year of Magical Thinking*, Fourth Estate 2005
Dave Eggers, *A Heartbreaking Work of Staggering Genius*, Vintage 2001
Annie Ernaux, *The Years*, 2000, Fitzcarraldo 2018
Linda Grant, *Remind Me Who I Am Again*, Granta 1998
Kathryn Harrison, *The Kiss*, Fourth Estate 1997
Jackie Kay, *Red Dust Road*, Picador 2010
Karl Ove Knausgaard, *My Struggle* (6 vols), Vintage 2012–19
Tim Lott, *The Scent of Dried Roses*, Viking 1996
Hilary Mantel, *Giving Up the Ghost*, Fourth Estate 2003
Hisham Matar, *The Return*, Viking 2016
Maggie Nelson, *The Argonauts*, Melville 2016
Lorna Sage, *Bad Blood*, Fourth Estate 2000
W. G. Sebald, *The Rings of Saturn*, Harvill 1998
William Styron, *Darkness Visible*, Cape 1991
Tara Westover, *Educated*, Hutchison 2018
Tobias Wolff, *This Boy's Life*, Bloomsbury 1989

ON MEMOIR

HIGHLY RECOMMENDED
James Baldwin, *Notes of a Native Son*, 1955, Penguin 2017
Alan Bennett, *Writing Home*, Faber 1994
Jo Brainard, *I Remember*, 1970, Granary 2001
John Burnside, *A Lie about My Father*, Vintage 2007
Marie Darrieussecq, *Sleepless*, Fitzcarraldo 2023
Seamus Deane, *Reading in the Dark*, Cape 1996
Edmund de Waal, *The Hare with Amber Eyes*, Chatto 2010
Jenny Diski, *Skating to Antarctica*, Virago 2005
Jenny Diski, *In Gratitude*, Bloomsbury 2016
Jennie Erdal, *Ghosting*, Canongate 2004
Annie Ernaux, *Simple Passion*, Seven Stories 1993
Michael Frayn, *My Father's Fortune*, Faber 2010
Helen Garner, *How to End a Story: Collected Diaries*, Weidenfeld 2025
Margo Jefferson, *Negroland*, Granta 2016
Mary Karr, *The Liar's Club*, Picador 1995
Chris Kraus, *I Love Dick*, 1997, Tuskar Rock 2015
Helen Macdonald, *H is for Hawk*, Cape 2014
Henry Marsh, *Do No Harm*, Weidenfeld 2014
Alexander Masters, *Stuart: A Life Backwards*, HarperCollins 2006
Mary McCarthy, *Memories of a Catholic Girlhood*, 1957, Vintage 2004
Philip Roth, *The Facts*, Cape 1989
Philip Roth, *Patrimony*, Cape 1991
George Szirtes, *The Photographer at Sixteen*, Maclehose 2019
Rebecca Stott, *In the Days of Rain*, Fourth Estate 2017

POETRY
Elizabeth Bishop, *The Complete Poems*, Chatto 1983
John Berryman, *The Dream Songs*, Faber 1990
Raymond Carver, *All of Us; The Collected Poems*, Harvill 1997

Seamus Heaney, *Poems*, Faber 2025
Tony Harrison, *Collected Poems*, Penguin 2016
Ted Hughes, *Birthday Letters*, Faber 1998
Philip Larkin, *Collected Poems*, Faber 1988
Patricia Lockwood, *Motherland Fatherland Homelandsexuals*, Penguin 2017
Sharon Olds, *Selected Poems*, Cape 2005
Claudia Rankine, *Citizen: An American Lyric*, Penguin 2014

REFLECTIONS AND GUIDANCE ON WRITING
Sally Cline and Carole Angier (eds), *Life Writing: A Writers' & Artists' Companion*, Bloomsbury 2013
John Gardner, *The Art of Fiction*, Vintage 1991
Vivian Gornick, *The Situation and the Story*, Farrar, Straus & Giroux 2001
Ernest Hemingway, *On Writing*, Scribner 1984
Philip Larkin, *Required Writing*, Faber 1983
Anne Lamott, *Bird by Bird: Instructions on Writing and Life*, Canongate 2020
Elmore Leonard, *10 Rules of Writing*, Weidenfeld 2010
David Lodge, *The Art of Fiction*, Penguin 1992
Mary Karr, *The Art of Memoir*, HarperCollins 2015
Cathy Rentzenbrink, *Write It All Down*, Bluebird 2022
David Shields, *Reality Hunger*, Hamish Hamilton 2010
Graham Swift, *Making an Elephant: Writing from Within*, Picador 2009

ALSO QUOTED FROM, DISCUSSED OR RECOMMENDED
J. R. Ackerley, *My Dog Tulip*, NYRB Classics 2010
Arifa Akbar, *Wolf Moon: A Woman's Journey into Night*, Sceptre 2025

ON MEMOIR

Decca Aitkenhead, *All at Sea*, Fourth Estate 2017
Svetlana Alexievich, *Chernobyl Prayer*, Penguin 2016
Martin Amis, *The War Against Cliché*, Vintage
Katherine Angel, *Unmastered: A Book on Desire, Most Difficult to Tell*, Penguin 2014
Katherine Angel, *Daddy Issues*, Peninsula Press 2019
Carol Angier, *The Double Bond: Primo Levi, a Biography*, Viking 2002
Jenn Ashworth, *Notes Made While Falling*, Goldsmiths Press 2019
Jenn Ashworth, *The Parallel Path*, Hodder 2025
Diana Athill, *Stet*, Granta 2000
Margaret Atwood, *Book of Lives*, Chatto 2025
Nicholson Baker, *U and I*, Granta 2011
Camilla Balshaw, *Named*, Bedford Square 2025
Patrick Barkham, *The Swimmer: A Life of Roger Deakin*, Hamish Hamilton 2023
Julian Barnes, *Nothing to Be Frightened Of*, Vintage 2009
Damian Barr, *Maggie and Me*, Bloomsbury 2013
Victoria Belim, *The Rooster House*, Virago 2023
Richard Beard, *The Day That Went Missing*, Vintage 2018
John Berendt, *Midnight in the Garden of Good and Evil*, Chatto 1994
Leila Berg, *Flickerbook*, Granta 1997
J. Bernlef, *Out of Mind*, Faber 1988
Thomas Blackburn, *A Clip of Steel*, MacGibbon & Kee 1969
Tony Blair, *A Journey*, Hutchinson 2010
Simon Boas, *A Beginner's Guide to Dying*, Swift Press 2025
Anthony Bourdain, *Kitchen Confidential*, 2000, Bloomsbury 2019
Constance Briscoe, *Ugly: The True Story of a Loveless Childhood*, Hodder 2006

Blake Butler, *Molly*, Archway 2023
Samuel Butler, *Notebooks*, 1912, Cape 1951
Gordon Burn, *Somebody's Husband, Somebody's Son*, Faber 1984
Gordon Burn, *Happy Like Murderers*, Faber 1998
Graham Caveney, *On Agoraphobia*, Picador 2022
Graham Caveney, *The Body in the Library*, Peninsula 2024
Michael Chabon, *Moonglow*, Fourth Estate 2017
Bruce Chatwin, *Songlines*, Cape 1987
Kate Clanchy, *Some Kids I Taught and What They Taught Me*, Picador 2019
Catherine Coldstream, *Cloistered: My Years as a Nun*, Chatto 2024
J. M. Coetzee, *Boyhood*, Vintage 1998
J. M. Coetzee, *Youth*, Vintage 2003
Mary Cregan, *The Scar*, Lilliput Press 2019
Laura Cumming, *On Chapel Sands*, Chatto 2019
Doreen Cunningham, *Soundings: Journeys in the Company of Whales*, Virago 2022
Rachel Cusk, *The Last Supper: A Summer in Italy*, 2009, Faber 2019
Rachel Cusk, *Aftermath*, Faber 2012
Rachel Cusk, *Outline*, Faber 2018
Rachel Cusk, *Transit*, Faber 2018
Rachel Cusk, *Kudos*, Faber 2019
Miriam Darlington, *Owl Sense*, Guardian-Faber 2018
Fred D'Aguiar, *Year of Plagues*, Carcanet 2021
Alan Davies, *Just Ignore Him*, Little Brown 2020
W. H. Davies, *The Autobiography of a Super-Tramp*, Parthian 2018
Roger Deakin, *Waterlog*, Vintage 2000
Rob Delaney, *A Heart That Works*, Coronet 2022
Anna Derrig, *What Became of Us? & Consent and Life-writing*, Goldsmiths, University of London doctoral thesis, 2019

ON MEMOIR

Joan Didion, *Slouching Towards Bethlehem*, Penguin 1968
Joan Didion, *The White Album*, Weidenfeld 1979
Joan Didion, *Where I Was From*, HarperCollins 2003
Joan Didion, *Blue Nights*, Fourth Estate 2012
Tove Ditlevsen, *Childhood, Youth, Dependency*, 1967–71, Penguin 2021
Robert Douglas-Fairhurst, *Metamorphosis: A Life in Pieces*, Cape 2023
Joe Dunthorne, *Children of Radium*, Hamish Hamilton 2025
Gerald Durrell, *My Family and Other Animals*, Penguin 2006
Andrea Dworkin, *Intercourse*, Basic Books 2006
Geoff Dyer, *White Sands*, Canongate 2016
Geoff Dyer, *Homework*, Canongate 2025
Geoff Dyer, *The Last Days of Roger Federer*, Canongate 2023
Annie Ernaux, *A Woman's Story*, Quartet 1990
Annie Ernaux, *Shame*, Seven Stories 1998
Annie Ernaux, *Happening*, Seven Stories 2001
Annie Ernaux, *Getting Lost*, Fitzcarraldo 2022
Annie Ernaux, *The Young Man*, Fitzcarraldo 2023
Annie Ernaux, *The Use of Photography*, Fitzcarraldo 2024
Annie Ernaux, *The Other Girl*, Fitzcarraldo 2025
Olaudah Equiano, *The Interesting Narrative of the Life of Olaudah Equiano, or Gustavus Vassa the African*, 1789, Mint Editions 2021
Bernardine Evaristo, *Manifesto: On Never Giving Up*, Hamish Hamilton 2021
William Finnegan, *Barbarian Days: A Surfing Life*, Corsair 2016
Richard Ford, *Between Them*, Bloomsbury 2017
Aminatta Forna, *The Devil That Danced on the Water*, HarperCollins 2002
Margaret Forster, *Hidden Lives*, Viking 1995
Miranda France, *The Writing School*, Corsair 2023

James Frey, *A Million Little Pieces*, John Murray 2004
Alexandra Fuller, *Don't Let's Go to the Dogs Tonight*, Picador 2015
Henry Louis Gates Jr, *Coloured People*, Viking 1995
Josie George, *A Still Life*, Bloomsbury 2020
Virginia Roberts Giuffre, *Nobody's Girl*, Penguin 2025
Sinéad Gleeson, *Constellations*, Picador 2022
Maxim Gorky, *My Childhood*, 1913, Penguin 1990
Simon Gray, *The Smoking Diaries*, Granta 2004
Simon Gray, *Coda*, Granta 2009
Lucy Grealy, *Autobiography of a Face*, 1994, Mariner Books 2016
Kate Gross, *Late Fragments*, HarperCollins 2014
Samantha Harvey, *The Shapeless Unease*, Vintage 2020
Joe Hammond, *A Short History of Falling*, Fourth Estate 2021
Sheila Heti, *How Should a Person Be?*, Vintage 2014
Sheila Heti, *Motherhood*, Vintage 2019
Richard Holmes, *Footsteps: Adventures of a Romantic Biographer*, Flamingo 1995
bell hooks, *Bone Black: Memories of Girlhood*, Women's Press 1997
A. M. Homes, *The Mistress's Daughter*, Granta 2007
Kerry Hudson, *Lowborn*, Chatto 2019
Langston Hughes, *The Big Sea*, 1940, Hill & Wang 1993
Zora Neale Hurston, *Dust Tracks on a Road*, 1942, Virago 1985
Siri Hustvedt, *The Shaking Woman, or A History of My Nerves*, Sceptre 2010
Howard Jacobson, *Mother's Boy*, Cape 2022
Kay Redfield Jamison, *An Unquiet Mind*, Knopf 1997
Leslie Jamison, *The Empathy Exams*, Granta 2014
Leslie Jamison, *The Recovering*, Granta 2018
Boris Johnson, *Unleashed*, Collins 2024

ON MEMOIR

Alan Johnson, *This Boy*, Penguin 2014
Alice Jolly, *Dead Babies and Seaside Towns*, Unbound 2017
Molly Jong-Fast, *How to Lose Your Mother*, Picador 2025
Paul Kalanithi, *When Breath Becomes Air*, Vintage 2017
Adam Kay, *This Is Going to Hurt*, Picador 2017
Rudyard Kipling, *Something of Myself*, 1937, Penguin 1977
Hanif Kureishi, *My Ear at His Heart*, Faber 2004
Hanif Kureishi, *Shattered*, Hamish Hamilton 2014
John Lanchester, *Family Romance*, Faber 200
James Lasdun, *Give Me Everything You Have*, Cape 2013
Tabitha Lasley, *Sea State*, Fourth Estate 2021
Damian Le Bas, *The Stopping Places: A Journey Through Gypsy Britain*, Chatto 2018
Tom Lee, *The Bullet*, Granta 2024
Benedicta Leigh, *The Catch of Hands*, Virago 1991
Deborah Levy, *Things I Don't Want to Know*, Penguin 2014
Deborah Levy, *The Cost of Living*, Penguin 2018
Deborah Levy, *Real Estate*, Penguin 2021
Joanne Limburg, *The Woman Who Thought Too Much*, Atlantic Books 2011
Amy Liptrot, *The Outrun*, Canongate 2016
Patrica Lockwood, *Priestdaddy*, Penguin 2018
Audre Lorde, *Zami: A New Spelling of My Name*, Penguin 1982
Mary Loudon, *Relative Stranger: A Life After Death*, Canongate 2006
Hannah Lowe, *Long Time No See*, Periscope 2015
Tom Lubbock, *Until Further Notice I am Alive*, Granta 2014
Thomas Lynch, *The Undertaking*, Cape 1997
Carmen Maria Machado, *In the Dream House*, Serpent's Tail 2020
Sheila MacLeod, *The Art of Starvation*, Virago 1981
Janet Malcolm, *The Journalist and the Murderer*, Knopf 1990

Sally Mann, *Hold Still*, Penguin 2024
Stephen Marche, *On Writing and Failure*, Sort of Books 2023
Adam Mars-Jones, *Kid Gloves*, Penguin 2015
Alexander Masters, *A Life Discarded*, Fourth Estate 2016
Noreen Masud, *A Flat Place*, Hamish Hamilton 2023
Mary McCarthy, *Memories of a Catholic Girlhood*, 1957, Vintage 2004
Frank McCourt, *Angela's Ashes*, HarperCollins 2005
Robert McCrum, *My Year Off*, Picador 1998
Robert McCrum, *Every Third Thought*, Picador 2017
Bernice L. McFadden, *Firstborn Girls*, Chatto 2025
John McGahern, *Memoir*, Faber 2005
Rose McGowan, *Brave*, HarperCollins 2018
Chanel Miller, *Know My Name*, Viking 2019
Jane Miller, *Crazy Age: Thoughts on Being Old*, Virago 2012
Sam Miller, *Fathers*, Vintage 2018
Jan Morris, *Conundrum*, Faber 2018
Helen Mort, *A Line Above the Sky*, Penguin 2023
Haruki Murakami, *What I Talk About When I Talk About Running*, Vintage 2009
Julie Myerson, *The Lost Child*, Bloomsbury 2009
Azar Nafisi, *Reading Lolita in Tehran*, HarperCollins 2004
Maggie Nelson, *Jane: A Murder*, Soft Skull 2005
Maggie Nelson, *The Red Parts: Autobiography of a Trial*, 2007, Vintage 2017
John Niven, *O Brother*, Canongate 2024
Katharine Norbury, *The Fish Ladder*, Bloomsbury 2015
Barack Obama, *Dreams from My Father*, Canongate 2007
John O'Donoghue, *Sectioned*, John Murray 2009
Maggie O'Farrell, *I am I am I am*, Tinder Press 2017
Andrew O'Hagan, *The Missing*, Picador 1995
Susie Orbach, *The Impossibility of Sex*, Allen Lane 1999

ON MEMOIR

Tony Parker, *The People of Providence,* Hutchison 1983
Tony Parker, *Studs Terkel: A Life in Words*, HarperCollins 1997
Tim Parks, *A Season with Verona,* Vintage 2003
Tim Parks, *Teach Us to Sit Still: A Sceptic's Search for Health and Healing*, Vintage 2011
Ann Patchett, *Truth & Beauty*, Fourth Estate 2020
Christina Patterson, *Outside, the Sky is Blue*, Headline 2022
Virginia Peters, *Have You Seen Simone?*, Nero 2014
Ruth Picardie, *Before I Say Goodbye*, Penguin 1998
James Rebanks, *English Pastoral,* Penguin 2020
Cathy Rentzenbrink, *The Last Act of Love*, Picador 2015
James Rhodes, *Instrumental,* Canongate 2014
Monique Roffey, *With the Kisses of His Mouth*, Simon & Schuster 2011
Becca Rothfeld, *All Things Are Too Small*, Virago 2025
Martin Rowson, *Stuff,* Cape 2007
Salman Rushdie, *Joseph Anton,* Cape 2012
Salman Rushdie, *Knife,* Cape 2024
Ignatius Sancho, *Letters of the Late Ignatius Sancho, An African*, 1782, Broadview Press 2015
Sathnam Sanghera, *The Boy with the Topknot*, Penguin 2009
W. G. Sebald, *The Emigrants*, Harvill 1998
W. G. Sebald, *Austerlitz*, Harvill 2001
Alice Sebold, *Lucky*, Picador 1999
Will Self, *Will*, Viking 2019
Lemn Sissay, *My Name is Why*, Canongate 2020
Lauren Slater, *Lying*, Penguin 2001
Nigel Slater, *Toast: The Story of a Boy's Hunger*, Fourth Estate 2003
Andrew Solomon, *The Noonday Demon*, Vintage 2016
Britney Spears, *The Woman in Me*, Simon & Schuster 2024
Lu Spinney, *Beyond the High Blue Air*, Atlantic Books 2017

Francis Spufford, *The Child That Books Built*, Faber 2003
Carolyn Steedman, *Landscape for a Good Woman*, Vintage 1986
Jessica Stern, *Denial*, HarperCollins 2010
Nell Stevens, *Mrs Gaskell and Me*, Picador 2019
Galen Strawson, *Real Materialism and Other Essays*, OUP 2008
William Styron, *Darkness Visible*, 1989, Vintage 2001
Catherine Taylor, *Stirrings*, Weidenfeld 2023
Michelle Tea, *Against Memoir*, And Other Stories 2018
Miriam Toews, *A Truce That Is Not Peace*, Fourth Estate 2025
Mark Twain, *The Autobiography*, University of California Press 2025
John Updike, *Self-Consciousness*, Andre Deutsch 1989
Carla Valentine, *Past Mortems*, Sphere 2017
J. D. Vance, *Hillbilly Elegy*, HarperCollins 2016
Bart van Es, *The Cut Out Girl*, Penguin 2018
Norah Vincent, *Voluntary Madness*, Viking 2008
Justin Webb, *The Gift of a Radio*, Doubleday 2022
Gabriel Weston, *Direct Red*, Cape 2019
William Wharton, *Wrongful Deaths*, Granta 1994
John Edgar Wideman, *Brothers and Keepers*, 1984, Canongate 2018
Binjamin Wilkomirski, *Fragments: Memories of a Wartime Childhood*, Picador 1996
Harry Windsor, Duke of Sussex, *Spare*, Penguin 2023
Raynor Winn, *The Salt Path*, Penguin 2019
Jeanette Winterson, *Why Be Happy When You Could Be Normal?*, Vintage 2012
Tom Wolfe and E. W. Johnson (eds), *The New Journalism*, Picador 1975
Tom Wolfe, *The Right Stuff*, 1979, Vintage 2019
Geoffrey Wolff, *The Duke of Deception*, Random House 1979
Tobias Wolff, *In Pharaoh's Army*, Bloomsbury 1994

ON MEMOIR

Tobias Wolff, *Old School,* Bloomsbury 2005
Naomi Wood, *Mrs. Hemingway*, Picador 2015
Virginia Woolf, *A Room of One's Own/Three Guineas*, 1929, Penguin 1991
Virginia Woolf, *A Woman's Essays*, Penguin 1992
Elizabeth Wurtzel, *Prozac Nation*, Quartet Books 1995
Louisa Young, *You Left Early*, HarperCollins 2018
Lea Ypi, *Free*, Allen Lane 2021

Notes and Acknowledgements

After fifteen years as a literary editor on newspapers, I spent another twenty as a professor at Goldsmiths University, and it's from those experiences, and from what I've been through as a writer, that this book is drawn. I'm immensely grateful to the authors I've read and the students I've mentored: the little I know I have mostly learned from them. My thanks also go to the editors for whom I've written over the years, including Ian Jack, Alison Samuel, Bill Buford, Frances Coady, Annalena McAfee, Liz Jobey, Jan Dalley, Clara Farmer and Craig Raine.

With this book I owe a huge debt to my agent Sarah Ballard and editor Ann Bissell, both of whom made great suggestions about what to include.

I'm also grateful to my friends and colleagues at Goldsmiths for their support over the years, among them Maura Dooley, Ardashir Vakil, Francis Spufford, Tim Parnell, Tom Lee, Adam Mars-Jones, Stephen Knight, Erica Wagner, Lavinia Greenlaw, Ross Raisin, Ros Barber, Alan Downie and Jane Desmarais. Many research students have been rewarding to work with too, including Virginia Peters, Anthony Joseph, Wendy Jones, Catherine Coldstream and Anna Derrig – for more on Anna's ideas about consent check out her BBC Radio Four programme *Other People's Stories*. Hermione Lee, Pamela Todd, Miriam

Darlington, Patricia Craig, Liz Oxley and Glynn Hugo were helpful too.

I've written pieces touching on themes in this book (including automatic writing, editors and permissions) for the *Guardian*, *The Times*, *London Review of Books*, *Times Literary Supplement*, *Quarto* and the *Independent on Sunday*. Other sections here draw on essays and forewords I've published in anthologies and monographs: for a fuller account of confession see 'The Worst Thing I Ever Did: The Contemporary Confessional Memoir' in Zachary Leader (ed), *On Life-Writing* (OUP, 2015), pp. 201–220; for a longer essay on Tony Harrison, see Edith Hall, *New Light on Tony Harrison*, pp. 3–12; and for more on James Agee see my introduction to the 2006 Penguin edition to *Let Us Now Praise Famous Men*.

'Marked with D' is taken from *Collected Poems* by Tony Harrison (c) Tony Harrison and reprinted by permission of Faber and Faber Ltd. The villanelle 'Life Writing' comes from my collection *Shingle Street* (2015).